GREAT HORSE RACING

Mysteries

True Tales from the Track

JOHN McEVOY

With LENNY SHULMAN

ECLIPSE PRESS

ESSEX, CONNECTICUT

An imprint of Globe Pequot, the trade division of
The Rowman & Littlefield Publishing Group, Inc.
4501 Forbes Blvd., Ste. 200
Lanham, MD 20706
www.rowman.com

Distributed by NATIONAL BOOK NETWORK

British Library Cataloguing in Publication Information available

Previous edition catalogued with the Library of Congress

Library of Congress Control Number: 00-101124
ISBN 9781493063215 (pbk. : alk. paper)
ISBN 9781493070138 (ebook)

∞™ The paper used in this publication meets the minimum requirements of
American National Standard for Information Sciences—Permanence of Paper for
Printed Library Materials, ANSI/NISO Z39.48-1992.

This book is
for my wife Judy,
and our children
Julia, Sarah, and Michael,
and our grandchildren
Madelaine, Colin, and Cecilia

Contents

Introduction

Editor's note: What follows is John McEvoy's introduction to the 2000 edition of Great Horse Racing Mysteries. *Because his introduction describes his approach to researching and writing this book, we have retained it for this updated edition. Summaries of the two new chapters, written by Lenny Shulman, appear at the end of the introduction.*

When I was asked by Eclipse Press editor Jacqueline Duke to write about great mysteries in the world of Thoroughbred horse racing, my first reaction was, "That's an intriguing idea. But I wonder if there is enough material for a full-length book?"

What a needless concern that turned out to be! The problem had nothing to do with a shortage of possible subjects, but an abundance of them from which to choose. Emerging from that selection process were a dozen chapters, involving horses, their owners, riders and trainers, and a racing official. Conclusions regarding "what really happened" in these notably mysterious cases are, in some instances, relatively clear-cut; in others, however, "the jury" remains out.

The twelve cases are presented in chronological order, beginning with the shocking death by poisoning — believed by many to have been intentional — of the great Australian champion Phar Lap, who succumbed in California in 1932 after winning his only American start in sensational style. Then follow chapters on these intriguing cases:

Albert Snider — On a day off from his riding duties at Tropical Park in the winter of 1948, Citation's regular jockey, who had never lost in nine starts on the Calumet Farm star, goes fishing with two friends in the Florida Keys. They are never seen again.

William and Ann Woodward — One of the Eastern establishment's most prominent married couples, these owners of the great horse Nashua are the central figures in a sensational case that saw the husband shot to death by his wife. Was it an accident, or was it murder?

Red McDaniel — A tremendously talented horseman who for five consecutive years (1950-54) topped all North American trainers in number of winners saddled leaves Golden Gate Fields one May afternoon and without warning jumps to his death from the San Francisco Bridge.

Dancer's Image — Toward the end of the turbulent 1960s, he becomes the only horse ever to be disqualified from victory in the Kentucky Derby. The cause: a medication violation. His owner continues to wonder who gave his horse the illegal drug — or if anyone actually did.

Hawthorne Race Course — In the autumn of 1978, one of the nation's oldest tracks is the scene of remarkable events on consecutive days: a "ringer" wins a race on Saturday, and on Sunday a major fire started by arsonists destroys the grandstand.

Shergar — In the winter of 1983, Europe's best-known racehorse and stallion is stolen from his stall at Ireland's Ballymany Stud, never to be seen again by his owners despite the most massive "horse hunt" in history.

David Joost — The Texas Racing Commission official is found dead along with his wife and their two children in March of 1990. This controversial case is ruled a murder-suicide, but Joost's relatives and others contend that this was the work of unknown killers who acted because of "something David knew."

Alydar — One of the world's most successful sires is euthanized as the result of an injury sustained in his stall at Calumet Farm, a death that leads to the scandalous financial collapse of the world's most famous Thoroughbred establishment.

Ron Hansen — The talented, controversial jockey, who had been accused but never found guilty of race-fixing, disappears after an auto accident he'd caused on a bridge near San Francisco, his remains going undiscovered for months.

Holy Bull — The 1994 Kentucky Derby favorite loses by eighteen and a half lengths in the worst performance of his otherwise excellent career. His owner-trainer becomes convinced that "the best one" he'd ever had — who would be voted Horse of the Year honors for that season — was drugged prior to the Derby.

William McCandless — Earns lasting infamy as the major figure in two of American Thoroughbred racing's most publicized cases: the 1977 theft from Claiborne Farm of the valuable broodmare Fanfreluche, and the "sponging" of horses at Churchill Downs twenty-one years later. Where is this man today?

Chris Antley — Just a year and a half after winning the Kentucky Derby and Preakness aboard Charismatic, the popular jockey was found dead in his California home in 2000. Police were unsure whether it was a case of foul play or if Antley's self-destructive behavior ultimately caught up with him.

Big Brown — The winner of the 2008 Kentucky Derby and Preakness was believed to be invincible and a sure Triple Crown winner by nearly every pundit of the sport. But instead of becoming the first Triple Crown winner in thirty years, he was pulled up and finished last in the Belmont Stakes. What happened to the robust colt?

Phar Lap's Last Race

It is rare that the death of a racehorse is reported on the front page of *The New York Times*, but it happened on Wednesday, April 6, 1932, under the headline "Great Australian Race Horse Dies in West After First American Triumph."

Other famous horses had died in the previous twelve months, including Man o' War's dam, Mahubah; McGee, sire of the great gelding Exterminator; and Sweep, who led the United States stallion roster in 1918. None, however, earned front page coverage in one of the world's most famous newspapers. Only the horse known as "the Red Terror of the Antipodes" warranted that distinction. His name was Phar Lap, and he was special.

And as rapidly as the report of Phar Lap's sudden demise circulated around the world, plunging the continent of Australia into mourning, so did the disturbing question that snapped at the heels of this shocking news: What killed this huge and hearty specimen of equine strength, power, speed, and courage?

———————

Bred by A. F. Roberts, Phar Lap was foaled on New Zealand's South Island in October of 1926, product of a mating of the stallion Night Raid with the mare Entreaty, a daughter of Winkie. His pedigree traced to the successful racehorse and sire Carbine, winner of Australia's most famous race, the Melbourne Cup, in 1890. Sold at auction as a yearling, Phar Lap brought a price that has been variously reported as being between 259 and 800 American dollars. Even at the top end of this scale, he was an extraordinary bargain. The buyer was a Sydney, Australia trainer named Harry Telford, who then persuaded one of his clients, David Davis, to go partners with him in the ownership of Phar Lap. Davis, an American businessman from San Francisco who had lived in Australia for twenty years, had raced other horses trained by Telford.

It was this partnership that came up with the horse's name, the origin of which has been as variously reported as his purchase price. Author Adrian Dunn wrote in *Crown Jewels of Thoroughbred Racing* that Phar Lap is "the Thai word for lightning, or wink of the skies." American racing historian William H. P. Robertson wrote that the horse's "name meant lightning in the language of the (Australian) aborigines." Another theory had it that the name was inspired by his maternal grandsire, Winkie, the connection being lightning as "a wink of light" in the night sky.

As a two-year-old, there was not much indication that this rawboned, growthy youngster would gain worldwide fame. Phar Lap finished out of the money in his first four races before breaking his maiden in his fifth and final start of the season. Phar Lap's three-year-old campaign also began modestly, but then he suddenly came into his own and entered a period of brilliance that would characterize the rest of his life.

Phar Lap made twenty starts at three, winning thirteen of them, including nine in a row at one point. Among his successes were the Australian Jockey Club and Victoria Derbys and St. Leger. In the sensational course of his nine-race winning streak, Phar Lap set four track records: 2:03 for a mile and one-quarter, 2:16 1/4 for a mile and three-eighths, 2:29 1/2 for a mile and one-half, and 3:39 1/2 for two and one-quarter miles. But this impressive campaign merely set the stage for more remarkable accomplishments to come.

After finishing second in his 1930-31 debut, Phar Lap began a fourteen-race victory skein that was bookended by another runner-up effort at season's end. The impressive string of triumphs was topped by his tally in the 1930

Melbourne Cup at Flemington racecourse. Carrying high weight of 138 pounds, or fifteen more than required by the weight-for-age scale, Phar Lap easily won this two-mile event by three lengths. It was a tremendously impressive performance in this premier race. Only three times previously in the history of the Melbourne Cup, which had its first running in 1861, had a higher impost been carried to victory.

His smashing success in the Cup certified Phar Lap's status as a national hero. Cup winners take on a cachet that the rest of the citizens of the world might find hard to comprehend, and great Cup winners do better than that. To most Australians (104,200 of whom turned out at Flemington to witness the 1999 running), the Cup is both a horse race and a signature event in life.

In the course of his world travels, author Mark Twain witnessed the 1895 renewal, won by a great filly from Adelaide named Auraria. Twain subsequently wrote: "The Melbourne Cup is Australasia's National Day. It would be difficult to overstate its importance. It overshadows all other holidays and specialized days of whatever sort in that congeries of colonies. Overshadows them? I might almost say it blots them out.

"Cup Day," continued Twain, "and Cup Day only, commands an attention, an interest, and an enthusiasm which are universal...Cup Day is supreme — it has no rival. I can call to mind no specialized annual day, in any country, which can be named that large name — Supreme...No one save this one."

Phar Lap won the 1930 Melbourne Cup at odds of 8-11; he

remains the only horse ever to start at odds-on in the long history of the classic. His tremendous popularity among Australians was explained this way by Adrian Dunn: "These were the Depression years. Times were bad. Hundreds of thousands were out of work. Many in the population were losers and the only light in their drab lives was the chance to associate themselves with a winner. That winner was Phar Lap. He was their psychological lifeline. Their principal and perhaps only pleasure was a day at their favorite racetrack to watch their beloved gelding with jockey Jim Pike — resplendent in his distinctive red jacket, black and white hooped sleeves, and red cap — win again."

But this popularity did not extend to all segments of the sporting population, and certainly not to all of the bookmakers Down Under. Many of them hated Phar Lap for negatively affecting their bottom lines: many people wouldn't bet on him because of the short odds available (often the bookmakers simply refused to offer a price on Phar Lap); others wouldn't bet against him because they were convinced he was so talented that he could not lose. As a result, bookmakers' business suffered.

Concern for Phar Lap's safety prompted Davis and Telford to hire armed security personnel and place a guard dog at the stable. Yet, only a few days before his November 4 Melbourne Cup tour de force, Phar Lap and his groom, Tommy Woodcock, chief assistant to trainer Telford, were targets of rifle fire by unknown gunmen near the Caulfield track in suburban Melbourne. Horse and handler were unharmed in this failed attempt to keep Phar Lap — who had attracted a lot of money in the pre-race wagering — from contesting the Cup.

Phar Lap's dominance of his Australian opposition continued the next year. By now the chestnut gelding with the distinctive white star stood slightly more than seventeen hands and had a girth measuring seventy-nine inches. He had a long stride — variously estimated at between twenty-four and twenty-seven feet — and for the most part he had his rivals over a barrel. His victories saw him lead his fields by huge margins. In their book on the Melbourne classic, *Cup Day*, Maurice Cavanough and Meurig Davies said that "The only time Phar Lap's opponents got near to him in a race was at the barrier (start)." The exception to this in 1931 came in the Melbourne Cup when Phar Lap suffered his only loss of the season while toting a record 150 pounds, conceding fifty-two to the winner.

Having seen their star rack up thirty-seven wins from his last forty-six starts, Phar Lap's owners looked for new worlds to conquer. They decided on an invasion of North America: Phar Lap would be pointed for the Agua Caliente Handicap of March 20, 1932, with subsequent assignments planned for northern California, Chicago, and New York. Davis and Telford's goal was to make Phar Lap the world's leading money winner. With his bankroll standing at $282,200, success in the Caliente "hundred grander" would enable Phar Lap to surpass Sun Beau. Australians were agog at this amazing undertaking. When he set sail, Phar Lap carried the hopes and well wishes of most of the seven million residents of the continent.

·

Phar Lap's audacious attempt to break the money mark was preceded by some arduous travel. Housed in a twelve-by-twelve-foot stall on the freighter *Monowai*, Phar Lap made the 10,000-mile trip in the company of young Tommy Woodcock and jockey Bill Elliott, the stable's second-string rider. The trip took three weeks. So confident of their gelding's prospects were Telford and Davis that they dispatched underlings (Woodcock was just twenty-six years old) to oversee Phar Lap's first race in North America.

Describing Phar Lap's arrival, William H.P. Robertson, in his *History of Thoroughbred Racing in America*, wrote that "… there appeared in the West an enormous gelding considered by many experts — including Eddie Arcaro, New York state steward Francis Dunne, and Marshall Cassidy, dean of American racing officials — as the greatest thoroughbred ever to race on the American continent. What is more striking is that the horse gained his lofty stature in exactly 2 minutes and 2 4-5 seconds."

The Phar Lap party landed in San Francisco on January 15, 1932, in a blare of publicity — probably more than any other horse had received in this country since Man o' War — and went to a nearby farm for a ten-day rest. Phar Lap was then shipped to Tijuana to begin preparing for the mile and one-quarter Agua Caliente Handicap.

According to Robertson, Phar Lap in Mexico "underwent the most peculiar training regime ever seen in America. No fast trials, no blowing out, none of the accepted works. In fact, much of the horse's exercise wasn't on the track… Woodcock rode Phar Lap over the countryside, much as a rancher would ride a cow pony, up and down sandy hills, over rocky ground, and through mesquite.

"Marshall Cassidy, who was the starter at Caliente, tried to persuade Woodcock to school Phar Lap out of the stalls with a Maxwell barrier (this was before the introduction of the modern starting gate), but although the horse had no experience at this type of start (being familiar only with walk-ups to a barrier), his trainer disdained the practice sessions. Phar Lap would come away properly, he said."

Many observers were not assured. Great pessimism persisted: How could a horse who had traveled so far be expected to run well over a strange track under conditions so alien to him?

Chronology has cut sharply into the corps of eyewitnesses to Phar Lap's days at Caliente. Among the few remaining are California horseman Noble Threewitt, who celebrated his eighty-ninth birthday on February 24, 2000. Threewitt was right on the scene, and he said there were some misconceptions concerning the way Phar Lap was trained up to the race.

Threewitt, a native of Benton, Illinois, was twenty-one years old in that spring of '32. "I was working as an exercise boy for trainer J. B. McGinn," Threewitt said. "I had met him at old Riverside Park in Kansas City, where I'd gone to race a filly I owned. When that meeting ended McGinn said to me, 'I'll ship your filly with the rest of my horses to Caliente if you'll come along to gallop horses and work for me there.' I said to McGinn, 'Where's Caliente?' I'd never heard of it."

(Later that year, McGinn died, and Threewitt, at the request of the widow, took over the training of the McGinn horses. Threewitt would go on to become one of the pillars of the Southern California training community, his numerous stakes winners including Correlation, Honeys Gem, and King of Cricket, and to serve as national vice president of the Horsemen's Benevolent and Protective Association for seventeen years).

The Caliente meetings in those days, Threewitt recalled, lasted "all winter. There wasn't much winter racing then — Caliente, New Orleans, Florida, Cuba, that was it. The meeting attracted a lot of big horsemen, big stables. Ben Jones and his son Jimmy (who would subsequently combine to saddle a total of eight Kentucky Derby winners) always raced at Caliente."

Threewitt lived at the track, in a tackroom he shared with Tom Smith, who later would become famous as the trainer of Seabiscuit. Threewitt well remembers the arrival of Phar Lap.

"News about Phar Lap had been in the papers for weeks," he said. "We were all pretty excited the day he shipped in and anxious to get a look at him. We were looking forward to the big race, which was supposed to have been $100,000 but was cut to $50,000 when business fell off at the track. But $50,000 was darned big to us — I was making $75 a month.

"I got to spend a lot of time around Phar Lap. His people had not brought a pony with them, so they arranged to borrow one from my boss, McGinn. That's how I met them —

Elliott, the jockey, and the groom, Woodcock, who was training the horse. They were very nice, very friendly people. But they were very suspicious of 'outsiders' and, I suppose you could say, a lot of Americans in general.

"Most of the backstretch workers at the Caliente meetings were Americans, and they preferred to live not in Tijuana but across the border in Chula Vista, or even farther up north near San Diego," Threewitt continued.

"In those days you were not permitted to come back into Mexico across the border until 7 o'clock in the morning. Well, by 7 o'clock each day Phar Lap's people had had him out on the track, exercised, and already cooled out before the Americans came down across the border. So, there was nothing really 'private' or 'secretive' about the way Phar Lap was handled. And it certainly wasn't true that they never worked him before the big race. I saw most of his training, and so did a few others of us who lived on-track, and it included both gallops and breezes. It is true that they took him up into the hills some mornings, and that they sometimes put a lot of weight on him — a couple of sacks of oats — when they walked him. But for the most part they worked Phar Lap over the Caliente strip in normal fashion.

"I was very nosy," admitted the good-natured Threewitt. "I had never been near a famous horse before. I knew Phar Lap's record — everybody knew he'd carried 150 pounds in the Melbourne Cup, which was quite something. I hung around his barn a lot, spent as much time there as I could, and I got to be friends with Elliott and Woodcock. From what I gathered from these fellows, the people back in Australia loved Phar Lap, but they weren't all that fond of his owners.

"Phar Lap was a big, grand-looking horse. Very impressive in appearance. And he was very kind; he never got hot. (Trainer Walter Kelley once recalled how he had seen "Phar Lap's people put three kids on him one day in the ring there at the winner's circle at Caliente and just walked him around with them on his back, schooling him. That shows you how calm and quiet he was. Anybody could ride him.") The day of the handicap they brought him over to the paddock two races before the big one. Can you imagine doing that with a horse today?" Threewitt asked.

Some time before the call to the post for the Caliente 'Cap — either two hours, or twenty minutes, the accounts differ — Phar Lap was saddled and Elliott boosted aboard him in the paddock under the hot Mexican sun. He was then walked "to get him accustomed to his weight," as Woodcock explained it (that impost of 129 pounds was top weight in the field, which meant Phar Lap was conceding from nine to thirty-nine pounds to his ten opponents). This development served to astound other horsemen present. Starter Cassidy came to the paddock and urged Woodcock to remove Elliott from Phar Lap, emphasizing that they were dealing with the highweight and betting favorite. But Woodcock declined, assuring Cassidy that Phar Lap was quite used to this routine and that it would not bother him in the least.

John I. Day, in his book *Call Me Horse*, wrote that "about 10 days before the race, Phar Lap sustained a quarter-crack and it was cut away and heavy bar plates put on his forefeet. On the day of the race, these were removed and he was shod with steel plates."

Phar Lap carried "a heavy Australian saddle," Day continued. "Jockey Elliott, weighing but 102 pounds, had to make up the difference to the assigned 129 with lead. Instead of carrying lead weights in the saddle, Elliott carried them inside his silk jacket.

"Before the horses were paraded to the post, Woodcock was overheard giving Elliott his riding instructions: 'When you leave the gate, canter down the stretch the first time, and when you get on the backstretch, gallop on home.'" This was the simple prelude to a performance never forgotten by those who witnessed it.

William Robertson later wrote that Caliente then "boasted the world's largest collection of starting chutes, one for every conceivable distance. The start of the Caliente Handicap was effected from the one and one-quarter mile chute, and true to his trainer's prediction, Phar Lap emerged with his field. However, he went immediately to the outside for an inspection tour of the one and one-eighth-mile chute which slanted into the track a furlong farther out, and passing the grandstand the first time he was fully fifty yards behind the pack.

"Having satisfied his (or his jockey's) curiosity, Phar Lap then bounded into the lead. From sixth place after a half mile had been run, he had moved to first before the end of 6 furlongs. Going around the home turn, Elliott permitted Reveille Boy to draw up almost alongside, then away went

Phar Lap again. He crossed the finish line eased up, two lengths clear of Reveille Boy, who was carrying 118 pounds.

"In his effortless romp, Phar Lap had set a new track record. The track was not exceptionally fast that day. Of the fifteen races on the program…none of the others was won in time anywhere near a track record. In the race immediately following Phar Lap's victory, Eddie Arcaro won on Wizardry in 2:07 1/5 for the same distance. The winner of the last race required 2:08."

Phar Lap's effort had, in the best sense, been scripted. As Walter Kelley recounted to racing writer Jim Bolus in 1988, the Phar Lap camp had announced their strategy to the world early on. "It was a peculiar thing, the orders they give on the horse," Kelley recalled. "They come on the radio three or four days before the race tellin' just how they were gonna ride him, what they were gonna do.

"There were newspapermen on the air one night," Kelley continued, "along with these reporters from Down Under. And Phar Lap's people said, 'We're gonna take him to the outside so he won't get dirt in his face and let him go slow-speed the first quarter. Now when he's at the mile pole, he'll be last, and we're gonna let him open up half-speed from the mile pole to the three-quarter pole. Then he'll be lapped on the last horse and runnin'. And we'll let him run full speed from the three-quarter pole to the half-mile pole. And he'll be in front and gallopin'.'

"That's exactly what he did," Kelley said, still amazed a half-century later. "And we had some horses in there that could really run three-quarters of a mile."

Riding a horse named Bahamas in that Caliente 'Cap was eventual Hall of Famer Johnny Longden. Bahamas carried ninety-nine pounds, thirty less than Phar Lap. "I was on a fast horse," Longden told Bolus, "and I was in front, and I looked back at the three-quarter pole and Phar Lap was at about the seven-eighths pole. When I hit the half-mile pole, he went right on by me like a freight train passin' a tramp. He was in the middle of the racetrack, and he just galloped around."

Another impressed observer that day (and future member of the Hall of Fame) was Charlie Whittingham. In a biography of him written by Jay Hovdey, the trainer stated, "I never got to see Man o' War. I was too young. But he'd have to be a helluva horse to be better than Phar Lap. He won that Caliente race running almost all the way around on the outside fence. His rider was convinced the other jocks in there were out to get them. He figured the best thing to do was not to give them the chance."

Of Phar Lap's winner's share of $50,050, Robertson wrote: "Caliente had run into financial troubles and had been forced to chop the planned purses in half, the 'hundred thousand' included. Had the race been run according to the original conditions, Phar Lap would have become the world's leading money winner — as it was, he boosted his total to $332,250 and was within what appeared to be striking distance of Sun Beau's record. Tracks all over the country were vying with one another to schedule rich races that would attract the super-horse, and Bowie offered $10,000 just to have him gallop around the track under silks."

None of these offers would ever be accepted.

———————

Following his amazing U. S. debut, Phar Lap's grand tour of this continent was initially delayed when he suffered a slight tendon injury. He was sent to the Edward Perry ranch near San Francisco to recover while plans for the rest of the racing season continued to be proposed. And it was not just action on the racetrack being discussed: On April 4, co-owner David Davis met with executives of the Metro-Goldwyn-Mayer film company and signed a contract to make a series of short films about horse racing, a series that would feature Phar Lap. One day later, all these grand plans turned to dust.

Reported *The New York Times* under a San Francisco dateline:

"Phar Lap, the sleek-coated, reddish-brown gelding brought to this country from Australia last January in the expectation of becoming the greatest money winner of all time, died of colic today on the Ed Perry Ranch at Menlo Park, near Palo Alto. Hours later sportsmen were so stunned at the suddenness of it they could scarcely believe the news.

"The 'Red Terror' was being conditioned on the Peninsula Ranch for an appearance at the Tanforan track, on the outskirts of the city, in the near future, following his sensational victory in the $50,000 added Agua Caliente Handicap.

"That race was Phar Lap's initial American appearance and it was anticipated it would be the forerunner of a season that would eclipse even the tremendous winning capacity of Willis Sharpe Kilmer's Sun Beau, greatest money winner of all time to date. Phar Lap needed only $45,000 more to pass the American champion, his total winnings being $332,250.

"The illness of the great Australian gelding was kept secret at the stable. Even a party of visiting newspapermen this morning were kept in the dark. But when they were refused permission to look at the horse suspicion was aroused and an investigation begun.

"It was afternoon, however, before an accurate guess was made as to the real trouble and the query was put directly. Attaches of the stable, with tears coursing down their cheeks, then confessed that death had claimed their charge.

"Later rumors flew the horse had been poisoned. This was immediately and emphatically discounted by Dr. Walter Nielsen, Australian veterinarian (subsequent reports identified him as Dr. Bill Neilson, or Neilsen); Trainer Tommy Woodcock and Jockey Elliott, but to remove any and all suspicion Chief of Police Frank Love of Menlo Park and Chief of Police Edward Farrell of Atherton announced that they would have Phar Lap's oats examined.

"About twenty sacks, the remainder of the original consignment brought from Australia, were stacked outside the stall. Little, if any, American food has been given to Phar Lap since his arrival.

"At the conclusion of an autopsy, Dr. Nielsen gave acute enteritis as the cause of death. He and Dr. Caesar Mascero of San Francisco found the stomach highly inflamed and perforated and agreed the fatal illness had begun at least two days before death. Dr. Nielsen said he believed alfalfa or barley covered with dew in the stable yard had been eaten by the

horse and caused poisoning because it was not properly prepared.

"David J. Davis, half owner of the horse...was in Los
Angeles at the time. Davis, a San Franciscan, started North
immediately.

"When the death had been confirmed and the restraint
had been lifted, Trainer Woodcock broke down. He threw
his arms around Phar Lap's neck and wept. Mrs. Davis, hur-
riedly called to the ranch, tried to comfort Woodcock, but
to little avail.

"Woodcock stumbled into the situation — and what
proved to be Phar Lap's fatal illness — this morning. When
he entered the stall upon awakening — he sleeps only a few
feet away, as does Jockey Elliott — the horse was lying
down. Woodcock was appalled and summoned Dr. Nielsen.

"Dr. Nielsen's cursory examination disclosed the ailment
and the veterinarian then plunged into the task of trying to
cure the condition. He bowed his head when Phar Lap drew
his last breath.

(Subsequent reports said that when Woodcock discovered
the horse in distress that morning, Phar Lap's temperature
was high. As the two veterinarians worked on him,
Woodcock later recalled, Phar Lap began to squeal with
pain. "Then he hemorrhaged terrible all over me and just
dropped down dead.")

"Davis," the account in the *Times* continued, "stated when
he came here that the horse carried no insurance as it was
impossible to place an accurate value on him. He had
expected the racer to win not less than $300,000 on the

American turf this year.

"...Among lovers of the thoroughbred few attain such a hold on the imagination that their names and fame penetrate to the general public...Man o' War was such a one a decade or more ago, and Phar Lap was rapidly gaining a similar distinction in this country after his name had become a byword from one end of Australia to the other."

(Some confusion arose over the fact that the aforementioned *The New York Times* story in its first paragraph identified colic as the cause of Phar Lap's death, then seven paragraphs later cited acute enteritis as the culprit. Actually, the two maladies are quite similar. According to Dr. Ronald C. Jensen, equine medical director of the University of California, Davis, "Colic is a general term for any kind of intestinal disorder. There are varieties of colic. Acute enteritis is an inflammation of the gut. Enteritis could be the cause of the symptoms of colic, which are abdominal pain and distress.")

In 1996, another of the few remaining witnesses to Phar Lap's final day was interviewed by racing writer Morton Cathro. Stuart Nixon, a retired newspaper executive, in 1932 had been a student at the Menlo School for Boys near the Perry ranch. He was sixteen at the time.

Nixon told Cathro: "We kids all loved Phar Lap. From our dormitory windows on the second floor we could watch him on the exercise track. And they let us pet him. He was gentle and intelligent. The day he died, several of us ran over after school just as they were finishing the post-mortem.

Men were shouting and cursing and weeping all at the same time. It was a terrible scene...Someone in the crowd said the exercise boy had let the horse graze on wet grass.

"My dad was in the dairy business at the time, and I was familiar with growing alfalfa. On those early spring mornings that year, the alfalfa was as heavy with dew as I'd ever seen it. The poor horse just swelled up and died."

The post-mortem performed by Drs. Nielsen and Mascero hours after Phar Lap's death found the horse's intestines to be inflamed, as well as his stomach and colon, and he was full of gas. However, there was no obstruction discovered in the digestive system as is usually the case with colic.

The following day, the United States Department of Agriculture launched an investigation that discovered arsenic to be present in leaves from trees on the Perry Ranch, trees that had been sprayed with insecticide. Traces of arsenic were also found in Phar Lap's liver and lungs, but in such minute quantities as not to suggest they caused the death of this large horse. The Department's report, issued April 27, identified colic as the cause of Phar Lap's death.

Co-owner Davis hired his own autopsy team headed by Dr. Karl Meyer of the University of California; it went to work on Saturday. By then, however, Phar Lap's heart — which weighed fourteen pounds, or five more than that of the average Thoroughbred — had been shipped to the Institute of Anatomy at Canberra, Australia (where it remains today), and his other organs had been buried. (Phar Lap's hide was sent to be displayed at the Melbourne Museum, where it was stuffed, put on display, and eventually served as inspiration for the poem by Peter Porter). The toxicologist on Meyer's team tested what remained for arsenic but found no trace of it. Meyer concluded that "an enormous accumulation of gas in the stomach and intestines probably killed the horse."

This conclusion did not satisfy everyone. Back in Australia, rumors persisted that Phar Lap had been intentionally poisoned. Serving to fan these flames was a story in the New Zealand *Referee* quoting one Dr. McKay as saying: "Phar Lap ate two clay pills containing arsenic, but the matter was hushed up...A well-known veterinary surgeon made investigations. It was then found that through a small window in the back wall of the stable four clay pills had been dropped on to the horse's bedding, and that Phar Lap had eaten the best part of two of these pills...The horse had begun on the third ball, but the fourth ball was untouched. When this fourth ball was taken away by the veterinary surgeon and analyzed, it was found to contain as much arsenic as would have killed two or more horses." No corroboration of Dr. McKay's version of events was ever produced

Were gangsters responsible for Phar Lap's death? Many people thought so, but owner-trainer Telford was not among them. In *The Sporting Globe* of April 13, 1932, Telford stated: "I refuse to believe that Phar Lap's end was brought about by poisoning. It would be a dreadful stigma to cast on Americans. There was no motive to kill him — and I am certain anyone who wished to would have to do it over Tommy Woodcock's dead body."

In the wake of the tragedy, Woodcock opted to stay in the States, accepting an offer from Willis Sharpe Kilmer, owner of Sun Beau, to train a string of his horses. But this association was short-lived. Woodcock returned to Australia late in the autumn of 1932. He subsequently recounted to J. M. Rohan of *The Sporting Globe* his version of the events. It was a shocker. Phar Lap had been poisoned by a mysterious criminal identified only as "The Brazilian," Woodcock stated.

"I have refused more than once to talk about it," Woodcock told Rohan, "but now…I have decided to speak the plain, ungarnished truth. I was placed in charge of a super horse who was a menace to owners and trainers of other horses — and to bookmakers as well. Phar Lap was a marked horse whose life through gallant deeds was forfeit."

Woodcock described how, from the time they first arrived in America, he feared for the safety of the horse he fondly called "Bobby." Woodcock said that "I was away from Phar Lap only for four days from the day he won the Victoria Derby until he died. I ate and slept with him. He went frantic if I was out of sight for a moment. Thus, you will understand me when I say I write of him with feeling…Phar Lap was my pal."

Woodcock had been given a letter of introduction to a Canadian farrier named Jim Smith, who worked the Caliente meetings each year. According to Woodcock, Smith "warned me to be careful of the dopers who would nobble a horse in quick time. 'Watch Phar Lap's water and feed' was Smith's constant advice. Smith said he did not know the actual doper, but he knew that a gang made it a practice, and got results…

"On the Sunday before the Handicap, Phar Lap earned

$5,000 for cantering down the straight before the crowd. When I was waiting for him to return to the enclosure, I noticed a flashily dressed fellow who had been hanging around our barn…and was known as 'The Brazilian.' He had the reputation of being a killer. 'The Brazilian' was with the toughest-looking bunch of men I have seen.

"One of Phar Lap's hoofs had split during exercise. It was bound up, and I noticed the gang watching him closely as he came into the enclosure. He was using the leg tenderly and, of course, they didn't fail to notice this."

Woodcock was with Phar Lap almost twenty-four hours a day, and his vigilance was rewarded with Phar Lap's great win. "I was much relieved," he told Rohan, adding: "There was a fearful din as he passed the winning post, and above it all I heard angry words behind me. On looking round I saw the gang, and it was evident that someone was telling 'The Brazilian' off.

"We packed our traps a few days later…Believe me, I was glad to see the end of Mexico. But we were a few days only at Menlo Park when who should I see snooping around but 'The Brazilian.' Straightaway I was on my guard, and never left Phar Lap, although I must admit I did not think it necessary to police the barn while the horse was out exercising. A few days later Phar Lap died of poisoning. I had little to go on, but I was certain that 'The Brazilian' had played a part in robbing the world of its greatest racehorse.

"The racing racketeers thought it impossible for a horse to win the Mexican classic without a solid preparation. They laid heavily against him and lost further on Dr. Freeland and others in the race…"

Woodcock said that before the Caliente race he had rarely slept more than three hours a night. The pressure of training Phar Lap had caused him to become tired and run-down. He began to take aspirin each night once they had reached California, "and I finally slept soundly at Menlo Park…With the big race over, I was inclined to relax a bit. While I slept, it no doubt was easy for 'The Brazilian' to mix poison with Phar Lap's feed.

"I knew in my heart that 'Bobby' was poisoned and had a fair idea of the perpetrator, but what was the use? Menlo Park…was inundated with analysts, inquiry agents, police, photographers, and pressmen. I realized that to voice my suspicions would involve me in endless trouble and nothing could bring 'Bobby' back to me…

"The analysts engaged by Mr. Davis declared that there was not sufficient poison found in Phar Lap to kill him, but Government analysts said that there was enough arsenate of lead found to bring about his painful end.

"…Gangsters are not placed behind bars in the States on evidence as flimsy as what I had, so I decided to keep my suspicions to myself. To have voiced them would have resulted in my following closely in the footsteps of the horse I loved."

It was during Woodcock's brief stint training for Kilmer that "The Brazilian" appeared again in the young Australian horseman's life. Woodcock described their meeting this way:

"One afternoon, while alone in the barn, I heard someone outside, and on looking up I nearly died of heart failure.

There was 'The Brazilian' in the doorway. He appeared to be taken aback. Evidently he was looking for someone else.

"I flew into a passion and rushed to the door, but he scarcely heeded my outburst. 'Get out, you murdering thief, or I'll pitchfork you,' I called out. With his right hand in his coat pocket he entered the barn and snarled, 'Another word from you and I'll drill you full of lead.'

"I was scared and speechless. I almost collapsed on a bundle of straw while he stood over me in threatening attitude and told me that if I thought I could come to America and upset his gang's plans, I had another thing coming.

"Then I was certain that my suspicions about Phar Lap's death (that he hadn't died of colic, but of poison) were well founded, but I was not prepared to hear the cool admission of a desperado who looked as though he would stop at nothing. Threatening to return if he heard of my squealing, he backed to the door, and his parting words were: 'I would have drilled you the night I fixed Phar Lap if you'd wakened.' " Shortly after this incident Woodcock's visa expired and he returned home.

Woodcock's recounting to Rohan, laden as it was with prose associated with American crime magazine stories of the '30s ("I'll fill you full of lead," etc.), caused a sensation in Australia. Nearly six decades later — fifty-seven years after Phar Lap's death, and four years after his own at age seventy-nine — another uproar arose involving Woodcock.

This occurred in September of 1989 when a story in Melbourne's The Age newspaper claimed Woodcock had *himself* accidentally killed Phar Lap by mishandling an arsenic-based appetite stimulant named Fowler's Solution.

An unnamed "source," who according to *The Age* report was "close to the Phar Lap stable," quoted Woodcock as having said, "It was a horrible mistake."

The fatal error supposedly came when Woodcock found himself running short of the feed additive which he had brought with him from Australia. To make it last longer, he mixed it with water, the source alleged. Toxicologists said that the water must be stirred well lest the arsenic base of the additive remain suspended; if not, there would be a build-up of pure arsenic. It was a concentrated dose of the poison which killed Phar Lap, according to this theory.

With Woodcock having passed away in 1985, it was left to others to defend him from this new charge — and many did. Australian trainer Bob Hoysted said, "I knew Tommy for a long time, and I can assure you he didn't poison Phar Lap." Another trainer, Geoff Murphy, termed it a "disgraceful suggestion." Richard Davis, son of Phar Lap's late owner, described it as being "sheer hogwash."

Australian racing writer Bill Whittaker commented: "I don't believe the likeable, modest Woodcock, whom I interviewed on his retirement, was a liar."

As an indication of the amazing interest in Phar Lap that still exists Down Under, this report led to the subsequent staging of a mock "trial" of Tommy Woodcock on prime time television. Evidence was presented by actors to a "jury" made up of members of the public. Their verdict: Woodcock was "not guilty." This exercise in sensationalism was deemed an embarrassment by most members of the racing community.

Another Australian who knew and admired Tommy Woodcock is Peter Tonkes, who after service in the Australian Army (attached to the American 173rd Airborne Brigade during the Vietnam War), became racing writer and form analyst for *The News* in his hometown of Adelaide. Tonkes now serves as Australian correspondent for a number of major Thoroughbred publications, including *The Blood-Horse* magazine. Said Tonkes: "Tommy had a resurgence in popularity in 1977 with a horse who was a maiden until it was 5, a wonderful old horse named Reckless. Tommy and Reckless seemed to do the 'grand tour,' winning the Sydney, Adelaide, and Brisbane Cups, all two-mile races, from March through early June.

"In the Melbourne Cup that year Reckless finished second, a length behind the Bart Cummings-trained Gold and Black. Despite Bart's enormous popularity, almost everyone wanted Woodcock's horse to win.

"Tommy Woodcock was one of the gentlest people I ever met in racing," Tonkes added. "He was not a man to be even remotely careless with the truth. His account of his experiences with 'The Brazilian,' shortly after Phar Lap's death, is entitled to be believed."

The televised "mock trial" was one indication of the continuing popularity of Phar Lap. Another, more dignified demonstration of it was the sale of a trophy in the autumn of 1999. The prize for the 1931 W. S. Cox Plate — in the form of a nineteen-carat gold cup, and the only trophy won by Phar Lap known still to be in existence — had been discovered five years earlier in a cupboard of a house belonging to one of co-owner Davis' grandchildren; it had then been shown in the Victoria museum (where Phar Lap's hide is displayed). The Davis heirs decided to sell it through Sotheby's auction house in Melbourne. Pre-sale estimates placed the trophy's value at 150,000 Australian dollars. On November 8, 1999, an unidentified Australian bidder paid 420,000 Australian dollars (about $270,000).

———————

Confronted with these the differing versions involving Woodcock, and speculations of all sorts from others of the many people fascinated by this puzzle, what is a student of the Phar Lap story to conclude concerning the cause of his death? The answer to that, probably, is that no definitive conclusion seems likely to be reached.

If the horse were intentionally poisoned, what was the motive? Revenge? That is doubtful. The only ones with such motivation might be bookies who got burned, but that seems most unlikely (they usually get it back another day, thank you).

Would some members of a potential rival horse's camp go to such vicious lengths? As Eddie Arcaro once put it, scoffing at that possible scenario, "I don't know why anybody would think that. Americans would have no reason to kill him. We like champions too much."

Was it colic-inducing feed, or an accidental arsenic overdose, or the fatal effects of an insecticide that killed Phar Lap? Severe bloat precipitated by the ingestion of the dew-heavy grass? Could it have been — as some current-day veterinarians have speculated — a case of Colitis X, rare now and even rarer and harder to recognize then, a disease characterized by colon inflammation and, eventually, hemorrhage of the colon wall?

As large as he was in life, the mystery that surrounded Phar Lap's death almost dwarfs even his reputation as a racehorse. (It is interesting to note that Noble Threewitt, to this day an astute judge of horses, is less profligate with accolades as other witnesses quoted above. Threewitt commented, "Phar Lap was a great horse at that time, but I'm not sure he would be considered a great horse today. There weren't as many good horses around then as there are now. But he had tremendous talent, he had a great presence, there is no doubt about that.")

Based on his knowledge of Woodcock's character and reputation, Peter Tonkes does not discount the tale of the mysterious "Brazilian." Yet, in Tonkes' opinion, "Few in Australia today believe that Phar Lap was poisoned."

But there are some, as Dr. Jack Robbins can attest. Robbins' tie to Phar Lap extends back to 1932, when he was a boy of ten living in northern California. For years, Robbins has been one of the nation's foremost veterinarians and is a past president of the American Association of Equine Practitioners.

"Phar Lap contributed enormously to me choosing the veterinary profession," Robbins said. "He was a great hero of mine. I was already interested in horses — in fact, a few years later, when I was fourteen, I started working on horse ranches during my summer vacations from school — and I was intrigued by what things might affect these beautiful animals. It is a subject that has fascinated me ever since," said the semi-retired Robbins, who still makes annual trips to Europe to examine potential purchases for major Thoroughbred owners.

"As to what caused his death," Robbins continued, "well, from everything I've read and heard over the years, the obvious conclusion is that he got sick from grazing in wet alfalfa. I don't think there is any reason to believe that he was intentionally killed.

"But you can't tell that to some Aussies," Robbins said with a laugh. "On Breeders' Cup Day of 1999, I met two visitors from Down Under at Santa Anita and spent quite a bit of time with them. In the course of the afternoon, the subject of Phar Lap came up. They were very pleasant people, mind you, but they were quite adamant — 'You Americans killed Phar Lap, no doubt of that.' There was no way of changing their opinion."

> *"In Australia children cried to hear the news...*
> *It was, as people knew, a plot of life:*
> *To live in strength, to excel and die too soon...*
> *It is Australian innocence to love*
> *The naturally excessive and be proud*
> *Of a thoroughbred gelding who ran fast."*

Strange Undercurrents

Lost at sea. Those three small words used in this combination make for one of the saddest sentences in any language, ranking with "died in childbirth," or "killed in action."

In the late winter of 1948, they were used to describe the combined fate of one of America's most prominent jockeys, a popular and successful trainer, and a Canadian industrialist with ties to Thoroughbred racing.

Their names, respectively, were Albert Snider, C. H. (Tobe) Trotter, and Don Fraser. On the evening of Friday, March 5, 1948, these three friends went fishing in the Florida Keys. They were never seen again.

The fishing party, made up of the missing trio and another three friends of theirs, had left Miami on the morning of March 3 aboard the yacht *Evelyn K.* They reached lower Matacumbe Key that afternoon, where they took on fuel. A skiff owned by Snider was carried on the bow of the yacht. At Matacumbe they rented a rowboat, which they towed behind the *Evelyn K.*, so all six men could fish off the yacht at the same time if they wished.

Shortly before 4 p.m. on March 3, the *Evelyn K.* left lower Matacumbe for Oxford Bank and Sandy Key, about twenty-seven miles to the northwest. The next morning, they moved to a point a half-mile or so from Marker 10. They fished all day, covering nearly all of the area in the flats where Snider, Trotter, and Fraser would disappear the next night.

On the fateful Friday, the men fished in the morning and napped in the afternoon. They were awakened by the radio broadcast of the feature race from Tropical Park. Almost immediately after the race had concluded, Snider, Trotter, and Fraser set out for some more flat-water fishing.

Their subsequent baffling disappearance was reported this way by *Daily Racing Form* in a story datelined March 8, 1948, from Miami: *

"At a late hour today hope was waning for the safety of Al Snider, Tobe Trotter and Don Fraser, who have been missing off the Florida Keys since Friday night.

"U.S. Navy, Coast Guard and civilian planes, blimps, boats and trucks continued their tireless search through the wide expanse of water and islands south of the tip of the Florida peninsula. The men were reported lost in a small boat Friday night, while 50-mile-an-hour winds churned the sea. They had set out from the yacht *Evelyn K.*, which had been anchored near Craig, a small town on the overseas highway, and no one has seen them since.

"The Coast Guard air-sea rescue service is directing the search. Commander Richard Baxter said dozens of private yachts joined the wide-spread operation. Baxter said there was little chance the party had been blown ashore on one of the many small keys in Florida Bay because 'we've looked over every yard of those Keys time and again.'

"Members of the Florida Air Pilot's Association volunteered to join the hunt and were assigned areas by the Coast Guard. Everglades National Park superintendent Daniel B. Beard placed Park Service boats into service and they are covering the Cape Sable and Shark River areas.

"Lawrence Boido, of Coral Gables, was aboard the yacht *Evelyn K.* when the three men shoved off in the small boat. Boido said he couldn't understand what happened to the men from the time the sun set at 6:30 Friday until the storm hit at 9 p.m. From where he was on the yacht, Boido saw them casting until the sun went down. 'Then they should have started to come back in,' Boido said. 'I just can't figure what they were doing for the two hours or more until the storm hit.'

"Snider, who recently supplanted Doug Dodson as the Calumet Farm rider, won the Flamingo Stakes at Hialeah Park aboard Citation. He was married to the former Miss Dorothy Wenzel. They have a daughter, Nancy, six, and live at 749 Pine Crest Drive, Miami Springs.

"Snider, a native of Calgary, Alberta, is a graduate of the Ontario racing circuit...He served his apprenticeship riding on Ontario tracks several years ago and later became affiliated with the Widener establishment, his first major assignment. Obviously an opportunist and not lacking in talent, he has remained among the top-flight ranks since that time.

"Trotter...is a partner in the ownership of the yacht *Evelyn K.* with John B. Campbell, the Jockey Club handicapper; C.

A. O'Neil Jr.; and others. A widely respected conditioner, he learned his trade from his father, the late Edward Trotter, who died in Miami two years ago. Trotter is about 49 years old and has four children. One son, Tom, is employed in the racing secretary's office at Tropical Park and also assists Campbell at the New York tracks.

"Trotter has 13 horses in his care at Hialeah for Alfred de Cozen's Short Brook Farm, Fair Stable, B. W. Miller, L. Lewis and W. W. Stone. His boyhood was spent in New Orleans and Kentucky, but in recent years Trotter has divided his time between New York, New England and Florida.

"Donald Fraser, proprietor of the Peerless Engineering Company which manufactures dies and gauges in Toronto, was a long-time devotee of the turf sport in Canada, according to his business associates, but otherwise was not an active participant as an owner. He was a member of the Ontario Jockey Club and the Thorncliffe Racing and Breeding Association.

"Churches in Greater Miami offered prayers yesterday (Sunday) for the safety of the three men. Warren Wright, owner of Calumet Farm, the employer of Al Snider, chartered several of the many planes which are searching for the missing trio."

Helping to finance the search was a fund established by the Jockeys' Guild, Horsemen's Benevolent and Protective Association, Hialeah Park, and the Gables Racing Association. Each organization contributed $10,000.

But the search — one of the most extensive ever carried out in waters off Florida — was finally abandoned at nightfall on Tuesday, March 9. Among those ordered by the Coast Guard to "cease further operations" in the rescue attempt was jockey Porter Roberts. A close friend of Snider's, Roberts had taken off his mounts at Tropical Park to join the fruitless effort, flying his own plane over a wide area. Roberts reluctantly resumed riding on Wednesday.

The jockey's wife refused to give up hope that her husband would be found. "I know he is alive," Dorothy Snider told the press on Wednesday. "He can swim like a fish. He is strong. Dieting to keep his weight down would permit him to live a long time without food. He was in an unsinkable plywood boat equipped with five life-saving pillows. I can't believe anything except that he is alive."

Two days later, *Daily Racing Form* writer Bob Horwood provided what the paper described as "the first complete and authentic account of the mysterious disappearance"[*] of the three men.

"Last Friday evening at 6:27 o'clock," Horwood began, "jockey Al Snider, trainer C. H. (Tobe) Trotter and Canadian manufacturer Don Fraser were visible from the deck of the yacht *Evelyn K.* as they fished from Snider's 13-foot plywood skiff in shallow water to the northwest. Lawrence Boido, George Woods and B. W. Miller all saw the flickering reflection of the setting sun on Snider's metal casting rod from the deck of the yacht as they watched the trio through powerful binoculars. Two minutes later, the three men vanished in the inky darkness.

"The mystery of their disappearance became increasingly impenetrable as Miller, in whose name the yacht is registered, and Boido gave *Daily Racing Form* their account of events leading up to the apparent tragedy.

"When last seen, Snider, Trotter and Fraser were only about a mile and a quarter from the *Evelyn K.* There was no wind and no rain. The winds began to rise at about 8:30 p.m., reaching a peak velocity of approximately 30 miles per hour two hours later. No rain fell in the vicinity that night or the next day.

"When the trio left the yacht a few minutes after 5 o'clock, Trotter said they would be back in a little more than an hour to partake of a fish chowder which he had been preparing during the afternoon while Miller, Boido, Snider, Fraser and Woods all napped after fishing all that morning.

"The skiff was powered by an outboard motor that was in excellent condition, and a five-gallon gasoline can in the boat contained about two and a half gallons of reserve fuel. Also in the skiff was a thermos jug containing water and it, like the gasoline can, would have floated.

"There were three life preservers in the boat, 75 feet of rope, and a small anchor which Trotter, an experienced fisherman, could have used to prevent the skiff from drifting... The skiff was equipped with good oars, extra spark plugs, and a coffee pot and large pail that could have been used for bailing.

"The men also had three cans of beer with them. There was no other drinking at any time on the trip. They were within easy swimming distance of land (in an estimated four feet of water, making even wading possible). Snider and Trotter were excellent swimmers, while Fraser could also swim but was suffering from a heart condition that was presumed to be mild.

"Darkness came suddenly and completely. Miller immediately turned on all the cabin lights (of the *Evelyn K.*), then went to the deck atop the deck house, where he operated a revolving searchlight casting a beam visible for several miles. Miller continued to operate the light, spelled by Boido and Woods, throughout the night. There were also three red flasher lights, strung some 18 feet above the water, in the space of 12 miles in the area. Trotter, who knew these waters thoroughly, was familiar with these red lights and their positions.

"Miller, Boido and Woods are completely at a loss to understand what happened in the two hours between sunset and the first impact of wind. Their first impulse as they waited for the missing men was mild anger, as it was understood that they would have an early dinner, and the aroma of the sauce Trotter had prepared had whetted their appetites. Anxiety came with the wind and the sauce was tossed over the side.

"There could be no question of moving the *Evelyn K.* that night, as it remained a beacon for the three fishermen. When there was no sign of Snider, Trotter or Fraser at dawn, the *Evelyn K.* was moved toward Sandy Key. Luther Weeks and his brother, two young mullet fishermen, were reached on Sandy Key and reported that they had seen the skiff just before sunset. Luther Weeks recalled that he remarked to his brother just before darkness fell: 'That little dude must have pulled back to the big boat in a hurry.' The sea was calm at the time. Captain C. F. Smith, of the motor vessel *Junalaska*, who was a half mile away, also reported that he had seen the trio before sunset, while a man on an ice boat anchored east of Sandy Key also said he had seen them at that time.

"Miller contacted the Coast Guard by means of a ship-to-shore radio on *Junalaska*...The first Coast Guard planes appeared in less than two hours. Later, planes appeared by the dozens, as well as blimps, and boats."

Horwood reported that none of the three surviving members of the fishing party — Miller, Boido and Woods — had any explanation of the disappearance which they accepted as plausible.

"John B. Campbell, a co-owner of the *Evelyn K.*, suggested that possibly Trotter had become confused and headed north up the West Coast, toward Ponce de Leon Bay. (But) they could not have drifted in that direction, as the wind would have taken them south toward Key West until Saturday, then carried them out into the Gulf of Mexico," Horwood concluded.

The only other possibly plausible explanation taken seriously was that the skiff had somehow vanished among the dense Mangrove Islands of the area.

George Woods, who was Al Snider's agent, later told friends that he had wanted to join the jockey and the other two men on the skiff that afternoon. "I tried to go with them," Woods said, "but Al wouldn't let me on the little boat. He told me, 'The boat would be too crowded. Besides, you were out fishing this morning.' "

Years later, Dorothy Snider told Turf writer Luther Evans of the *Miami Herald* that "Al had missed the boat (the

Evelyn K.), the previous time that a group went down into the Keys on it. And he told me, 'If it wasn't for Tobe, I wouldn't be going on this fishing trip. But I disappointed he and the others the last time.' My daughter Nancy and I kissed Al goodbye at the pier," Mrs. Snider said, "and that was the last we ever saw of him."

Missing the trip was Snider's fellow reinsman, Eddie Arcaro. He told Evans, "Albert had phoned me in California and urged me to fly back and make this fishing trip with them. But I had to ride a horse in a stakes the Monday that they shoved off from Miami — it was closing day at Santa Anita," Arcaro said.

On March 13, eight days after the mens' disappearance, the empty skiff was found on tiny Rabbit Key, some ten miles south of Everglades City. It was undamaged. The outboard motor and oars were missing. There was no trace of the men.

––––––––––

Besides jockey Porter Roberts, there were other racetrackers involved in the search. Flying his own plane over the area was Jimmy Jones who, along with his father, Ben, trained the Calumet Farm horses. Calumet owner Warren Wright had only recently signed Snider to be regular rider of this powerful string that was headed by Citation.

More than a half-century later Jimmy Jones, who turned ninety-three in 1999, remembered Snider with fondness and respect. "Albert was a great rider, just as good as Eddie Arcaro," Jones said. "He had a good personality; he was always very congenial. He conducted himself like a professional. Albert fit Citation real good and Doug Dodson, who was Calumet's contract rider, didn't like that. When it became clear that Albert was going to be Citation's rider, Dodson got mad and turned in his papers. That's when Albert was signed to ride for us."

Snider rode Citation nine times — five races when the Bull Lea colt was two, four the next year — and never lost on him. They first joined forces in Citation's career debut at old Havre de Grace in Maryland on April 22, 1947. Next came an allowance score at Pimlico, also in Maryland, then another one back at Havre de Grace. On August 16 Citation made his stakes bow at old Washington Park near Chicago. Steve Brooks was aboard that day, and Citation finished second to his stablemate Bewitch, eventual two-year-old filly champion. It was Citation's only loss in nine starts as a juvenile.

Snider then was aboard Citation for winning trips in the Futurity Trial and Futurity at Belmont Park in New York, but Dodson rode him in the final start of his first championship season, the Pimlico Futurity.

When the 1948 racing season got under way, Snider guided Citation to four straight wins at Hialeah, including the Seminole Handicap and Everglades and Flamingo Stakes. The latter event, which Citation captured by a widening six lengths, was run on February 28 — less than a week prior to the fatal fishing trip.

Recalled Jimmy Jones, "Albert had considerable experience before he came to us. He was a very intelligent rider, very polished. After Dodson quit, I moved pretty quick to get Albert on the payroll. He could ride a front-runner; he could come from behind — whatever fit the situation or the horse, he could do. I also liked him as a person. He was real clean-cut, a nice-looking young fella with great work habits.

"Albert rode Citation better than anybody," Jones continued. "He fit him perfect. Albert rode with his hands close together on the horses' manes, Arcaro did, too; neither of them used a wide cross. Most jockeys do use a wide cross of the reins, and some horses don't like that, and Citation was one of those horses. When Steve Brooks rode Citation as a two-year-old, Citation didn't like it at all."

After Snider had guided Citation to victory in his seasonal debut on February 2, 1948, Calumet owner Wright put some pressure on Jones. "Mr. Wright got into an argument with a friend of his, another owner and breeder, Eddie (Edward S.) Moore," Jones said. "Mr. Moore had a nice horse he was pretty high on, one who had won very impressively on a day that Mr. Wright and I were both there. Mr. Moore was proud of his horse, and he said so. Mr. Wright said to him as we were walking out of the track that day, 'Wait till you see what we're going to do with *our* horse.' He meant Citation. What he had in mind was to run Citation in the Seminole Handicap for just his second start of the season.

"Well, these horses next ran on February 11. Mr. Moore's horse, Mahlima, was in the fifth race on the program, an allowance race. Citation was in the sixth, which was the Seminole. I told Albert before the race, 'Citation won't win. Just take care of him.' I wanted to get a race into Citation before the Flamingo. My thinking was, hell, Citation wasn't even three years old yet — he was a foal of April 19 — and here he was going seven-eighths against some top sprinters, older ones, too — Delegate (who would be voted co-champion sprinter the following year), Buzz Fuzz, horses like that. No matter what Mr. Wright wanted, I didn't think Citation could do it that day.

"I was wrong. Citation won. He broke good, and Albert had him up between a couple of those good old horses, and Citation left them after the first quarter and went on to win very easily.

"After the race, I said to Albert, 'How did you get along with those tough old sprinters?' Albert said, 'Mr. Jones, after the first quarter of a mile we were just playing with those horses.' That is when I really started to think that Citation was going to be a great horse. He also showed up Mr. Moore's horse, who lost his race, and that made the old man (Wright) very happy.

"It was just a shame Albert couldn't have gone on with Citation to win the Triple Crown and Horse of the Year and all those races. Losing a fine young man like that when he was in his prime, well, it just made us all sick."

———————

Slightly more than one year after the tragedy, New York newspaper columnist Dan Parker produced a speculative piece for *The American Weekly*. Parker's specialty was sensationalistic stories, and this one fit the bill. He suggested that Snider and his two companions had been victims of an underworld plot.

Wrote Parker in July of 1949: "Over a year has passed since Jockey Albert Snider and two companions on a fishing trip were swallowed up by the Florida Keys, and the mystery of their disappearance, darker than ever, now has taken on sinister angles. Miami's underworld is whispering stories that Citation's jockey met his death through gangland vengeance because he wouldn't obey the orders of a gambling syndicate when riding the Calumet Flier. Far-fetched as this may seem, there are aspects of this strange case which lend support to the foul-play theory.

"The only light ever thrown on the mystery," Parker continued, "was the scant testimony of the last men to see the fishing party before it was swallowed up, as if by a sea monster (Luther Weeks, the man on the ice boat, and Capt. Smith of the *Junalaska*)...Two months later, Mrs. Snider's maid (Rosa Doon), engaged in packing the missing jockey's clothes for shipment, found $4,000 in cash and a check for $295 in a shirt Snider had worn. Mrs. Snider had no knowledge of its (the money's) existence. Where this came from has never been explained."

(Actually, it *had* been explained by Dorothy Snider, who told *Daily Racing Form* on May 18, 1948, that "Al was always hiding money around the house.")

Parker concluded his provocative piece with this paragraph: "With the nation's underworld concentrated in the Miami area during the winter racing season, jockeys are constantly being approached by gangland betting syndicates and offered big money to ride to their orders. Al Snider was a straight shooter. Did his honesty cost him his life in that baffling triple tragedy?"

———————

Jimmy Jones put no credence in Dan Parker's gangland theory. Neither did Thomas E. (Tommy) Trotter, son of Tobe Trotter, who was twenty-one years old when his father disappeared. Tommy, who was working for racing secretary Francis P. Dunne at Tropical Park that winter, went on to have a long and distinguished career as a racing secretary, director of racing and steward at major tracks all over the nation.

"When he was lost, my dad was just forty-seven, not older as reported in some places," Tommy told the author in 2000. "He had trained for twenty-five years in the Midwest, New England, and Florida. He had a public stable and he trained a few stakes-placed horses, including Michaelo and a horse named Silent Witness that at one point was considered a Kentucky Derby prospect."

Trotter said that he did not know Snider well, but that his father did, "and liked him a lot. Snider had a good reputation and was quite popular and a very, very good rider. Dad was good friends with a lot of jockeys and ex-jocks, like Eddie Arcaro and the Hanford brothers, Ira and Carl. The other man lost, Don Fraser, was another real gentleman. He and his wife came to Florida each winter. That is where they met and became friends of my parents."

Tommy said his father's experience with boats "went back to his childhood. He was raised in New Orleans, where his father, who was quite a successful trainer, kept a boat. My dad grew up around boats and horses. After training hours in Florida, if Dad wasn't running a horse that afternoon, he'd be down at the boatyard. My late brother Jake (Tarlton) and I spent a lot of time on the water with my father."

This background, said Tommy, "makes it even more of a mystery as to what happened that day. The fellows on the *Evelyn K.* could see them fishing from the skiff, see them quite well. My father was very, very conservative and cautious about boating. He respected the sea. Anytime he saw a storm coming up — at the first sign of even a minor one — he would tell us, 'We're going in.'

"I was at work at Tropical Park that day and I saw that it was a bad storm coming through, kind of an unusual one in that it came up so quickly. The sky turned dark in a hurry.

"Later, I tried to picture them in the skiff. I tried to imagine what happened. I had been in that skiff with my dad many, many times. Their options would be trying to get back to the *Evelyn K.*, or heading to one of the nearby islands. There was an island quite close to where they were fishing.

"Maybe the outboard motor didn't work. But, even if that were the case, why didn't they row to an island? Al Snider and my dad were both in excellent physical condition. I know Don Fraser had a heart ailment. Maybe something happened to him that caused Snider and Dad to concentrate on that problem and lose sight of the impending danger. The water is shallow in that area of the Keys, but the locals will tell you that it can get very rough."

Trotter's boss, Francis Dunne, told his young assistant to "go ahead and take whatever time off you need from work," Tommy recalled. Tommy was soon joined in Florida by his brother Charlie, a student at Notre Dame.

Said Tommy, "Al de Cozen, an auto dealer and owner-breeder from New Jersey who was a great friend of my father's, chartered two boats to aid in the search. Even after the Coast Guard declared Dad and the others lost after a very large area had been combed, we kept searching. My brother Charlie and I were in one boat, while de Cozen, C. J. Edwards, and my Uncle Hap (Harold Trotter) were in the other.

"We searched every day, from morning till night, for two straight weeks. We just did not want to give up hope. We never found anything. It was extremely hard on the families, when there were no answers, no closure.

"Dorothy Snider hired a private investigator. He was from Miami, I believe, and he kind of took over supervision of the searching along the coast lines. As it turned out, he was a crook — he pretended to discover evidence every now and then, stuff that he had actually planted himself, just to keep his salary coming in. He was finally found out and then fired. That was a pretty mean trick on all the survivors, rais-ing false hopes as he did."

(Also during those days, some so-called prankster signed notes "Al S." and placed them in a bottle that supposedly washed ashore in the search area, causing a flurry of excite-ment until the notes were established as being phony.)

"Dad had a life insurance policy," Trotter went on, "not a big one, but enough to warrant investigation by the insur-ance company. Al Snider was known to carry a lot of cash with him, and there were rumors of foul play. But there was never anything remotely resembling proof of that. The investigator from the insurance company was very thorough. He couldn't find anything to support any of the 'sinister' theories that Dan Parker came up with. We just will never know what happened to those men that day."

There was another mysterious occurrence, Trotter said, "the day after the disappearance. I got a phone call at the house. The operator said the call was from Havana, Cuba. The phone connection was terrible, and all I heard was a voice — one that I did not recognize — ask, 'Are you Tommy Trotter?' I said 'Yes.' But before I could ask who was calling, or anything else, the line went dead. I didn't know anybody in Cuba. We waited for days, but whoever that was never called again."

On May 17, 1948, Dorothy Snider received a check for $4,170 from Eddie Arcaro and Calumet Farm owner Warren Wright as her late husband's "share" of Citation's purse from the Kentucky Derby. Arcaro gave half of his riding fee; Wright matched that amount in this gift to the widow.

As Arcaro pointed out to Luther Evans in 1980, "If that boat hadn't gone down, it would have been Al Snider winning the Kentucky Derby and Triple Crown on Citation, not Eddie Arcaro. He would have been the top rider in money winnings for at least the next four or five years, not Eddie Arcaro.

"I wound up with all of Albert's horses — Citation, Coaltown, Bewitch, all of them. It was a cruel fate for Albert."

————————

Unfortunately, Albert Snider was not unique among jockeys as the victim of a waterway mishap. In 1986, Martin Arnold, a one-time leading rider at old Latonia who had been in action at the River Downs meeting, died in a grisly boating accident. The twenty-seven-year-old Arnold and trainer Jocko Rosello were killed on the Ohio River. Said *The Blood-Horse* report at the time: "It is believed the men left on an 18-foot motorboat from a riverfront restaurant late on Aug. 11 and that the boat collided with a barge early on Aug. 12. The motorboat submerged under the barge on impact and was not discovered until the barge was uncoupled in Louisville, Ky."

Then there was the mysterious case of former jockeys William McKeever, age twenty-nine, and Steve Miller, thirty-six, who were killed in a boating accident in Florida in late February of 1982. The men, both of whom had been exercising horses at the Florida Downs (now Tampa Bay Downs) meeting, were sailing in Tampa Bay when the accident occurred. There were no witnesses to this event.

McKeever was the first apprentice to ride in the Preakness Stakes, finishing third aboard Nodouble in the 1968 renewal won by Forward Pass. He had won the Arkansas Derby earlier in the year with Nodouble. After increased weight cut short his jockey career, McKeever turned to training. He was subsequently involved with two notable horses.

Tom Morgan, who for years has been the agent for Chicago riding mainstay Randall Meier, was making his living as a racetrack publicist in the late 1970s. That is when he got to know McKeever, who, Morgan said, "looked just like Charles Manson. But he was nothing like that madman. Billy was extremely personable and likeable.

"Billy bought a horse named Good La Quinta for the Chicago owner Augie Stella," Morgan continued. "Stella was his major owner. They bought the horse from Marion H. Van Berg in 1977, and he went on to win two or three stakes at Washington Park. But Good La Quinta was more famous for drinking a six-pack of Strohs beer every day. I was working in publicity at Washington that meeting, and we got a lot of mileage out of 'the beer-drinking horse.' Actually, most horses would drink beer if you let them — they like the taste of the hops and barley."

Before his success with Good La Quinta, Morgan recalled, "Billy had a brush with the Boston Mafia, something that was a complete surprise to him. I was doing publicity at Hazel Park then, and Billy was training there. A horse shipped in from Suffolk Downs, where she'd lost the only start of her career, a race for $5,000 maidens. She was entered at Hazel in a $5,000 maiden claimer. Billy saw this filly in the *Racing Form* and noticed that the jock who had ridden her first time out was coming all the way in from Suffolk to ride — in a maiden claimer, mind you! Billy said to me, 'I think they held this horse at Suffolk, but they're going for the money here — that's why they're bringing in their jock. She might be worth something.' Billy dropped in a claim for the filly on Augie Stella's behalf.

"There was no betting action on the horse that day, and she ran out of the money again. The jock had evidently come in to hold her again. Billy puts the halter on her and gets the horse back to his barn where, a few minutes later, a big black car rolls up. The window opens, and a guy says to Billy, 'Mr.____ (mentioning the name of a Boston Mafia bigshot) wants his horse back.'

"Billy is stunned, but he recovers, and gives this guy a story about how he can't possibly give up the horse — that he's just claimed it for his main owner, he's obligated to Augie and can't do this to him, and so on. Then he says to the guy, 'Let me take her to Chicago and you can bet her next time out there. I'll still have the horse, and your boss can get his money.' The guy thinks over this proposition and gives Billy the okay. But before he drives away, he emphasizes, 'Mr.____ don't want no excuses.'

"So Billy ships to Sportsman's Park and finds a race for her a couple of weeks later. She wires the field and pays $11, and Billy never heard from Mr.____ or his representatives again. Which was pretty amazing, because this horse was Powerless, who went on to become a stakes winner of about a quarter-million dollars for Augie Stella. Augie later sold her as a broodmare prospect, got a good price, too. Powerless was the best horse Billy McKeever trained."

In Morgan's opinion, "Billy McKeever's death was surrounded by a cloud of mystery. There were storm warnings out that day in Tampa. Nobody could ever figure out the reason why he and Steve Miller would have just gone out fishing in that kind of weather. They found Miller's body right away, Billy's about four days later.

"Nobody has ever come up with a good explanation of what happened that day in Tampa Bay."

Red McDaniel's
Sudden Leap

———◇———

"They said Red McDaniel had everything to live for, and it sure looked like it. But I guess he didn't think so."

After offering that observation Robert Lee (Bobby) Baird leaned back in his chair in the Hawthorne racing secretary's office, shaking his head from side to side. Although he was many years removed from the spring afternoon during which he'd last seen the man who was then one of America's best-known and successful trainers, Baird's memory was as fresh as the next day's racing entries that were being recorded behind the nearby counter.

"To this day I don't understand why Red McDaniel jumped off that bridge," Baird said. "It was the damnedest thing then, and it's still the damnedest thing now."

On May 5, 1955, Baird was a veteran jockey in his fourth year of campaigning on the West Coast racetracks. His career interrupted by service in World War II with Gen. George Patton's U. S. Third Army ("I drove the first Jeep onto Utah Beach in the Normandy invasion," he proudly recalled), the tough little Texan was just starting to come into his own as a rider. Amazingly enough, Baird would chalk up more than 2,000 winners after he turned forty-two — an age by which the vast majority of reinsmen have long retired. Baird concluded his thirty-nine-year career at age sixty-two in 1982 with a total of 3,749 wins from 24,822 mounts. Since 1985 Bobby has served as agent for his son, E. T. (Eddie) Baird, a prominent member of the Chicago riding colony.

"I went out to California in the fall of 1951," Bobby Baird continued. "I got to know Red McDaniel not long after that, but I never rode a horse for him until the day he died. I wish I could have hooked up with him, though — the man won a ton of races. He was a top, top trainer, a guy like Bob Baffert or Wayne Lukas today."

Baird's deeply lined and usually animated face was momentarily still, his lively eyes narrowed as he reflected on the events of that May day in 1955 at Golden Gate Fields in Albany, California.

"I rode a filly for Red McDaniel in the third race that day. In the paddock Red told me, 'Bobby, this little filly hasn't done much running, but she could be alright.' He was just as calm, as normal as could be when he talked to me. I think the filly finished fourth — I know I didn't win with her — and I didn't see Red after the race.

"That was my last mount of the day, so I got dressed and drove over to Trader Vic's to have an early dinner. A waitress I knew came up to my table and said, 'I thought you'd want to know about Red McDaniel.' I just looked at her. I had no idea what she was talking about. Then she told me he had killed himself jumping off the San Francisco Bay Bridge.

"I think I dropped my drink. I said, 'That can't be, I just saw the man an hour or so ago and he was fine.' I went up to the bar and the bartender let me use the phone there. I called the *San Francisco Examiner*, and sure enough, that's what had happened. I don't believe I tasted any of my dinner that night."

———————

McDaniel's shocking death was front-page news in many newspapers across the United States, including *Daily Racing Form*, whose northern California correspondent, Kent Cochran, reported the story on May 6, 1955:*

Robert Hyatt McDaniel, 44, America's leading trainer for the last five years, is dead. He destroyed himself late yesterday afternoon by leaping from the highest span of the San Francisco Bay Bridge only minutes after saddling a winner at Golden Gate Fields.

McDaniel's suicide stunned California racing circles, as it must have stunned horse people everywhere. Scores of friends had chatted with him during the afternoon and found him as quiet, retiring and smilingly pleasant as usual. They were dumfounded on hearing the report of his self-destruction — so much so that they believed the report a tragic error or canard — until grim confirmation forced its acceptance. Then their dazed confusion turned to mingled bewilderment and perplexity, for no tenable motive was at once apparent.

The fabulously successful trainer had saddled

horses in the first, second and fifth races and watched them lose. He then saddled Aptos in the sixth, the Sinaloa Pagent Purse, climbed the stairs through the grandstand to the clubhouse, nodding pleasantly to acquaintances in the big crowd, walked out the gate to his car and drove away — to death.

Aptos, under jockey Ralph Neves (whose nickname was one of the most ringing in racing — "The Portuguese Pepperpot"), won the sixth race. As Neves guided Aptos into the winner's circle at about 4:30 that afternoon, McDaniel was driving his beige 1954 Cadillac south along the East Shore Freeway to the great bridge that connects the cities of Oakland and San Francisco. He paid the toll and headed west across the bay, above the shallow stretch of water east of Yerba Buena and then past the mid-bay point of Treasure Island, site of a world's fair fifteen years earlier.

When McDaniel's car reached the high point of the bridge, above the Bay's deepest channel, he brought it to a halt in the outside lane. Moving rapidly, he exited the car and headed for the nearby railing of the bridge. Then, without any hesitation whatsoever, McDaniel climbed on top of the railing and propelled himself into space. Moments later he hit the waters of the Bay hundreds of feet below, dead upon impact. The time was 4:35 p.m. — exactly fifteen minutes after he had tightened the girth on Aptos and departed the Golden Gate paddock.

Looking on in horrified amazement as McDaniel committed suicide were three men whose cars had followed his Cadillac onto the bridge. The third car in line belonged to trainer W. J. (Buddy) Hirsch, who recognized McDaniel as he moved from his car to the railing. But McDaniel acted so quickly that neither his fellow horseman nor the other two witnesses had an opportunity to try and stop him. "Buddy Hirsch said he couldn't believe what he was seeing," Bobby Baird recalled. "He said they never had a chance, it all happened so quick." One of the men used an emergency phone located on the bridge to alert the authorities. Twenty-four minutes after his fatal leap, McDaniel's body was retrieved from the Bay by the U.S. Coast Guard.

Police removed McDaniel's Cadillac from the bridge, which had become laden with curious onlookers. The car's windshield bore a Golden Gate Fields parking sticker. In the car they found papers which identified the owner, as well as a reported $3,000 worth of good, uncashed mutuel tickets from the previous day's races. There was no suicide note. By early evening, other friends of McDaniel had officially identified the body. A search of the dead man's clothes revealed that he had jumped to his death with his stopwatch in his pocket.

Surviving America's leading trainer, whose net worth was later estimated to be nearly a million dollars, were his wife, Evelyn; and their five-year-old son, Terry Lee, and daughter, Carole Ann, four.

Red McDaniel's rise to the top of American racing was hardly meteoric. The native of Enumclaw, Washington, a small town some forty-five miles southwest of Seattle, was by no means born with a silver halter in his hand. Member of a family of very modest means, McDaniel left home as a young teenager to seek employment. Years of hard work and scuffling on the racetracks of the West preceded his arrival at the pinnacle of his profession.

McDaniel's first job in racing was as an exercise rider. The freckle-faced, redheaded youngster eventually grew to be five feet, eight inches, very tall for a professional jockey, and his brief riding career was cut short by increasing weight. It was followed by a stint as a jockey's agent. McDaniel subsequently took out a trainer's license and put together a small public stable, the nucleus of one that would grow increasingly powerful in the years following World War II and dominate in number of races won.

The first of McDaniel's five consecutive national training championships — only Hirsch Jacobs (seven in a row) and H. Guy Bedwell (six) had earned more successive titles — came in 1950 when he saddled the winners of 156 races. McDaniel upped the ante after that, winning 164 races in 1951, 168 in 1952, a then-world record 211 in 1953 (the first year any trainer had exceeded the 200-win mark), and 206 in 1954.

In addition to the 905 victories during that span, McDaniel's purses-won totals also placed him high in the national rankings each year. From 1950 through 1954 his trainees earned $3,140,978, which was major money in those days. At the time of his death in 1955, McDaniel's stable had won forty-eight races and $343,850 — in other words, a typically good year in progress. (McDaniel's career totals were 1,143 wins and purses of $4,072,725).

McDaniel's second of five championships, in 1952, was the

hardest won. He had battled for the lead with Willie Molter (who would later train the great Round Table) for most of the season. It wasn't until the last two days of the Santa Anita meeting in late December that McDaniel edged away, finishing five wins ahead of his arch-rival.

"That was a very exciting competition," recalled Leon Rasmussen in a 1999 interview. Rasmussen launched *Daily Racing Form*'s widely read "Bloodlines" column in 1950 and contributed to its popularity for nearly four decades before his retirement in 1987. Co-author of the 1999 book *Inbreeding to Superior Females*, Rasmussen was not only an expert on equine genetic patterns and influences but a keen observer of California racing. He well remembered Red McDaniel's abruptly abbreviated career.

"McDaniel had a large stable — he probably carried an average of at least fifty head for as many as a dozen and a half owners — but his strength wasn't just in numbers," Rasmussen said. "McDaniel believed in 'running 'em when they're ready', and they were usually ready.

"In 1952, when he beat Willie Molter by five winners, McDaniel campaigned two of the hardiest horses in training. One was named Stranglehold, the other was Horsetrader-ed. Both were owned by Mr. and Mrs. N. G. Phillips. And both of those horses made thirty-seven starts that season, if you can even imagine that! One or the other of them seemed to be entered on almost every card during that year in California.

"Both horses raced with the best of their divisions," Rasmussen continued. "Stranglehold won a stakes and he placed in several others. Horsetrader-ed didn't win stakes, but he earned a part of the purse in many. McDaniel had a lot of good horses over the years. Poona II, a multiple stakes winner (who ran fourth in the Golden Gate Handicap two days after his trainer's death), was probably the best, but he had such other good ones as Stitch Again, Great Dream — a knockout of a horse — Blue Reading, and Apple Valley.

"The season that McDaniel went head-to-head with Molter, every one except one of his owners made money. (Despite, or perhaps because of, their intense rivalry, McDaniel and Molter became good friends. Molter was one of the people McDaniel spoke with at Golden Gate the afternoon he would die; he evidenced no hint of any depression, no forewarning of what he would later do, Molter said). McDaniel had an uncanny ability to 'improve' his claims. He also had the rare ability to keep his stock going month in and month out without them becoming jaded or track-weary. The man was an outstanding horseman," Rasmussen said.

———————

Following the funeral services in San Mateo, California, where he had made his home, Red McDaniel was buried in Forest Lawn cemetery in Los Angeles on May 11, 1955. Speculation as to why McDaniel chose to take his life continued to be wide-ranging long after his interment.

With the possible exception of the backrooms of Washington, D.C. or the boardrooms of Hollywood, America's racetracks have no rival as the source of rumors. This was emphasized in the case of Red McDaniel. What drove him to kill himself in his professional prime? The theories were numerous and varied.

Sam Swartzberg served as agent for the McDaniel stable, which had thirty-eight employees, an annual payroll of $125,000, and was run with a business-like efficiency relatively rare in racing at that time. While there was a considerable revenue flow — product of a twelve dollars per day training rate, and ten percent of the purses earned — there were great pressure and responsibility as well. Swartzberg said his employer had been in ill health in 1955, suffering from what had been diagnosed as bleeding ulcers. Turf Club regulars reported that McDaniel had been spending more time than usual at the bar. Known to imbibe only on rare occasions in the past, he reportedly had begun to drink quite heavily that April. McDaniel had confided to a close friend that he was depressed over his inability to resist the desire to drink, even though alcohol exacerbated his gastrointestinal condition.

Many of McDaniel's colleagues believed that an excess of extremely hard work may have exacted a terrible toll. The trainer invariably arrived at the barn at dawn and remained at the track until well after the last race each day. Besides the fifty to sixty horses stabled at the track under his care, McDaniel usually had another thirty or so undergoing freshening or recuperation at nearby farms. The demands upon him by the eighteen to twenty owners he normally had were also strong. McDaniel maintained close associations with almost all of his clients, celebrating their victories with them and commiserating with them after losses. Such a strenuous routine could well have led to a case of nervous exhaustion, threshold to a fatal fit of despondency, or so it was thought by several of those who knew him best.

There was no question of financial troubles being a factor. Indeed, McDaniel was doing so well that he had begun to acquire blocks of stock in both Golden Gate Fields and Bay Meadows Racetrack, and had indicated he was interested in further expanding those holdings. (He did not live long enough to see the potential conflicts of interest issues be addressed regarding those investments.)

Some observers had noticed a change in McDaniel that spring. While considered a relative "loner" on the racetrack, polite and convivial with all but close to few, he was a famously "soft touch" for those down on their luck. Stable agent Swartzberg estimated that when he died McDaniel was owed some $30,000 in unsecured loans.

However, in the months leading to his death, McDaniel's normally placid demeanor occasionally gave way to angry flareups that startled those who knew him best. Still, even though he lost at least two of his owners because of disagreements during this period, he remained friendly with them and continued the business partnerships he had with them in non-racing ventures.

One man close to McDaniel was his stable foreman, Ray Scott. Theirs was described as a "father-son" relationship. *San Francisco Examiner* writer Abe Kemp interviewed Scott shortly after his employer's demise. Had McDaniel given any sign that he was contemplating suicide?

Scott replied "yes and no" to the question, Kemp wrote, adding that the young horseman fought to hold back tears as he talked. "When I say 'yes,' I mean he did drop hints in a kidding moment…The other day he remarked that I would outlive him by many years. I just didn't like the way he said it. At the time, though, it didn't mean anything to me. But now I wonder.' "

There were actions on the morning of his death that gave evidence McDaniel had something on his mind besides his four Golden Gate starters that Thursday. He instructed two of his employees to take a large sum of cash he had with him and deliver it to his wife, Evelyn. One of the men offered to drive McDaniel to his San Mateo home after the races, so that he could deliver the money himself. McDaniel declined the offer. He said he wasn't going home.

––––––––

As success brings fame, so does it attract detractors, and Red McDaniel's career was not without a cadre of those carpers. For years, jealous rivals whispered that the redhead's success was traceable to his alleged use of an illegal stimulant on his horses, some form of "juice" that chemists were unable to detect. He was secretly importing it from Mexico, some claimed. Others claimed the source was Australia. Stewards at every California track at which the McDaniel stable raced were aware of these allegations. As a result, McDaniel's runners were closely scrutinized, their patterns monitored. However, no positive results ever emerged from his runners' post-race urine or saliva tests.

No official investigation of any of these completely unsubstantiated charges was ever made. The man led the nation in wins for half a decade, and there was no logical reason to believe he had done so any other way than on the up and up.

Another rumor circulated that some powerful underworld

figures "had the goods" on McDaniel and the alleged illegal practices, were "putting the squeeze" on him, and that that was what led to his leap into the Bay's cold waters.

Leon Rasmussen, for one, dismissed these scenarios as having no basis in truth. "Red McDaniel's success," he said, "was as legitimate as his life — the way it ended was unfortunate."

Also refusing to put any credence into the sinister implications of those long ago rumors regarding Red McDaniel was Bobby Baird. "Magic drugs!" Baird scoffed. "What a bunch of baloney. He was one of the most watched guys in California racing. And he just kept getting better, winning more races and improving his stock every year.

"If you would have known Red McDaniel you would laugh at the idea that he was cheating or anything like that. Red never looked real healthy when I knew him — he was real pale-skinned, kind of a skinny guy — but he was just the nicest and politest type person. He carried himself like a deacon...like a pastor. You know what I mean?

"Believe me," said Bobby Baird, seated in the Hawthorne racing secretary's office, miles and years from his last meeting with Robert Hyatt McDaniel, "this guy was the real goods, a terrific trainer. Why he did what he did — we'll never know."

* Copyrighted ©2000 by Daily Racing Form, Inc.
Reprinted with Permission of the Copyright owner.

Woodward's Smoking Gun

When they first met, in a posh Manhattan nightclub, he was dressed in white tie and tails. She wore a white bathing suit, black net stockings, pink and white rabbit ears, and cottontail. The year was 1942. He was twenty-two years old; she was nearly five years his senior.

Thirteen stormy years later when they parted for the last time, he was lying naked in a hallway of their plush Long Island home and she was wielding the twelve-gauge shotgun that killed him.

In the ensuing period, prior to the bloody event that *Life* magazine termed the "shooting of the century," William (Billy) Woodward and his wife Ann had combined to become nationally famous as owners of the Preakness and Belmont Stakes winner Nashua. Their emergence as very public figures in 1955, Nashua's three-year-old season when he would earn Horse of the Year honors and win one of America's most famous match races, was what made the tragic happenings of October 30, 1955, all the more shocking.

On its front page one day later, in a lengthy article datelined Oyster Bay, L.I., *The New York Times* reported this sensational event:

A shotgun blast early Sunday morning took the life of William Woodward Jr., financier, sportsman and owner of the great racehorse Nashua.

District Attorney Frank A. Gulotta of Nassau County said the gun was fired by the victim's wife, Ann Eden Crowell Woodward, who told investigators she thought she had aimed it at a prowler.

After preliminary questioning...she was taken to Doctors Hospital, Manhattan. She arrived there on a stretcher in a private ambulance.

Mr. Gulotta said that, pending further inquiry, the death would be considered accidental. Inspector Stuyvesant Pinnell, chief of the Nassau County detectives, described the case as 'more likely to be accidental than homicide.'

The pellets, from a 12-gauge, double-barreled British model gun, were fired across an 18-foot hall between the door of Mrs. Woodward's bedroom and that of her husband. Mrs. Woodward told the police she had been awakened by the barking of a poodle called Sloppy, which slept in the kitchen.

The crash of the shots did not disturb the couple's two sons (William III, age 11, and his seven-year-old brother James) who were sleeping upstairs.

According to the story assembled by Mr. Gulotta and Inspector Pinnell, the Woodwards had attended a party last night in honor of the Duchess of Windsor at nearby Locust Valley. Their hostess was Mrs. George F. Baker, widow of the chairman of the First National Bank of New York.

At the party, according to other guests, the Woodwards mentioned recent incidents suggesting that someone had been trying to break into their home.

Mr. Woodward had spoken to Lieut. C. Russell Haff of the Oyster Bay Cove police only yesterday afternoon about an apparent attempt to enter a bathhouse (on the Woodward property). Mr. Haff subsequently confirmed that reports of such a prowler...were well founded.

At any event, the Woodwards drove to their home on Berry Hill Road here. It is in one of the most fashionable sections of the North Shore, a wooded and coved area long associated with the Theodore Roosevelt family...

The Woodwards went to bed soon after returning from the party. It was 2:08 a.m. Standard Time when a telephone operator, answering a call from the Woodward number, heard a woman screaming incoherently. That started the alarm...After Lieut. Haff arrived he found the body, with the widow embracing it, on the floor.

Mr. Woodward had fallen on his face. He was unclothed; the shot had caught him in the right temple, killing him instantly. The charge from the second barrel, fired immediately after the first according to the police technicians, had sprayed the door frame.

An unlikely series of developments led to the Woodward marriage, whose contrasting principals hailed from America's Eastern aristocracy and an area of its impoverished midlands.

Billy Woodward was the only son of William Woodward Sr. and Elsie Cryder Woodward, leaders of New York society (the couple had four daughters as well). The senior Woodward, who served as chairman of The Jockey Club for more than twenty years, took over the presidency of the powerful Hanover Bank of New York upon the death of his bachelor uncle, James, and headed it for nearly two decades. A director of the Federal Reserve Board, he evidenced his wealth by at one time owning five homes as well as one of the world's major racing stables.

Young Woodward followed his father's educational path by going to Groton, then Harvard. After service as a lieutenant in the United States Navy in World War II, the "handsome young sportsman," as he was frequently described, served on the boards of several businesses and indulged his passion for tennis. When President Dwight D. Eisenhower in July of 1955 convened a White House conference to discuss athletic programs to be designed for the country's young people, Billy Woodward was among the thirty-two sports leaders invited.

Billy Woodward's wife was born Angeline Luceil Crowell on a farm outside Pittsburg, Kansas. Her road to a role in international café society was an unlikely one. The child of an impoverished family, she had lived in eight different houses by the time she was fourteen. What she had going for her was brains (a grade school I.Q. test found her scoring 139), ambition, and very good looks.

Now calling herself Ann Crowell, she arrived in New York City at age twenty-two. She soon became involved in a relationship with actor Franchot Tone. The tall, attractive young blonde worked as a showgirl, appearing in the chorus of a Noel Coward musical review. She then launched a career as a radio actress, appearing on numerous soap operas. She was once voted "the most beautiful girl in radio." (In 1952, she was voted one of six "Great American Beauties" by *Vogue* magazine.)

It was in 1942, when she was dancing under the name of Ann Eden in the Monte Carlo nightclub in New York City that she met both Billy Woodward and his father. Some of the senior Woodward's friends believed that Ann was his mistress. This was never proven, but there is no question that Ann several times accompanied The Jockey Club chairman to the racetrack prior to marrying his son.

The relationship between Ann and Billy Woodward was strenuously opposed by Woodward's mother, Elsie, who once famously stated, "These girls from nowhere can be dangerous to (good) families." Elsie urged her husband to cut their son off financially unless he gave up Ann. But, emboldened by a healthy and untouchable trust fund that supplied him with $4,000 a month, young Woodward defied his mother. He and Ann were married in 1943 in Tacoma, Washington, near where Woodward was stationed. He subsequently served on a U.S. aircraft carrier that was torpedoed in the

South Pacific by the Japanese. More than 600 crewmen died, but Billy emerged unscathed. After the war, his father gifted Billy with the rest of a trust made up of blue chip stocks, thus boosting his monthly income to $10,000. At the time of his death, his personal fortune had escalated to more than $10 million.

––––––––––

Major among the Woodward family's holdings was Belair Stud, which was founded in 1741 by Maryland Governor Samuel Ogle. It would change hands several times, but nevertheless set a record for continuous operation extending more than two centuries. A subsequent Maryland governor, Oden Bowie, acquired part of Belair, and later that portion was sold to James T. Woodward, the brilliant financier who put together the Hanover National Bank empire. When James Woodward died in 1909, he left both the bank and the breeding farm and racing stable to his nephew, William Woodward.

An avid racing patron and student of bloodlines, William Woodward proceeded to build Belair into a Turf colossus. In 1925, he joined with A. B. Hancock Sr. in a syndicate to acquire the French stallion Sir Gallahad III and import him to America. Profitable results soon followed: Gallant Fox was a member of Sir Gallahad III's first U.S. crop. The famed "Fox of Belair" in 1930 became America's second Triple Crown winner. He also contributed to the lore of the Turf when, as the heavy favorite, he lost that year's Travers Stakes at Saratoga to 100-1 shot Jim Dandy. Gallant Fox retired as the world's leading money winner with $328,165 and Horse of the Year. (Sir Gallahad III would rank as America's leading sire four times and leading broodmare sire a dozen times.)

At stud Gallant Fox sired Omaha, who in 1935 became the third winner of the Triple Crown. This remains the only father-son Triple Crown combination and is about as likely to be matched as Wilt Chamberlain's record of 100 points scored in a National Basketball Association game. Like his sire, Omaha was trained for Belair by the legendary James E. (Sunny Jim) Fitzsimmons, also known as the "Sage of Sheepshead Bay," whose career with the stable began in 1923. Fitzsimmons retired in 1963 at age eighty-nine, having saddled 148 stakes winners in an incredible career that spanned three-quarters of a century. He is still the only man to develop two heroes of the Triple Crown. (Ben Jones is credited with training two Triple Crown winners — Whirlaway (1941) and Citation (1948), although Jones' son, Jimmy, actually conditioned Citation.)

Other stars raced by William Woodward Sr. in the white and red polka-dotted Belair colors included two Horses of the Year: Granville (a son of Gallant Fox) in 1936 and Johnstown in 1939, as well as champion three-year-old filly and handicap distaffer Vagrancy (1942). But William Woodward Sr. never got to see race perhaps the most famous Belair champion, Nashua. Woodward died when this bay colt was a yearling.

The senior Woodward also had enjoyed great success with the English division of his international stable. His stakes winners abroad included 1936 St. Leger winner Boswell, and

Flares, hero of the 1938 Ascot Gold Cup.

While William Woodward Sr.'s racing stable was going well, the marriage of Billy and Ann was not. The marriage was preceded by Elsie Woodward's hiring of a private detective to follow Ann. After the nuptials had occurred, both husband and wife employed investigators to spy on each other. Billy's detective even managed to succeed in tapping Ann's phone.

In the fall of 1946, Billy began seeing Princess Marina Torlonia, wife of international tennis star Frank Shields. Ann became aware of this, and her already well-developed capacity for jealousy increased, leading to numerous public spats between her and her husband. During this period Billy altered the terms of his will, reducing Ann's share of his estate.

Ann's defenders after the shooting often cited this point in her defense, noting that she would have been monetarily far better off divorced from Billy than as his widow. When Billy's will was filed weeks after his death, it showed he had waived large tax savings by withholding Ann's control over her share of the fortune. According to a story in the November 10, 1955, *Chicago Tribune*, tax experts "said the estimated $10 million value of the estate will shrink to $2.5 million when federal and state taxes are deducted from it."

In the winter of 1948, some five years after they'd been joined together, Billy announced he was opting for "asunder." He formally requested a divorce from Ann, offering a $2 million settlement, evidently intending to marry the princess. A separation agreement was signed. If Billy could establish that his wife had committed adultery, he would not have to pay the agreed upon $2 million. But he and his detectives were never able to do so, although Ann reportedly journeyed abroad and had a tryst in France with Prince Aly Khan, perhaps the Continent's (if not the world's) most famous womanizer at the time.

Although separated, the embattled Woodwards were not always apart, and they engaged in some verbal and occasionally physical squabbles that several times resulted in the police being called by concerned neighbors. After approximately a year of such tumult, they reconciled and moved back in together. Proximity, however, failed to produce lasting peace.

It was after this reconciliation that Ann began to join Billy on various hunting trips. She became an ardent convert to this sport: on an excursion in India, she bagged two Bengal tigers and a pair of leopards. In 1954, her husband gifted her with a custom-made shotgun crafted in England. It was the gun she would kill him with the next year.

Author Susan Braudy, whose eight-year investigation of the Woodward case led to publication in 1993 of her book *This Crazy Thing Called Love* (Alfred Knopf Inc.), quotes Jack James on this subject. James was a Harvard classmate of Billy Woodward and served as best man at his wedding. According to James, "There was nothing more important to Billy than chasing women. Sometimes he had been in love with Ann and loyal to the boys (their sons) — but it was not his way of life. He felt that extracurricular activity was his prerogative as a man. There were three words to describe Billy Woodward:

selfish and egotistical and well-mannered. I don't recall Ann
ever being at peace with herself. Everything was always a crisis. She was insecure, but he gave her that feeling."

Cleveland Amory, in his 1960 book *Who Killed Society?*,
wrote of the Woodwards that "even judged by the loose
standards prevailing in their Society, their marriage was a
tenuous one; their public scenes had given grim indication
of what their private life must have been."

On September 26, 1953, William Woodward Sr. died at
age seventy-seven. His thirty-three-year-old son inherited
Belair Stud (now expanded to 3,000 acres), $1 million, and
the racing stable. The majority of the deceased's estimated
$30 million estate went to his wife, Elsie.

His father's passing marked a sea change in the younger
Woodward's life — at least as far as his public interests were
concerned. Growing up, Billy had shown little interest in racing, only occasionally accompanying his father to the track.
Now, however, reportedly encouraged by Ann, he developed a
new enthusiasm for what had been his father's passion.

In the words of *Daily Racing Form* columnist Joe Hirsch, "If
anything brought him closer to the Turf, kept him in racing,
provided the spark that touched off a deep and sincere interest in the welfare of the sport…it was the colt Nashua."

(Billy once told another *Daily Racing Form* columnist, Tom
O'Reilly, that he had been readied to become master of
Belair "by a process of osmosis. Although I was not directly
involved with the stable, I couldn't help picking up a certain
amount of horse lore, and it was impossible not to contract
my father's enthusiasm." Ann's interest was also apparently a

factor in Billy's new involvement with the horses.)

Woodward Sr.'s original plan had been for Nashua to be sent to the English division of the Belair stable and try for the Epsom Derby, a prize his owner had never won. But after his father passed away, Billy, instead, decided to keep the beautifully-bred colt (Nasrullah—Segula, by Johnstown) in the United States and in the talented hands of trainer Fitzsimmons.

Nashua, who was foaled April 14, 1952, at Claiborne Farm in Kentucky, was an awkward specimen as a yearling, primarily because he was growing so fast. But he developed into a striking individual at two, measuring more than sixteen hands and having the musculature of an older horse.

In his debut, at Belmont Park on May 5, 1954, Nashua impressively broke his maiden by three lengths, beating no less than twenty rivals down the straight Widener chute going four and a half furlongs. Nashua's first defeat came in his third start, the Cherry Hill Stakes at Garden State Park, when he dropped a neck decision to Royal Note. Eddie Arcaro, long the country's leading jockey, was hired as Nashua's regular rider. Fitzsimmons equipped the young horse with blinkers. Nashua finished his juvenile campaign with six wins (four of them in stakes races) from eight starts, the finale being his Futurity Stakes score at Belmont Park on October 9.

Following the Futurity, Billy Woodward told a *Daily Racing Form* writer: "This is the greatest thrill I've had in racing to date...It's a shame papa wasn't here to see it."

Also notable among Nashua's races that 1954 season —

and contributing to his being voted champion two-year-old colt — were the Cowdin, in which his regular rival Summer Tan beat him while setting a track record of 1:16 for six and a half furlongs; and a subsequent allowance race in which Nashua set a track record of his own — six furlongs in 1:08 1/5 down the Widener course.

After a winter respite in Florida, Nashua launched his three-year-old campaign in smashing style. He easily annexed his seasonal debut going a mile and one-sixteenth at Hialeah, then captured the Flamingo Stakes there. When Fitzsimmons went north to prepare the rest of his stable (in addition to the Woodwards, Sunny Jim also had a lengthy and terrifically successful association with the Phipps family) for the opening of the New York season, Billy remained in Florida. He visited the barn every morning as Nashua was being prepared for the Florida Derby.

The Gulfstream Park strip was extremely muddy on Florida Derby Day. As Arcaro later recalled, he and Woodward "walked out on the track to check it personally. After we'd done so, I thought for sure he'd scratch Nashua. But he turned to me and said, 'Hell, Eddie, I can't scratch Nashua. Look at all those people in the stands who have come out here on a day like this to see him run.' " Woodward, added Arcaro, was "a real credit to racing."

Nashua prevailed by a neck in the Florida Derby, then took the Wood Memorial at old Jamaica. As a result, he was the 6-5 favorite in the Kentucky Derby on May 7, but fell a length and a half shy of catching the front-running Swaps. Arcaro later took the blame for this defeat, saying he had paid too much attention to Summer Tan (who finished third) and not enough to the victorious colt from California. But Swaps, it should be remembered, ran a terrific race, and his final time of 2:01 4/5 for the mile and one-quarter under young Bill Shoemaker was the fourth fastest Derby up to that point.

Swaps was returned to California following his Churchill conquest, the Derby being the only Triple Crown race to which he had been nominated by breeder Rex Ellsworth, who owned the Khaled colt in partnership with his longtime friend and fellow Mormon, trainer Meshach A. (Mesh) Tenney.

Back East, Nashua rebounded with a vengeance. After annexing the Preakness Stakes by a length in track-record time of 1:54 3/5 for the mile and three-sixteenths, he rolled to a nine-length triumph in the Belmont Stakes. This margin of victory delighted Billy Woodward, who shouted after the finish, "He won off!" Woodward had been accustomed to the usually much narrower margins that marked the finishes of Nashua's races, win or lose.

Three weeks after the Belmont, Nashua won the Dwyer Stakes at old Aqueduct. Two weeks later he shipped to Chicago to capture the Arlington Classic. Then came the exciting news that Nashua would be back in Chicago the next month to meet Swaps in a $100,000 match race arranged by Benjamin F. Lindheimer, owner of Arlington and Washington Parks. It was to be at a mile and one-quarter, each colt carrying 126 pounds, winner take all.

Fitzsimmons chose to get Nashua in match-race shape by

training him over the deep surface at Saratoga in upstate New York. Billy Woodward visited the track nearly every day, becoming increasingly subject to the pressure of the public's interest combined with his mother's stated disapproval of the race. (The previous year at Saratoga, Billy met author Ian Fleming. The two men, of similar backgrounds, became fast friends. Fleming was so impressed with Woodward and his lifestyle — which now included frequently having a martini with his breakfast — that he patterned a character in one of his popular novels after him: Felix Leiter, a former Secret Service agent who is James Bond's partner in *Diamonds Are Forever*. Like Woodward, Leiter drove a souped-up auto called a "Studillac," which housed a Cadillac engine in a Studebaker body. Fleming dedicated the book to Woodward.)

Elsie Woodward's opposition to the match race may have stemmed from her resentment of Ann's increasingly public role as horse owner. Ann was photogenic, friendly to members of the press and the photographers, and as a result was frequently pictured in the newspapers and magazines. Her career as a showgirl and actress had prepared her for this sort of exposure. She made a point of acknowledging all of Nashua's connections — trainer, rider, and groom — and this impressed the media representatives.

Although Ann seemed to garner more than her share of the spotlight, Billy was nevertheless somewhat enjoying his new fame, even though he often appeared stiff and uneasy in the limelight's glare. Both he and his wife began to receive fan letters from all over the country. (There were hundreds of them, but Nashua got more mail than either of his owners).

Despite — or perhaps because of — the fact that *Sports Illustrated* magazine in the summer of 1955 ran a photo spread on Ann's outfits at the racetrack, and termed her the "best dressed woman in sports," both Billy and his mother advised Ann to choose conservative clothing for these very public appearances, especially the upcoming match race which was to be nationally televised.

According to author Susan Braudy, Ann had ten outfits with her when she and Billy arrived at the Lake Forest, Illinois, estate of their friend Charles Wacker Jr. Billy stated that he would be the one to select her ensemble for the day of the match race. They fought over this subject while Wacker's helicopter waited on the lawn of the estate, ready to transport them to Washington Park. Finally, after a long delay, Billy pointed at the array of clothing choices, and dismissively said, "Oh, wear that." As a result, Ann wound up wearing the most inappropriate attire imaginable — a clinging, low-cut, black cocktail dress. (A kinescope of the match race includes several shots of the Woodwards; although seated or standing together, they apparently hardly looked at each other at all during the course of this exciting afternoon.)

Although it was held on a Wednesday afternoon — August 31, 1955, almost two months to the day before Billy Woodward was to die — the "Great Match Race" was viewed an enthusiastic Washington Park crowd of 35,262 and the CBS telecast of it was seen by an estimated 50 million people. On hand were such diverse luminaries as Louisiana Governor Earl Long; boxing champion Sugar Ray

Robinson; and hotel magnate Conrad Hilton.

In addition to the attractiveness of the two very talented horses, the event sizzled with sociological contrasts: Nashua, owned by the tradition-steeped Belair, a pillar of the Eastern Turf establishment, versus Swaps, pride and joy of a couple of former range-riding cowboys. Finally, there was the contrast of the thirty-nine-year-old Arcaro, widely known as "The Master," riding against the twenty-four-year-old Shoemaker, his heir apparent.

Nine previous starts that year had seen Nashua beaten only once — by Swaps in the Derby. Swaps, meanwhile, was riding an eight-race winning streak. After his Kentucky Derby victory, Swaps had kept busy, winning the Will Rogers and Westerner at Hollywood Park, setting a stakes record in the latter. In between those efforts, Swaps beat a field of good older horses in the Californian Stakes, establishing a world record of 1:40 2/5 for the mile and one-sixteenth.

In his final start before the match race, on August 20, Swaps made his first start on the turf and set a new track record that also equaled the American record of 1:54 3/5 for a mile and three-sixteenths while winning the American Derby at Washington Park. Swaps, a beautifully-made individual, demonstrated convincingly that he could transfer his fluid action from dirt to turf, for he won that day under a firm hold applied by Shoemaker, who was evidently determined to save some horse for the match race eleven days later.

Confronted with these glistening credentials, racing experts found it impossible to arrive at a full-fledged consensus regarding the match race. By a slight majority, the experts believed that Swaps would win. His margin of victory in the Derby, a length and a half, was clear-cut enough to suggest he was capable of again beating Nashua.

The Washington Park punters reflected the same opinion, but with more conviction: they made Swaps a strong 3-10 choice, while Nashua closed at 6-5.

The track was holding and soggy after the previous night's heavy rains, but it was considered no disadvantage to either horse. They entered the gate — Nashua in the No. 2 stall, Swaps in No. 4 — at 5:18 p.m. and were off almost at once.

As the starting gate doors opened, Arcaro, yelling like a banshee and using his whip with all his strength, shot Nashua to the front. Swaps, away on the outside and a bit tardily, veered farther out toward the outside rail. Nashua remained in front as they passed the stands for the first time, and he was to be in front for the entire ten furlongs, Swaps making repeated thrusts at him, all of which fell short.

On the clubhouse turn, once on the backstretch, and again on the final turn, Shoemaker, racing on the outside and in the worst going, brought Swaps almost level with Nashua. But at each of these bids Nashua drew away, always in complete control. Even before they reached the top of the stretch, it was obvious that Nashua was going to win.

Reaching the wire in 2:04 1/5, good time considering the track condition, Nashua had six and a half lengths on his rival, a hundred grand coming to his owners, and Horse of the Year honors in his immediate future. Both horses (Swaps would be voted Horse of the Year the following season) earned the respect of the generations. Both would eventually enter the Racing Hall of Fame.

Following the match race, Billy and Ann Woodward were pictured in newspapers all over the country as they stood smiling with Nashua in the Washington Park winner's circle. The next time their photos would appear was two months later, in the aftermath of the sensational shooting in their home, called the "Playhouse," on Oyster Bay, Long Island.

———————

The day after Billy Woodward's death, Inspector Pinnell told *The New York Times* that the Woodwards had agreed, when they returned from the dinner party for the Duchess of Windsor, to arm themselves for any emergency involving the suspected prowler. Billy took from their gun case an automatic pistol, which investigators subsequently found in a bureau in his bedroom. Ann took the shotgun Billy had given her, loaded it with No. 7 shot (birdshot) and rested it against the wall at the side of her bed.

"They went to bed," Pinnell recounted. "with the understanding that they would execute the plan — the plan being that either of them who heard a prowler would take a gun and go after him."

After hearing the dog barking, Ann grabbed the shotgun, opened her bedroom door and, she told the inspector, "saw a figure which I failed to recognize." Acting on instinct, she said, she brought the gun up and rapidly pulled both triggers. The second shot ricocheted off Billy's bedroom door and hit him, causing flesh wounds on the right side of his face and neck. Amazingly, just one of the small pellets entered his brain, but that was what killed Billy Woodward.

"Almost immediately," Inspector Pinnell said. "Mrs. Woodward recognized him (her husband). She realized what she had done. She ran to him and embraced him. Then she picked up the phone."

Under subsequent questioning, Ann told investigators that she had not seen "anything. I just heard the noise and fired in the direction of the noise. I really didn't intend to even hit anybody. I just intended that they would know that, you know, we were protected. And whatever it was would go away."

Identifying the body was the victim's nephew, William Bancroft (of the family that later raced the great Damascus). Susan Braudy says in her book that "Bancroft tapped on Ann's bedroom door: her shame and wretched grief touched him. It is a curious fact that nearly everyone present that morning believed Ann was innocent. In years to come, the Woodward family would be split. Bancroft believed Ann (to be) innocent, while his grandmother Elsie did not."

On November 1, Nassau County police picked up a twenty-two-year-old German alien, Paul W. Wirths, near a stolen car that contained a gun. He was held on burglary charges after admitting he had attempted to break into the Woodwards' mansion the previous week. Wirths said he also had wandered around the estate two nights during the week preceding the shooting, had failed in an attempt to break into the home, but did enter the estate's six-car garage.

Only a few days later, Wirths changed his story. He admitted he not only had been on the Woodward estate at the time of the shooting, but was attempting to break into the house at the time.

An Associated Press story said Wirths had climbed a tree onto the roof "terrace directly above the Woodwards' first-floor bedrooms. Police quoted Paul W. Wirths as saying he wrestled noisily with a glass-paneled door leading from the roof into an unoccupied guest room. It was unlocked but dampness made it sticky and caused a noise when he forced it open. When the door was flung open, a curtain blew out and swept across Wirths' face, startling him and causing him to drop the loaded shotgun he was carrying on the roof over Ann Woodward's bedroom. When he heard shots, he fled. 'It sounded like a cannon,' Wirths said. 'I didn't wait. I got the hell out of there.' "

Wirths' revised version of his story served to support Ann's claim that a noise in the night had led to the fatal shot. Physical evidence also backed up her story. Billy Woodward was not shot in his shower, then moved, as some rumors had it. As an assistant medical examiner noted, the six-foot, two-inch Woodward weighed approximately 180 pounds, making it "impossible" for Ann to move him. The medical examiner also reported no traces of blood anywhere but the place where the victim lay. He pronounced himself "amazed" that the single shotgun pellet had caused this death.

Newsday's Pulitzer Prize-winning reporter Bob Greene wrote: "The Woodward family would like the investigation over with as quickly as possible. Even if the shooting was in doubt, the family would want to see Ann cleared because of the possible scandal involved."

While the investigation was being conducted, a former Woodward employee, Ingebourge Sorenson, told the *Los Angeles Times* that the couple had numerous arguments. "She described Mrs. Woodward as a suspicious, hysterical type who relied heavily on sleeping pills to calm her nerves," the report continued, adding:

"Mrs. Sorenson, who had been hired June 6, said 'both of them used to sleep behind locked doors...she (Ann) would get up sometimes during the night and pound on his door. She would hammer and scream for him to open the door... She could never sleep without taking sleeping pills...She would walk until 5 or 6 a.m. in the garden before she would go to bed. She usually drank about three beers after she went to bed.'"

A member of the Woodwards' social circle years later was interviewed by author Braudy. In refuting the theory that Elsie Woodward had worked to "cover up a murder in order to save the family from embarrassment," she commented that there was "nothing to hide" about the tragic incident "except the fact that Billy and Ann were not happily married." No fight at the dinner party the night of the shooting had occurred, she continued, adding: "Truman Capote and Nick Dunne (Dominick Dunne in his best-selling novel *The Two Mrs. Grenvilles*) tried to establish a fictional motive for murder. But that fight never happened...Of course, they fought every day, but there was no big fight that night."

Billy Woodward's funeral was described as the "biggest in New York since Babe Ruth's." Thousands of people crowded the blocks near St. James Episcopal Church at 71st Street and Madison Avenue, and some 900 mourners jammed the church. The widow was not among them. Reportedly at the urging of her mother-in-law, who feared a funeral spectacle, Ann remained hospitalized; she was permitted to order the flowers that covered the casket — an arrangement of white chrysanthemums and red carnations, representing the Belair racing colors.

In *Who Killed Society?*, Cleveland Amory wrote that "the night before the funeral...Michael Butler, described in the gossip columns as the Duchess of Windsor's 'latest favorite' (Butler would later produce the hit musical "Hair"), gave a dinner. Wednesday, the day of the funeral, Mrs. Harold Brookes gave still another dinner." The Woodward shooting was the main course of discussion at numerous other events, Amory continued. A sizeable segment of New York society, Amory quoted an "awed onlooker" as saying, "seemed to treat the whole thing like a rather successful floor show."

On November 25, Ann Woodward appeared before a Nassau County Grand Jury. She appeared voluntarily to tell her story of the shooting and was therefore required to sign a waiver of immunity. Prior to her appearance, the twenty-two-member jury panel that included five women had heard testimony from twenty-five witnesses.

That night the jury deliberated for thirty minutes before telling County Judge Norman F. Lent it would not indict Ann Woodward. Said the jury chairman, "We found that no crime had been committed in the Woodward case."

Before taking up the Woodward matter, the Grand Jury heard testimony in the case of accused burglar Paul Wirths.

When the jury reported to the judge on the Woodward case, it handed up an indictment naming Wirths on several counts of burglary. Wirths was eventually convicted of the charges, spent nearly six years in prison, and upon his release in 1961 was deported to Germany.

Elsie Woodward prevailed upon Ann to send her sons abroad to an international boarding school and there they remained, separated from their mother, for years.

A month and a half after Billy Woodward's death, with no family members having expressed a desire to continue the Belair tradition, the executors of his estate decided to disperse his racing and breeding interests via an unusual, sealed-bid auction. The bids were opened on December 15 at the Hanover Bank in New York City.

Nashua easily proved the biggest attraction. The best of the five million-dollar-plus bids for him came from a syndicate headed by Spendthrift Farm's Leslie Combs II. The Combs syndicate's combined successful bid was a world-record $1,251,200. (The total brought by the rest of the Belair Thoroughbreds — nine horses of racing age in addition to Nashua, sixteen weanlings, twelve yearlings and twenty-four broodmares — was $2,237,200.)

Campaigning for the Combs syndicate at four, still trained by Fitzsimmons and ridden by Arcaro, Nashua won six of ten outings, including the Widener, Grey Lag, Camden, Monmouth, and Suburban Handicaps before closing out his racing career with a memorable flourish — setting an American record of 3:20 2/5 in winning the two-mile Jockey Club Gold Cup. That brought Nashua's record to thirty starts, twenty-two wins, four seconds, one third, and world-record earnings of $1,288,565.

In his career, Nashua won from four and a half furlongs to sixteen furlongs, and retired perfectly sound, making him an extremely attractive stallion prospect when he arrived at Spendthrift Farm in Kentucky.

In the years following her husband's death, Ann Woodward traveled the world. She reportedly engaged in several affairs, all with younger men and primarily in Europe, but she never remarried. In September of 1975, Ann was informed by a friend that a short piece of fiction by Truman Capote was to be published in the November issue of *Esquire* magazine; the story, she was told, would depict her, not by name but recognizable to many people neverthe-less, as a murderous vamp. On October 10, 1975, Ann's body was discovered in her Fifth Avenue apartment. Her death by means of a drug overdose later was ruled a suicide. She was fifty-seven. Her funeral on October 14 was described as "sparsely attended."

Less than a year after his mother's suicide, James Woodward jumped to his death from the window of a hotel overlooking Central Park. He was twenty-nine and a bache-lor. A Vietnam veteran who became addicted to drugs, James four years earlier had leaped from a fourth-floor win-dow but survived.

The last member of the family, William Woodward III, known as "Woody," worked as a *New York Post* reporter fol-lowing his graduation from Harvard. He later used some of his fortune to finance *More*, a liberal magazine of media criticism, and after serving in the administrations of New York Governor Hugh L. Carey and New York City Mayor Edward I. Koch, he ran unsuccessfully for the State Senate from the East Side's "silk stocking district." Shortly thereafter, he dropped out of the public eye.

On May 2 of 1999, "Woody" Woodward dropped to his death out of the kitchen window of his fourteenth story New York City apartment. It was ruled a suicide, and termed a "terrible tragedy" by a friend who said of Woody that "his desire was to give something back, to try to do good. But there was always a shadow of sadness. It seemed to emanate from him." Woody was fifty-four. He left a wife and a daughter.

————————

To this day, the question remains unanswered in the minds of many: Did Ann Woodward mean to murder her husband? Making a monumental effort to answer the question was Susan Braudy.

Wrote Braudy, "It was clear from (newspaper and magazine) clippings that most Americans believed Ann Woodward was guilty of murder, despite the fact that she had been cleared by a Nassau County grand jury three weeks after the shooting had occurred.

"In 1975, I read Ann Woodward's obituary in *The New York Times*, and a week after that I read Truman Capote's thinly disguised fictional description of her in his 'Answered Prayers.' In the piece, Capote had characterized 'Ann Hopkins' as a...cold-blooded murderess...Several society people told me with intimidating authority that the Capote story was 'positively factual.'

"In 1981, when Ann's mother-in-law, Elsie Woodward, grand dame of New York society, died (at age 97), I set out to prove Capote's fiction had foundation in fact...I wanted my research to support the myth that Elsie Woodward had covered up the murder of her only son for the sake of her grandsons...According to myth, Elsie never swerved in her view that the bold and attractive Kansas girl (Ann) ruined Billy's life with her powers of sex. Elsie fueled the story by declaring that her son's tragic shooting was rooted in the fact that Ann was not his social equal...As Elsie's friends saw it, Capote had accused Ann in print and she had responded like a guilty person by committing suicide.

"(However) I came to see that Ann Woodward was innocent of the murder of her husband...From reading hundreds of pages of police documents and interviewing police officers and over 1,100 people...it became clear to me that Ann Woodward had killed her husband Billy by mistake," Braudy concluded.

Nearly seven years after the death of Ann Woodward, the great Nashua's extremely successful stud career came to an end at Spendthrift Farm. Suffering from what a farm spokesman described as muscular problems, Nashua was euthanized at age thirty. (The previous breeding season, he had gotten twenty-four of his thirty-three mares in foal.)

Nashua's numerous offspring, champion mare Shuvee among them, included eighty stakes winners — none of which Ann and Billy Woodward, his famously rich and glamorous former owners, ever saw run.

Scandalous Image

Peter Fuller felt uneasy as he watched his three-year-old colt, Dancer's Image, lag in last place during the early stages of the mile and a quarter race. Fuller's discomfort increased when Dancer's Image continued to lope along as the trailer in the fourteen-horse field.

Fuller, forty-four, was standing amid a party of sixty-five friends and family members he had invited to Churchill Downs for the Kentucky Derby. With his pride and joy some sixteen lengths off the lead, Fuller began to feel emotionally seasick in the waves of apprehension that were emanating from his guests. As he said later, "Some of them were looking at me questioningly, as if thinking, 'He's brought us here for this?' I couldn't blame them. I was starting to get a bit nervous myself."

But then the big colt got rolling and the mood changed dramatically in the Fuller party. Dancer's Image split horses as he advanced toward the frontrunners in the final turn. Then he snatched the lead with an eighth of a mile to go — under a hand ride, no less, jockey Bobby Ussery having dropped the whip.

From that point, Dancer's Image extended his advantage, arriving at the wire a length and half to the good of Forward Pass. His thrilling last-to-first effort brought a roar from the crowd of 92,617 Churchill Downs patrons on that first Saturday in May of 1968.

Fuller whooped with joy in the center of the now jubilant entourage of friends and family members. Then Fuller and his wife, Joan, accompanied by some of their eight children, hustled their way to the winner's circle to greet Dancer's Image and his grinning jockey. It was approximately 3:45 on that May 4 afternoon.

Thirty-six hours later, Peter Fuller's world changed with all the decisiveness of a massive Arctic ice floe separating. His life careened from the thrill of a classic victory to the agony attached to an announcement that, although Dancer's Image had finished first in the Kentucky Derby, and his backers had collected $9.20, $4.40, and $4 across the board, he was not indeed the winner of the race because of a positive drug test. The winner would be Calumet Farm's Forward Pass, the 2-1 Derby favorite on whom no bettor collected a dime from a win wager (his place and show backers received $4.20 and $3.20).

Then began one of the most expensive and protracted legal battles in racing history, one designed to determine what alchemy of events had turned Peter Fuller's golden triumph into dross.

"Let us have wine and women, mirth and laughter, sermons and soda water the day after," urged 19th Century

English poet George Noel Gordon, better known as Lord Byron. Peter Fuller, a successful Boston, Massachusetts, businessman and prominent civic figure, was a teetotaler. The only women he had celebrated with at a post-Derby party at Churchill Downs on Saturday, then that night at a dinner for the delighted sixty-five guests, were his kin or old friends. But in that Derby's aftermath, Fuller would have happily settled for "sermons and soda water" instead of the bitterly disappointing experience he had while attempting to "clear my horse's name," as he put it.

In what was a truly momentous year in American history — one that included assassinations of major figures, violent political protests and reactions to them (including Chicago Mayor Richard J. Daley's ordering his police force to "shoot to kill" looters), a massive anti-war march on the Pentagon, black power salutes by U.S. track stars at the Mexico City Olympics — Dancer's Image became the first and only horse ever to be disqualified from victory in the world's most famous horse race.

This "worst scandal in the 300-year history of American horse racing," as the *Chicago Tribune* termed it, received widespread media coverage, some of it in sensational form, such as *The New York Post* headline that blared "Derby Horse Drugged." Recalled Fuller, "It was the biggest headline I ever saw. It took up the whole front page. You would have thought we had gotten into another war."

When Peter and Joan Fuller flew home from Louisville, two men seated in front of them in the plane were reading newspaper reports of the medication finding. The Fullers overheard one man say to the other, "They'll do anything to win a Derby, won't they?" Joan Fuller turned to her husband and asked, "Who's he talking about?" Replied Peter Fuller, "He's talking about thee and me."

Peter Fuller entered racing as an owner in 1953 with the purchase of a horse named Michikee at a Belmont Park horses-in-training sale. Michikee won four days later, and Fuller was hooked. By the mid-1960s he had raced ten stakes winners, including the good fillies Sonny Says Quick and Main Pan, but his stable never housed anything approximating that most sought after of American Thoroughbreds — "a Derby horse."

Fuller's breeding operation grew to include more than thirty mares. The most money he had ever paid for a stallion service, $20,000, went to Alfred G. Vanderbilt's Sagamore Farm in Maryland, home of the Hall of Fame racehorse Native Dancer. Fuller sent his mare Noor's Image (a daughter of Noor, four-time conqueror of Citation) to the court of Native Dancer, the gray speedster whose dominating talents and dramatic running style had made him a darling of television viewers in the early 1950s. Native Dancer, known as "The Gray Ghost of Sagamore," lost just one race in his sensational twenty-two-race career: the 1953 Kentucky Derby, in which he was second, beaten a head by longshot Dark Star.

On April 10, 1965, Noor's Image produced a robust gray colt. Fuller liked his looks and at first considered naming him A.T.'s Image in honor of his late father, Alvan Tufts Fuller, the Republican governor of Massachusetts from 1924-28.

(Governor Fuller earned a place in the nation's history books when, in the face of a public clamor to do otherwise, he refused to commute the death sentences of the anarchists Nicola Sacco and Bartolomeo Vanzetti; having been convicted of murder, they were executed in 1927. This stance probably cost Fuller the Republican vice-presidential nomination in both 1928 and '32.)

However, Peter Fuller finally settled on the name Dancer's Image because of the youngster's physical similarity to his sire and the hope that he might have a heartening measure of paternal brilliance. One less desirable aspect of the resemblance was the foal's underpinnings. "He had Native Dancer ankles," Fuller said. In other words, they were prominent and potentially troublesome when exposed to the stress of racing.

Dancer's Image spent most of the first year of his life at Fuller's Runnymede Farm near North Hampton, New Hampshire. He was later broken at Tartan Farm in Ocala, Florida, where he was first observed by Fuller's trainer, forty-four-year-old Lou Cavalaris Jr. The colt's ankles were a cause of concern to the Ohio-born, Canadian-based conditioner who had led all North American trainers in number of wins in 1966 with 175 and saddled some 400 winners over the three previous seasons. Cavalaris advised Fuller to sell the youngster.

As a result, Dancer's Image was entered in the Fasig-Tipton Company's horses-in-training sale in February of 1967 at Hialeah. The decision to sell was opposed by Joan

Fuller, who said to her husband as the bidding began, "He's so beautiful. Why do you want to sell him?" The bidding came to a halt at $25,000. Fuller, who had believed the colt would bring at least $35,000, then bought him back for $26,000 and turned him over to Cavalaris to train. Serendipity dripped all over this decision.

In his first year of competition, the hardy Dancer's Image saw action at eight different racetracks in the United States and Canada. From his fifteen starts he garnered eight victories (four of them in stakes) and four seconds. His seven wins in Canada earned him the two-year-old colt championship of that nation.

Dancer's Image launched his three-year-old season on New Year's Day of 1968, running second in a mile stakes at Laurel. But it wasn't until late March that Fuller began to entertain thoughts of the Kentucky Derby. Jockey Bobby Ussery, who had replaced Phil Grimm as the colt's regular rider, suggested to Cavalaris that the blinkers be taken off Dancer's Image. In his first start with Ussery and without the hood, Dancer's Image defeated Elmendorf Farm's well-regarded Verbatim.

The next race on Dancer's Image's schedule was the mile and one-sixteenth, $100,000 Governor's Gold Cup at Bowie on April 6. On April 4, Dr. Martin Luther King was assassinated in Memphis, an event that sparked riots and demonstrations in many of the nation's major cities, including Baltimore. Bowie racetrack officials considered postponing the Governor's Cup, one of the major races of the meeting, but finally decided to go ahead with it. The race was run without incident. Dancer's Image came from the clouds to win going away by three lengths.

Peter Fuller was deeply affected by the death of Dr. King, whom he had met at Boston University. Fuller was a trustee of Boston U., which both Dr. King and his wife, Coretta, had attended. "I didn't agree with all of Dr. King's positions," Fuller said, "but I admired many of the things he stood for, especially his advocating social change through non-violent means, and I wanted to do something for his family after this tragedy occurred."

What Peter and Joan Fuller decided to do was donate the winner's share ($62,500 after the trainer and jockey percentages had been deducted) of the Governor's Cup purse to Coretta King. This was no exercise in the brand of "radical chic" prevalent in some portions of American society at the time. Peter Fuller had black friends, many of them made during his youthful career as a successful amateur boxer (fifty-five bouts, fifty wins, New England Golden Gloves and AAU heavyweight champion). His boyhood hero had been Joe Louis. The only fight Fuller lost by knockout was to Coley Wallace, who went on to a fine professional boxing career and eventually portrayed Louis in a biographical movie of that champion. His loss to Wallace convinced Fuller that he did not have a future as a pro, and in 1949 he joined his father's firm, which at the time was the largest privately owned Cadillac-Oldsmobile dealership in the United States. Referring to the man who so forcefully diverted him from boxing to business, Fuller said in an interview early in 2000 that "Coley and I remain friends to this day."

The Fullers flew to Atlanta where they met "Mrs. King at her church," Fuller recalled, and there they gave her the check. "She was very appreciative," Fuller said. "Joan and I didn't want any publicity out of it. Harry Belafonte (the noted entertainer) was acting as an adviser to Mrs. King and he was at our meeting. He said they would prefer to keep it quiet, too, that it wouldn't look good for them to be accepting such a gift from us at that time. I said 'fine.' "

Next on Dancer's Image's agenda was Aqueduct's Wood Memorial Stakes on April 20. Some ten days before the Wood, Fuller was offered $1 million for his now very much prized colt. He discussed this with his family, who urged him to refuse the offer, and that he did. Dancer's Image won the mile and one-eighth Wood by three-quarters of a length in his best performance yet. "After the Wood, Lou (Cavalaris) turned to me and said, 'You might have a Triple Crown winner,' " Fuller recalled. "The shakes went right through me. It was a tremendously thrilling thought."

As Fuller's excitement level rose, so did the value of Dancer's Image. Fuller had him insured with Lloyd's of London for $1.5 million. After the Wood Memorial, Fuller turned down another offer to buy Dancer's Image, this one for $2 million. Friends of Fuller's in the Kentucky horse industry told him that if Dancer's Image won the Triple Crown, he could be syndicated for possibly as much as $7.5 million. These were dizzying numbers when bandied about in connection with Fuller's $26,000 "buy back."

It was the afternoon of the Wood Memorial that Fuller's gift to Mrs. King was made public. Announcer Win Elliot, privy to what the Fullers had done with the Governor's Cup purse, had some airtime to fill in the course of the radio broadcast of the Wood and did so by reporting the story of Fuller's selfless act. This was not greeted by universal applause across the nation and certainly not in Kentucky.

One year earlier, in the spring of 1967, Dr. King had led a widely publicized open-housing demonstration in Louisville a couple of weeks prior to the Derby. Midway during Derby Week that year some young blacks ran across the racing strip at Churchill Downs in front of a field of horses, creating great consternation and television footage, though no injuries. Dr. King urged restraint and argued against any Derby Day actions by his supporters. None occurred, either as a result of Dr. King's plea or the plethora of Kentucky National Guardsmen who were deployed prominently around the track as Proud Clarion swept to his smashing upset ($62.20) victory under none other than Bobby Ussery.

Many Kentuckians reacted coolly to having such "real life" issues impinge on the Derby. It was not a popular thing in 1967, and Peter Fuller's gift to Mrs. King a year later elicited expressions of scorn and resentment from many citizens of the Bluegrass State.

Public reaction elsewhere, at least as measured by the mail and phone calls Fuller received, "was for the most part very positive," Fuller said, "although some were vicious. I got a phone call from one guy referring to the 'nigger horse' I owned, and a few letters from the lunatic fringe. But the overwhelming majority of the responses were in support of what we'd done. In the black community Dancer's Image

became kind of a symbol for some, and he had a lot of supporters there. Many of those people said they didn't know
much about racing, but that they would be rooting for
Dancer's Image in the Derby."

In the wake of the publicity regarding the gift to Mrs.
King, Fuller — who once described himself as "the new guy
in the game, from abolitionist Boston" — said he called
Warner Jones to talk about possibly bringing extra security
from Boston to Louisville. Jones told Fuller, "Oh, don't do
that. That will just exacerbate the situation. We have plenty
of security." As Fuller later noted, "Obviously, that was not
the case."

The road to the Kentucky Derby is rarely trouble free, and
it certainly was not smooth for Dancer's Image. On Sunday
of Derby Week, a clear, crisp morning, the problem of
Dancer's Image's always problematical right front ankle
came to the fore.

After arriving in Louisville, Dancer's Image was vanned to
Churchill Downs and housed in Barn 24, headquarters of
forty-three-year-old Dr. Alex Harthill, the man known as
"the Derby Vet" because he had treated so many Derby horses in the past. Harthill was considered one of the most talented, successful, and controversial equine practitioners.
The suggestion that Fuller hire him came from owner-breeder Warner L. Jones, master of Kentucky's Hermitage Farm
and a director of Churchill Downs, who described Harthill
as "the best vet in the country." Over the years many others
have termed him "a genius" in the treatment of equine leg

ailments.

A third-generation veterinarian, Harthill, upon graduating from Ohio State's school of veterinary medicine in 1948, soon took on some Calumet Farm horses as his first patients and continued to treat Calumet stock through the years. On several occasions Harthill had his license suspended for various infractions but won it back upon appeal. He was frequently under scrutiny by the *Louisville Courier-Journal*. In 1972 that paper, calling for the veterinarian's removal from Barn 24 at Churchill, editorialized that "The faith of bettors shouldn't be abused by allowing a veterinarian who has been under suspicion in case after case, here and elsewhere, to enjoy unique accommodations in a key security area of the Downs..."

"I needed a vet for my horse at Churchill in the days before the Derby," Fuller said. "Warner (Jones) recommended Harthill to me."

In an interview early in 2000, Harthill said he agreed to treat Dancer's Image at Churchill "at the request of an old friend of mine, Odie Clelland, who trained for Fuller in New England. I didn't know anything about the horse before then. The horse meant nothing to me. I didn't even know he had won the Wood. I never met Fuller until the day before the Derby."

That Sunday morning before the Derby Harthill and trainer Cavalaris concentrated on the colt's ankle condition, which had become aggravated after the Wood and the joint was inflamed and swollen. This was not a career-ending condition, but with only six days left before the Derby to have it treated successfully was crucial. Daily tubbing in ice water had not done the job. (Hall of Fame trainer Marion H. Van Berg got a look at Dancer's Image when Harthill took him on a backstretch tour to see the Derby horses. According to Harthill, Van Berg, after observing Dancer's Image, remarked that he had "$2,500 claimers that aren't as sore as that colt." Van Berg said he could not understand how "they can be thinking of running him in the Derby.")

At the end of the Sunday morning examination of Dancer's Image, Cavalaris and Harthill agreed that the best prescription was to treat the colt with Butazolidin, or "Bute." Butazolidin, the trade name for phenylbutazone, is a commonly prescribed anti-inflammatory agent-not a stimulant, or depressant, or form of "dope." Under the Kentucky rules of racing in effect in 1968, the use of this U.S. Food and Drug Administration-approved medication was permitted for training, but not for racing. Any trace of it in a post-race test would be cause for disqualification. Bute usually clears a horse's system in thirty to seventy-two hours, so giving it to Dancer's Image was believed to be safe enough. A four-gram dose of Bute was thrust into Dancer's Image's throat with a balling gun. "That was the only time that week that I gave the horse Bute," Harthill said.

In a post-Derby statement made to Churchill Downs security director Alvin Schem, Dr. Harthill said that "on Sunday morning, April 28, Mr. Cavalaris and I inspected the right fore ankle of Dancer's Image. We agreed the horse, obviously, had slightly sprained the ankle while at exercise on Saturday and that he should receive four grams of phenylbutazone. I administered it. This was approximately 152 hours before the running of the Derby. It is my professional opinion, and I believe the consensus of the veterinary profession, that a normal dose (as was four grams in this case) of phenylbutazone will be completely expelled by a horse's system within a maximum of 72 hours after administration."

Horses had been allowed to run on Butazolidin in Kentucky until 1962, when the racing commission outlawed it. In 1974, the commission reversed itself and permitted Bute once again; it continues in widespread use in Kentucky as well as in most other American racing jurisdictions. Dancer's Image in 1968 fell into one of those dozen "gap years."

Dancer's Image had been treated with Bute "a few times before," said Fuller, adding that the horse's physical reaction to the medication was "very predictable. He showed signs of colic and 'spewed,' or had terrible diarrhea, each time. He had the same reaction after getting a dose that Sunday before the Derby. But he didn't have anything like it at any other time later in the week, before or after the Derby. As far as I know," Fuller said, "the only Bute my horse got in Kentucky was given to him that Sunday morning of Derby Week."

The treatment was wonderfully effective. The next morning, Monday, April 29, the fluids in Dancer's Image's ankle were gone. Cavalaris sent him to the racetrack and, after galloping a couple of miles, Dancer's Image breezed three furlongs in :36 and looked fine doing it. On both Thursday and Friday, Harthill treated Dancer's Image with vitamins and Azium, the latter another anti-inflammatory medication.

Cavalaris' original plan had been to run Dancer's Image in

the Derby Trial on Tuesday, April 30. But the trainer knew that was out of the question because of the race-day ban on Bute. So, he had Dancer's Image galloped each day the rest of the week, lengthy exercises designed to increase stamina while not putting undue pressure on the ankle. In midweek, Cavalaris departed Churchill, leaving Dancer's Image in the care of assistant trainer Robert Barnard and groom Russell Parchen, and returned to Canada to check on the string he had stabled there for his major patron, George Gardiner. Fuller said he "wasn't too happy about" Cavalaris' absence during that period, but that he understood it from a business standpoint.

Cavalaris was at Churchill Downs on Derby Day morning to watch Dancer's Image again gallop strongly. After the exercise, he told *Daily Racing Form* executive columnist Joe Hirsch that "I've looked for the slightest possible excuse to scratch this horse from the Derby. He is a very valuable animal. There is a syndication in the process of being completed, and I wouldn't want to take the slightest chance of running him if he wasn't 100 percent. But I can't find a single small reason not to run him, so he goes."

(The previous day, veterinarian Harthill was far less sanguine about Dancer's Image's condition. In the presence of witnesses he told Cavalaris that he should scratch the colt from the Derby. "There's nothing I can do for you now," Harthill said.)

Dancer's Image went to the winner's circle Saturday afternoon. On Monday, Peter Fuller received a phone call from his friend Warner Jones at Louisville's Brown Hotel.

"They've got a problem with your horse's test," Jones told an incredulous Fuller. "It's very serious," he added. That it was.

——————————

The "problem" was tied to a $9.50 laboratory test, one of the urinalyses done on each of the ten winners on the Derby Day program. Nine of the tests were clear. The one that wasn't belonged to the winner of the Derby.

The historical significance of this was not lost on Red Smith, the first sports columnist to win a Pulitzer Prize for commentary and a writer who regularly covered the Run for the Roses. The ninety-three previous runnings of the Derby had not produced a disqualification of any sort despite numerous incidents of blocking, bumping, and impeding, nor any punishment for the use of an illegal medication. But, wrote Smith, "Almost surely, horses have been doped for the Derby." Sir Barton, the 1919 Derby hero and first winner of the American Triple Crown, Smith wrote, was reputed to be one of racing's great equine hopheads, supposedly "coked to the eyes whenever he ran."

In bygone days, Smith continued, "touching up" was not uncommon: "Ethics only forbade double-crossing form players by running an animal 'hot' one day and 'cold' the next... (Members of) the old school never accepted the notion that it was wrong to help a horse out. Old-timers still tell gleefully of seeing Derby horses enter the paddock 'with all their lights turned on' long after Sir Barton's day."

The urine sample had been taken from Dancer's Image in the Churchill detention barn about an hour after the Derby. It was tagged with the number 3956 and the letter U, denoting urine sample. Half the tag, with the horse's name and number on it, was sent to the stewards' office where it was locked up. The other half of the tag was applied to the bottle containing the urine. This tag bore only the number, not the horse's name. The bottle was sent to the racing commission laboratory located in a trailer at the track. The idea was for lab technicians to run "blind" tests in which they had no knowledge of the identity of the horse undergoing scrutiny for illegal medications.

Specimen 3956U was tested by technician Jimmy Chinn. When it began to change color, Chinn suspected he was dealing with a positive. He notified his immediate supervisor, who then telephoned Kenneth Smith at a post-Derby party he was attending at Audobon Country Club. Smith's company, Louisville Testing Laboratory Inc., was under contract to the Kentucky Racing Commission to handle all its testing. After running his own tests on the urine sample Chinn pinpointed, Smith late that Saturday night called Lewis Finley Jr., the commission steward, to report that there was a positive from Derby Day. Smith was told to follow procedure and submit the written report of his finding on Monday, which was the next racing day at Churchill.

Fuller and his family on Sunday had been hosted by Warner Jones at Hermitage Farm, where Jones told Fuller he was looking forward to a syndication of Dancer's Image that could be valued at some $3 million; he said the deal was "nearly done." That same day, chemist Smith returned to his lab in downtown Louisville. He packed up some of the 3956U sample and airmailed it to prominent chemist Lewis

Harris in Lincoln, Nebraska. Smith had telephoned Harris, asking him to run a routine check on the sample and to inform Smith of his findings.

Monday morning steward Finley and his colleagues opened the envelope that contained the horses' names and tag numbers of their urine samples. To their amazement, they saw that sample 3956U belonged to Dancer's Image. Smith had not yet submitted his written report to Finley. He informed the steward that he was awaiting a report of the findings by Lewis Harris. Smith said he was convinced it was a positive.

The stewards said they did not want to wait for "any findings from Nebraska" and ordered Smith to write up his report. They informed racing commission Chairman George Egger of the positive test and dispatched security guards to search Dancer's Image's stall at Barn 24 for evidence of Butazolidin, but none was discovered. The next day Cavalaris was officially informed of the lab finding, and the first public announcement of it was made.

(Lewis Harris' tests on the urine sample Smith sent him proved negative, a fact that Smith kept to himself. In September of 1968, Smith told Harris that the portion of Dancer's Image urine he had shipped to him had had all the Bute extracted from it. One of Fuller's attorneys termed this revelation, which was given in sworn testimony, "unbelievable.")

––––––––––––

The 1968 Derby first departed the racetrack for hearing rooms and courthouses on May 12, when the Churchill stewards began a closed hearing that encompassed forty-three hours over three days. On Wednesday, May 15, the stewards ruled that Dancer's Image was disqualified from his Derby win for racing with a prohibited substance. Forward Pass was declared winner of the $122,600 purse. Cavalaris and his assistant, Robert Barnard, were each suspended for thirty days for failure to safeguard the condition of the horse. Slightly more than two weeks later, Fuller formally entered an appeal of the stewards' rulings to the racing commission.

Dancer's Image, meanwhile, had been shipped to Pimlico for a rematch with Forward Pass in the Preakness Stakes on May 18. With Cavalaris under suspension, the colt was under the care of Runnymede Farm manager Bob Casey. Maryland, like Kentucky and New York (where Dancer's Image had won the Wood), prohibited the use of Butazolidin on race day. After the Derby ruling, Lloyd's of London abruptly terminated the $1.5 million policy Fuller held on Dancer's Image, so the colt ran uninsured in the Preakness.

Recalled Fuller, "Bobby (Ussery) had him too far back early, but he came on strong. He looked like (football great) Jim Brown running through traffic." Dancer's Image closed well to finish third, six lengths behind the victorious Forward Pass. But his "Jim Brown" running style cost him. The *Daily Racing Form* chart footnotes said Dancer's Image "finished gamely to just miss the place," but that he had "bullied his way through a narrow opening at the furlong pole," bumping Martins Jig. The stewards disqualified Dancer's Image and placed him eighth.

"There's no question he deserved to have his number

taken down," Fuller said after the Preakness, adding that he did not blame jockey Ussery for the disqualification. "This is the chance you must take with a come-from-behind horse," Fuller said. "We have gotten through the hole before. In other races it has opened up for us; this time it did not. That's just racing."

(Forward Pass' bid for a Triple Crown sweep ended when he ran second to Stage Door Johnny in the Belmont Stakes.)

Two weeks later, Dancer's Image worked six furlongs in 1:13 2/5 in preparation for the Belmont. But he came back sore in his right front ankle and Fuller decided that was it. "I didn't want to risk any serious injury to this horse who had given us so much," Fuller said.

Veterinarian Mark Gerard, who treated Dancer's Image at Belmont, said the colt had "distension of the joint capsule of the right ankle," or a strained ankle joint. X-rays did not show any bone chips or calcium buildup "or anything of a really serious problem," Dr. Gerard said, adding that "normal treatment would find a horse with this condition returning to racing after a rest of six months."

Announcing his colt's retirement, Fuller said Dancer's Image was "too honest and game to allow him to race in the Belmont and not be in perfect physical condition to give his best." He said it would not be "economically sound" to bring Dancer's Image back the next year, thus "We will not be able to...prove that this colt could have won (the Derby) without any assistance at all."

Fuller told *Daily Racing Form* columnist Herb Goldstein that "the horse's condition has always been first with me no matter what you may have read or heard. It was always my understanding with Lou Cavalaris that no matter how many people I had invited to see a race, if Lou didn't think the horse was ready to run, he wouldn't run. That's how it has always been."

Dancer's Image retired with a career record of twelve wins in twenty-four starts (including seven stakes wins) and earnings of $236,636. Despite the post-Derby brouhaha, Fuller was able to syndicate Dancer's Image at $62,500 per share, making for a total valuation of $2 million. "Some of the biggest names in racing who had shown an avid interest in buying into the syndication before the Derby dropped out of the picture afterwards," Fuller said. "But others, including some very good friends, stepped in."

On June 3, 1968, Fuller appealed the decision of the Churchill Downs stewards to the Kentucky Racing Commission. The next day the commission issued citations to Cavalaris, Barnard, Harthill, trainer Doug Davis Jr., and Fuller's attorneys, Arthur W. Grafton Sr. and Edward S. (Ned) Bonnie, to show cause why they should not be ruled off for involvement in one of the most bizarre chapters of the Dancer's Image saga.

Two days after the Derby, and shortly after word got out about the positive test, Davis (who died in 1976) and his longtime friend Harthill met with Cavalaris and Barnard in Davis' motel room in Louisville near Churchill Downs. Davis and Cavalaris had been friends for years, having raced against each other in Canada.

According to subsequent testimony before the racing commission, all the men said they were at a loss to account for the positive test. Harthill and Barnard left for the track. Cavalaris was distraught, Davis said, wringing his hands and pounding on a table, "and then he asked me if I thought Alex could have made a mistake, got the wrong bottle or something; I told him there was no chance of that...He began pacing again, very upset, and then he...looked me in the face real serious and he asks point blank, did I think Alex gave that horse Bute? I told him again that was ridiculous, that Alex had nothing to gain.

"Now, in my opinion," Davis continued, "...he was accusing Alex. I thought Lou was looking for someone to put this thing on, to share the blame."

After Davis met with Harthill later that day, the two men came up with a scheme to "test Cavalaris' honesty, to try to smoke him out," Davis testified. Davis informed Harthill about Cavalaris' asking him if Harthill had perhaps inadvertently given Bute to Dancer's Image too close to the race. Davis told Harthill that while Harthill "might not be elected (by Cavalaris to be the fall guy), you're damn sure nominated...My motive was to protect my friend Alex from a false accusation," Davis testified.

Harthill said he then came up with a scheme, "a sort of half-ass brainstorm we had in a sort of panic, I was thinking of it as a matter of self-preservation" — to "test" Cavalaris. That evening they placed a foreign substance — ground-up aspirin — in Dancer's Image's feed at the barn. They told Barnard, who was present, that it was crushed tablets of Bute. Harthill testified that he thought if Cavalaris was guilty of giving Bute to Dancer's Image shortly before the Derby, he (Cavalaris) would seize upon the doctored feed as an excuse to pin the blame for the positive test on someone else. On the other hand, if Cavalaris were honest, Harthill said, he thought the trainer would refuse to play along with the scheme and would dispose of the feed.

"What Doug said to me," Harthill said in an interview early in 2000, "was that he was trying to protect his friend, Cavalaris. 'Why don't we just say the damned stuff (Butazolidin) was in the feed?' Doug said. The idea was to suggest that somebody else could have slipped it to the horse. It was a well-meaning but foolish idea...a phantasmagoria."

Cavalaris told the commission that after he discovered the "salted" feed in Dancer's Image's ration of bran, he poured it out on the ground and called his attorneys, Grafton and Bonnie. After arriving at the barn, Grafton put the doctored feed in his car and drove away to dump it alongside a rural road outside of Louisville. They all paid for this: once the commission learned of this it issued citations charging that the men had interfered with the Dancer's Image investigation. Harthill and Davis each chose to pay $500 fines in lieu of thirty-day suspensions. Fines of $300 each were meted out to Cavalaris and Barnard. It was only the fourth infraction of Cavalaris' career, which began in 1946 and was capped by his 1995 election to Canada's Racing Hall of Fame; the other three were $25 fines for entering ineligible horses.

(In a 1969 interview with *Daily Racing Form* columnist

Don Grisham, Harthill said he and Davis "have been abused throughout this thing. I came under a lot of fire following the Derby. Unfortunately, we veterinarians have little recourse after treating a horse. We can be crossed up by anyone having access to the animal."

(Davis told Grisham he and Harthill were both "disturbed" about a printed report hinting that a $50,000 bank withdrawal played a role in the 1968 Derby. "The money," Davis said, "was...from an actual sale...of the horse Northern Pride." Proceeds from the sale, Davis said, had been deposited in the horsemen's account at Churchill, then withdrawn on May 10. "This was six days after the Derby and not three days before the race as falsely stated, which intimated the money was withdrawn from a bank account and used to engender a betting coup.")

The Kentucky Racing Commission hearing on Fuller's appeal commenced November 18, 1968 in Louisville's Freedom Hall. Fuller was one of the first witnesses, stating, "I am making this appeal because I know I didn't do anything wrong, I believe the members of my organization didn't do anything wrong, and I feel that I should...find out what did go wrong.

"This horse (Dancer's Image) was to be syndicated down here in Kentucky," Fuller continued, for "$2.5 to $3 million after the Derby, and now, all of a sudden, this horse is... libeled. This is a...very strong part of the reason that I have appealed. This horse is no phony horse. This horse won races on his ability, without the help of anything..."

The commission questioned Harthill at length, including

asking him if he had bet on Dancer's Image in the Kentucky Derby. Replied Harthill, "You couldn't have given me a ticket on him...sore as he was..." (In an August, 1968 interview with the *Chicago Tribune*, Harthill referred to Dancer's Image as "a walking drugstore" during the week leading up to the Derby. He denied giving the horse Bute after the Sunday, April 28 treatment and speculated, intriguingly, that if someone else had not, then because "all four of the tests given for the drug by the racing chemist were nonspecific for Butazolidin...it is possible that what they discovered is the buildup of the Azium...a drug twice administered to Dancer's Image during Derby Week...which is not prohibited in Kentucky...and has many of the properties of Butazolidin.")

In his testimony before the commission, Harthill recounted the medications he had administered to Dancer's Image at Churchill Downs. He repeated what he had said at the stewards' hearing — that on Thursday before the Derby Dancer's Image appeared to him to be so sore that he advised against having the horse galloped, but that the horse's condition improved tremendously that afternoon, and that by Friday he was sound. The ailing ankle at that point in time, Harthill said, "was beautiful."

Harthill and two other veterinarians, including the man representing the Kentucky Racing Commission, Dr. L. M. Roach, were asked if such a marked improvement in a horse's condition was consistent with his having received Bute, and all three men said "yes." But under cross-examination by Fuller's attorneys, all three vets also said that it was possible for a horse to "dramatically recover" in this fashion without *any* medication. Stated Roach: "That a horse was lame one day and sound the next doesn't prove he had any medication."

Prominent chemists called by Fuller's attorneys said that, in their opinion, the post-race tests done by commission chemist Smith were incomplete, inconclusive and ineptly conducted. Kentucky Attorney General John B. Breckenridge and George Rabe, his assistant representing the racing commission, countered with their own expert witnesses who backed up Smith's expertise and supported his findings.

After some eighty hours of hearings over three weeks, involving a parade of chemists, veterinarians, horsemen, stewards and trainers, the commission announced its decision on December 23, 1968: it upheld the ruling of the Churchill stewards in both disqualifying Dancer's Image and ordering the Derby purse redistribution, concluding "as a matter of law that phenylbutazone and/or a derivative thereof was present in the urine of the horse Dancer's Image, following the seventh race on May 4, 1968, in violation of Rule 14.04 of the Kentucky Rules of Racing...Regardless of the amount of phenylbutazone...its presence...shows that the administration affected the health and speed of the horse by enabling him to run racing sound."

On December 11, 1970, Fuller's fortunes took a temporary turn for the better when Franklin Circuit Judge Henry Meigs set aside the racing commission's ruling against Dancer's Image "for lack of substantial evidence to support it." Meigs

ruled that the tests on which chemist Smith based his finding of phenylbutazone were "inadequate and contradictory."

"It is undeniably apparent from the record," Meigs concluded, "that misunderstanding, misconception, and mis-
chance have attended every unraveling thread of this case
since Kenneth Smith retired to his laboratory Saturday
evening following the 1968 Derby." Meigs ordered that the
Derby purse should be distributed according to the original
order of finish and that Fuller should "recover the costs
incurred in seeking to receive the winner's purse."

None of what Meigs ordered ever happened. Assistant
Attorney General Rabe on March 9, 1971, filed an appeal to
the Kentucky Court of Appeals which, on April 28, 1972,
overturned Meigs' ruling. Dancer's Image was again disqualified, Forward Pass declared the winner of the 1968 Derby —
the eighth for Calumet, a record unlikely to be matched.

The unanimous decision of the seven-member panel stated
that "The Racing Commission, as trier of facts, saw each
witness and was in superior position to evaluate the situation as well as the conduct and demeanor of each witness as
he testified; to consider the credibility of the witness; and to
determine the weight as between conflicting statements of
witnesses or even a single witness.

"This court, after having considered the entire record and
the law of the case...finds and now holds that there was an
abundance of substantial evidence supporting the findings
and rulings of the Kentucky State Racing Commission."

When, on June 30, 1972 Fuller's petition for a rehearing
was refused by the Court of Appeals, the former boxer fig-

ured he had "lost his last round." His expenses in this case had mounted to nearly a quarter of a million dollars, he said, which was on top of the lost Derby purse ($122,600) and the diminished value of Dancer's Image as a stallion in the eyes of commercial breeders because he was not a Kentucky Derby winner. Fuller hung up his gloves.

––––––––––––––

Dancer's Image began his stud career at Glade Valley Farm in Maryland in 1969 and remained there until 1973 when he was sent to Ireland, leased by prominent French owner-breeder Daniel Wildenstein. In July of 1976 Fuller sold twenty-five of the thirty-two shares in the eleven-year-old stallion to a group of European breeders headed by Wildenstein. Dancer's Image then stood in France before moving to Japan late in 1979, where he died at age twenty-seven on December 26, 1991. The thirty stakes winners sired by Dancer's Image included three European champions: the colts Godswalk and Saritamer (both of whom became successful stallions), and the filly Lianga.

(After beginning his stud career at Calumet Farm, Forward Pass was sold to Japan where he died at age fifteen on December 1, 1980. He was the sire of six stakes winners.)

Fuller remained in the sport. In 1985 his three-year-old filly Mom's Command, ridden by Fuller's daughter Abby, wrote a memorable chapter of racing history when she won the New York Triple Crown for fillies and an Eclipse Award as champion of her age and sex. Fuller continues to "race a few horses," but nothing of the quality of Dancer's Image.

Fuller said early in 2000 that he still had "no idea how

Dancer's Image was given Butazolidin prior to the Derby — "if he was" — or if his selfless gift to Coretta King somehow had backfired on him and his horse. Fuller said he had come to believe that the threat by Calumet owner Lucille Markey to "never again race in Kentucky if Forward Pass isn't declared the winner of the Derby" had a strong influence on the outcome of his battle. "She made good on a similar threat in California after her filly Miz Clementine was disqualified in a race out there, you know," Fuller said. "And Kentucky without Calumet, well, that's pretty unthinkable."

He recognizes the irony in the fact that the official winner of the 1968 Derby, Forward Pass, was not tested for medication after the race (fifth-place finisher Kentucky Sherry, selected at random, was the only horse besides Dancer's Image to be tested). And, he said, "If anything good came out of all this," Fuller said, "it's that security for the Kentucky Derby horses was improved tremendously after that year."

Harthill also remains active in racing, with a thriving veterinary practice based in Kentucky. Asked if he thought Dancer's Image had run on Bute in the Derby, he replied, "I got no idea." If the horse did have Bute in his system, Harthill added, he had "no idea" who might have given it to him. Could Dancer's Image have won without Bute? "Yes," said Harthill. "Some horses can run sore. Some big horses have big motors. He could have run and won with just hay, oats, and water, yes."

As to the various fingers of suspicion that have been pointed his way regarding the Dancer's Image case, Harthill was philosophical. "I can't do anything about that," he said. "All I know is that I was as innocent as a new-born babe."

Fuller looks back, he said, with bitterness — "not for me but for the horse. Dancer's Image was a terrifically game and competitive animal. He ran a great Derby, going from last to first and winning going away. This thing hurt his reputation terribly. I don't care what people think," Fuller said, "I still consider Dancer's Image to be the winner of that Derby."

All these years later, no one has been able to solve the mystery of who administered Butazolidin to Dancer's Image, as chemist Smith, the Kentucky Racing Commission, and Kentucky Court of Appeals concluded was done. As commission Chairman George Egger commented nearly three decades ago, "How are we ever going to find that out? Will the party who did it admit it? Why, he would be ruined for life."

Hot at Hawthorne

It was a cold autumn day in Chicago — Saturday, November 18, 1978 — and one of the Midwest's major horse players, having checked out the weather, decided to pass up his regular visit to Hawthorne Race Course.

Usually, the big bettor known as "Milwaukee Lou" never missed the weekend programs at what he called his favorite track. When the two men who normally accompanied him on the ninety mile drive south from their Milwaukee homes dropped by for him that rainy morning, Lou waved them off. "See you tonight," he said. "Good luck."

That evening, Lou and his wife were just ordering dinner in a downtown Milwaukee restaurant when Lou's horse-playing friends returned from their trek to Hawthorne. "Who won the double?" Milwaukee Lou asked.

"Nervous Tortilla took the first; Charollius won the second," one of the men replied. Hearing this, Milwaukee Lou almost choked on his brandy and soda.

"Charollius!" he exclaimed. "Impossible! A guy I know used to own that bum — the horse can't stand up on an off-track. Couldn't have been Charollius."

Milwaukee Lou was absolutely correct. As was later established, it definitely was not the $2,500 claimer Charollius who skipped six furlongs over the sloppy Hawthorne strip in 1:12 4/5. Rather, the horse who won the second race that day before a crowd of 13,788 was a ringer produced by Charles Lee (Charlie) Wonder — a horse named Roman Decade, whose previous start had been in allowance company at Beulah Park in Ohio and who in the winter of 1977 had raced in $20,000 claiming races at Meadowlands in New Jersey and in early 1978 had raced for an $18,000 claiming tag at New York's Aqueduct Racetrack.

The real Charollius had made his previous start at Thistledown in Ohio, an undistinguished effort in $2,500 claiming company. Entered to be claimed for $3,500 on November 18 at Hawthorne, and having won just one of his twenty-one previous starts that season, "Charollius" was a longshot, both on paper and in the track program (30-1). But there was action on him early. After his odds had plummeted to 8-5, they drifted back up to 4-1 (he went off as the third choice in the field of eleven). After Roman Decade, performing as Charollius, reported home one and three-quarter lengths to the good, the win payoff was $10.80.

The daily double — betting on which, of course, had closed before the money began to show prior to the second race — was completely out of line, 2-1 shot Nervous Tortilla combining with the second race winner for a return of $113.60. A parlay would have resulted in about half that figure.

One day after Charlie Wonder and colleagues pulled off

this illegal wagering coup, old Hawthorne burned to the ground.

Prior to the November 19 blaze that leveled it, causing property damage originally estimated at between $10 and $14 million as well as forcing the cancellation of twenty-eight remaining racing dates, Hawthorne had been hit by a series of small conflagrations. A concession stand burned in October of 1975; there was a small fire in an area of the clubhouse the following February; a small barn fire in April of 1977; then an electrical fire in the clubhouse on October 29 of 1978. The last one was the most serious in this series, causing some $40,000 in damage to an area housing cables and wiring used for the totalizator board. This Sunday morning blaze — exactly three weeks before the big one — was discovered by a *Daily Racing Form* clocker who was on duty timing horses and smelled smoke a little before 7 a.m. There was no loss of life in any of these cases.

(On the Monday following the fire that affected the tote system, many of Hawthorne's win, place, and show betting machines were out of action. As a result, the track received permission from the Illinois Racing Board to offer gimmick betting — anything other than straight wagering — on all of the nine races that day, a first in Illinois.)

This was a period of great concern for owners of American racetracks, many of whose plants were of ancient vintage and susceptible to fire. Fairmount Park in downstate Illinois had its stands destroyed in 1974. In 1977, Washington Park, in the Chicago suburb of Homewood, burned to the ground, and that same year the clubhouse and grandstand of Garden

State Park in New Jersey went up in flames. In Massachusetts, Rockingham Park's grandstand was destroyed in 1980, five years before Arlington Park in Arlington Heights, Illinois, fell victim to an all-encompassing fire. All of these tracks with the exception of Washington Park were rebuilt; the site of the famed 1955 match race in which Nashua defeated Swaps was sold and then converted into a shopping center.

Constructed on a 119-acre site purchased by Edward Corrigan in 1890, Hawthorne first opened on May 20, 1891. The ties of the Carey family to Hawthorne extend to 1905, when the property was acquired by brick manufacturer and Thoroughbred owner Thomas Carey, a former Chicago alderman. He bought it from Ed Corrigan, who had suffered financial reverses tied to the failure of two other tracks: Ingleside Park in San Francisco and City Park in New Orleans. Six months before he formally petitioned for bankruptcy, Corrigan turned Hawthorne over to Carey for $2,000 in cash and $26,000 in notes.

When Thomas Carey died in 1925, Hawthorne was then leased by the Thomas Carey Estate to the Chicago Business Men's Racing Association, an arrangement that lasted until 1946. That year, control of the track's operation returned to the Carey Estate, whose managing director was Robert F. Carey. Hawthorne has been operated by the Estate ever since.

The November 19, 1978 fire broke out a few minutes after 5 a.m. near a wooden wall in the grandstand area, the same general area as the blaze three weeks earlier. This one, however, proved uncontainable, despite the efforts of firefighters from Chicago and four neighboring suburbs. Fortunately, no one was injured, and the 1,300 horses stabled at Hawthorne and adjacent Sportsman's Park all were unharmed. Lost were the racing silks and riding equipment that had been used at the meeting, worth a combined total of $90,000, as well as personal belongings of members of the press corps, estimated values of which ranged widely.

"My father (Robert F. Carey) ran Hawthorne for more than thirty years," said current track president and general manager Thomas F. Carey, grandson and namesake of the alderman. "He was devastated by the fire. Fortunately, he lived to see the track rebuilt, but he passed away during the week after we reopened in the fall of 1980."

Carey, who has headed Hawthorne since his father's death (and whose son, Thomas III, now assists him in management of the track), remembers that day very clearly. He received a phone call at his northside Chicago home alerting him to the situation, jumped into his car, and "drove like a madman" down the Dan Ryan Expressway toward the track. It was still dark, a little before dawn. When Carey's car reached the rise in the highway where the Ryan connects with the Stevenson Expressway, he looked to the west and was immediately stunned. "It was like when you were a kid," he said, "and piled up cardboard boxes for a big bonfire out in an open field — a huge fire, flames way up in the sky. When I saw that, I knew it was all over for the old Hawthorne."

Carey was a close friend of Chicago's Fire Commissioner,

Robert J. Quinn. The two men played handball together every week. Even though Hawthorne is located outside the Chicago city limits, units of the Chicago Fire Department arrived to work alongside suburban firefighters in trying to combat the blaze.

But it was too far gone by the time they began their efforts. Actually, with a structure of that kind — all hardwood floors, beadboard ceilings, 450-feet long, built that long ago — it was amazing that something hadn't happened before, even though Hawthorne had one of the best sprinkler systems of any track in the country. As Commissioner Quinn told Tom Carey, "Sprinklers are fine, but a strong fire will run over them every time."

After he had reached the scene, one of the fire captains asked Carey if there was anything he especially thought they should try to remove from the burning structure. Carey immediately replied, "Yes, the foal papers." Then Carey, the fire captain, and another firefighter hurried to the outside wall of the racing secretary's office and cut a hole in it. Carey was given fireman's protective gear — leather coat, hat, and gloves — and the three of them crawled through the hole into the office. Carey knew the location of the safe that contained the foal papers. He tied a steel cable around the heavy safe, and the three men managed to haul it out of there not long before the roof caved in.

Carey termed the whole thing "a numbing experience." When the fire was finally extinguished, there was a pile of ashes between fifteen and eighteen feet high. For months after, Carey said, he could not sleep at night for thinking of the events of that day. "I started to exercise more than usual, trying to exhaust myself so that I could sleep," he said. "I was probably in the best physical shape of my life during that period," added the former University of Notre Dame quarterback, "but it wasn't doing any good. I finally wound up going for treatment by a doctor who specialized in sleeping disorders, and he helped me."

Carey's father, Bob, announced to the press almost immediately in the wake of the fire that "we will rebuild Hawthorne." Said his son, "the fire had a terrible effect on my dad...it was very sad. But he was determined to go ahead and we did.

"The way the insurance was structured, we would have gotten almost nothing had we not rebuilt. Almost right away, we had an architect my father and I knew start taking bids. That was when we got a call from Florida from Gust Newburg, an old friend of ours who owned a huge construction business in the Chicago area. Gust had a thick Norwegian accent. I can still remember him saying to me, 'What's going on up there? I hear you are taking bids. You know who is going to rebuild for you, don't you? Stop taking bids.'

"It was Gust and his company," Carey said, "who did the work, and he gave us terrific breaks on the costs. He put his top people on it but never charged us for their services. He charged us just for the basic costs of materials and labor. There were other friends of ours whose companies helped out, too, including those owned by guys I had played ball with.

"We probably got Hawthorne rebuilt for about half the

cost it could have been had somebody else done it. That was the one rewarding aspect that came out of that disaster — the kindness that people showed us, especially Gust Newburg."

While the cause of the Hawthorne fire was being investigated in Stickney, Illinois, other investigations were going on at five tracks in five other racing states. Their focus was ringers — faster horses illegally substituted for slower ones — and the gang of criminals who controlled them.

Years before this period of chicanery, there had been a notorious ringer mastermind named Paddy Barrie, a native of England who had illegally entered the United States from Canada. Operating in the late 1920s and up to the mid-1930s primarily on the East Coast, Barrie pulled off numerous betting coups.

Barrie's modus operandi was to alter a horse's appearance by the judicious use of colors. His predecessors who were caught usually failed because they used water-soluble dyes that sometimes washed off, revealing the horse's true hue and, ultimately, his identity. The extremely innovative Barrie, on the other hand, employed henna dyes which withstood repeated washings and even liniment applications. As a result, Barrie's ringers stayed "rung."

In 1933, Barrie succeeded in substituting a horse named Aknahton for other horses at least three times. Using his considerable artistry, Barrie managed to convert Aknahton, a three-year-old dark chestnut gelding who could run, into Shem, a two-year-old light chestnut with a white stripe, who couldn't. Barrie collected at odds of 6-1 at old Havre de

Grace. He was finally nabbed by Pinkerton Agency detectives, tried and convicted, and deported by the U.S. Department of Labor in 1934.

In contrast to Paddy Barrie, the ringer criminals of the 1970s pulled off their coups without, for the most part, altering horses' appearances. Instead, they used counterfeit foal papers to slip their faster horses past officials. In a statement issued in November of 1978, Clifford W. Wickman, president of the Thoroughbred Racing Protective Bureau (the security arm of the Thoroughbred Racing Associations of North America), said, "TRPB agents in several East Coast and Midwest states have been engaged in virtual round-the-clock duty in order to complete all logical leads as swiftly as possible. It has been established that all of the horse substitutions have been accomplished by means of counterfeit foal certificates.

"Results of TRPB's investigations," Wickman continued, "will be presented to appropriate racing and law enforcement authorities in order that persons behind these schemes may be brought to justice...There definitely appears to be a common thread of involvement by several licensees, or former licensees, in racing."

It was subsequently discovered that what members of the ring were using were some of the estimated twenty-five to thirty partially blank foal papers that had been stolen in the early 1970s from The Jockey Club's offices on Park Avenue in New York City. These purloined papers did not bear the distinguishing water marks that appeared on the bona fide documents; neither did the foal papers found to be in use for these ringers in the late '70s — including the papers used for

"Charollius," né Roman Decade, on November 18, 1978, at Hawthorne.

At one point during the post-ringer, post-fire probes at Hawthorne, an Illinois Racing Board official stated that the team headed by Charlie Wonder and William Combee had "hit" on twenty-seven of thirty-two attempts to run ringers. Their profits did not accrue so much from purses won — usually the vehicle for their thievery was a cheap claiming race — as from bets cashed. As depressingly impressive as that percentage of success was, it was still clear these fellows were not perfect criminals. And they did not always resort to the use of phony papers.

According to one source close to the case at the time, the group once bought an "old, broken down horse for $500 and sent him down to one of the Ohio tracks and entered 'him' in a race for $2,500 claimers. Then they substituted a $15,000 claimer after changing the horse's markings and altering his lip tattoo.

"The day after the race in question, the man who had sold them the $500 horse called the Ohio authorities. He had seen his old horse's name in the racing results. He knew that it was just not possible for his broken down campaigner to be back on the racetrack and running.

"What happened in the race was that the ringer got beat! He ran second. The gang members, who fled town without being apprehended, were in shock. One of them supposedly said, 'We better send somebody back down there to Ohio to buy that winner — he's a bargain at $2,500.'"

As the November 19 fire was being fought, two Hawthorne-based horsemen, well aware of the vital importance of the foal papers, tried to save them. Reported *Daily Racing Form* columnist Don Grisham, "At the outset of the blaze, trainer Ernie Poulos and assistant trainer Dave Adwell rushed to racing secretary Thomas P. Scott's office on the east end of the grandstand. They intended to carry out the metal file cabinets that they thought held the papers. The foal papers are documents recording the horse's registration; no horse can start in any race unless his papers are in the hands of the track's identifier.

"Poulos and Adwell found the office locked. They were advised by a security guard not to break down the door because the fire appeared to be under control. Poulos and Adwell returned to their barns. Within minutes, the office of the racing secretary was ablaze." (And within minutes of that, Tom Carey and the two firemen launched their quick and successful rescue operation of the safe containing the papers.)

Another Hawthorne trainer, John (Jumbo) Gural, an average-sized fellow whose nickname traced to his reputedly having "a memory like an elephant," told reporters that the firefighters' response had been quick and their efforts initially seemed to be containing the blaze. "But," said Gural, "suddenly we heard a low rumble, and the thing was gone."

Among those surprised by the Hawthorne catastrophe was William Masterson, then executive secretary of the Illinois Racing Board. As he noted at the time, "Of all the Illinois tracks, Hawthorne had the best record of compliance with fire codes."

The racing board had been "concerned" by the series of small fires that preceded the November 18 blaze, Masterson said. But, he told the author in late 1999, "there appeared to be nothing intentional about them. The biggest one, the one that caused the $40,000 damage to the clubhouse on October 29 that year, was apparently accidentally started by a workman — a welder who negligently laid down his torch.

"One of the things I recall most vividly," Masterson said, "was the effect of this disaster on Bob Carey Sr. He was just devastated at the destruction of his beloved track. We all felt very, very sorry for him."

It was initially reported that the valuable foal papers had been lost (it was also erroneously broadcast on several Chicago radio stations that $2 million in cash in the track's money room had gone up in smoke).

Recalled Masterson, "Long before the Hawthorne fire the racing board at the urging of member Ray Freeark, I believe, or perhaps Herb Channick — both were horse owners and breeders, and really knew the sport — insisted that all Illinois tracks install fireproof safes to contain and protect the horses' registration papers. The safes were installed about a year before the Hawthorne fire. That was part of a national fire protection program for racetracks created by Illinois Racing Board member Lucy Reum, who later served as its chairman." All the foal papers in use at that Hawthorne meeting were found undamaged in the asbestos-lined safe that had been hauled to safety by Tom Carey and the two fireman.

On November 29, ten days after the fire, suspicions were officially confirmed: Hawthorne had been the victim of expert arsonists. Said Illinois Law Enforcement Director Tyrone C. Fahner, "The fire was the result of some sort of liquid accelerant or propellant...being set ablaze after having been poured on three separate floors of Hawthorne's grandstand. They knew what they were doing," Fahner said. "The fire was definitely planned."

Damage to the plant was estimated at between $10 and $14 million. Because of its age and wooden structure, the track was insured for only $3.4 million; the Careys had been unable to obtain more coverage than that. The only way for the policy to produce more was if the track were rebuilt. The new facility opened to much fanfare on September 29, 1980.

Lost because of the blaze were twenty-eight racing dates, which was costly to the Careys, the owners and trainers of horses stabled at Hawthorne, jockeys, 500 backstretch employees, and the state of Illinois, deprived of some $3 million in pari-mutuel tax revenue that would have been collected. Also lost was the forty-third running of the Hawthorne Gold Cup, the track's most prestigious event, which had been scheduled for the following Saturday. (The attempt to transfer Hawthorne's twenty-eight days to Sportsman's Park was thwarted by a lack of available mutuel machines.)

———————

After investigators had determined that a switch in foal papers had permitted Roman Decade to run as Charollius on

November 18, the Illinois Racing Board in December suspended Charlie Wonder, then fifty, a native of Washington, Indiana; and William Combee, thirty-two, of Lakeland, Florida, for twenty-five years each. Banned for six months was trainer Michael L. Reavis, thirty-two, in whose name the ringer had run.

Neither Wonder nor Combee appeared at the Illinois hearing. Reavis, who cooperated fully with the board after initially lying to them about his role in the affair, admitted to a charge of false ownership. However, Reavis contended that he was not aware until well after the second race on November 18 that he had saddled a ringer. The horse had disappeared from his barn on November 21, he said.

Racing board counsel Jewel Klein said the substitution of Roman Decade for Charollius was made possible by a forged foal certificate provided by Wonder. She also presented evidence showing that Combee delivered Roman Decade to Reavis' barn at Sportsman's.

In his testimony at the hearing, Reavis said that Wonder, whom he described as "a friend" who had done him "favors in the past," asked him on November 3 if he would take over the training of a horse that was due to be shipped to Chicago, a horse that Wonder said "should win." Reavis agreed to do so and also agreed to falsify the horse's ownership, putting himself down as the owner because, as he put it, "the odds would be better if he ran in my name instead of Charlie's."

(Wonder had enjoyed steady success for several years after taking out his first training license in 1953. In the 1960s his clients included such prominent Midwest owners as W. Archie Lofton and Gene Goff. For the latter's Verna Lea Farm, Wonder conditioned eventual multiple stakes winner Nodouble when the horse was a two-year-old. That same year, 1967, Wonder sent out Goff's Strate Stuff to win the Hawthorne Juvenile.)

Reavis testified that Wonder promised to bet $200 for him on the shipped-in horse. Reavis added that he did not himself bet the horse and didn't know whether Wonder had, either, since he had received no money from him. A woman described as Reavis' "girlfriend," Wilma Lewis, testified that she had bet $370 on "Charollius" but not at Reavis' suggestion; rather, she said, she "always bet" Reavis' horses.

The jockey named to ride "Charollius" on November 18 was seventeen-year-old apprentice John A. (Johnny) Johnston, member of a prominent Chicago racing family. After increasing weight brought his promising career to an early conclusion, Johnston became a Chicago harness executive.

Johnston told the board that he had absolutely no knowledge his mount was a ringer. He said he had received his pre-race instructions from Wonder, not Reavis, but did not find that to be surprising because he knew Wonder and Reavis were friends.

According to Reavis, he first learned the horse was a ringer on the morning of November 21 at Sportsman's when Wonder informed him that the horse had "been moved" from his stall and that "possibly he was a ringer." At Wonder's urging, Reavis attempted to pick up the foal papers on the horse from Hawthorne racing secretary F. G. (Pat)

Farrell, but was rebuffed.

Reavis added that Wonder instructed him to tell investigators that the horse was owned by a man named George Bowers. Reavis said that Wonder met him on the night of November 21 and tried to construct a story involving two "fictitious persons": one who had delivered the horse to Reavis, another who had removed him from Reavis' barn. It was the morning following this conversation, Reavis said, that he "decided to tell the truth." He then went to the Hawthorne stewards, who summoned state investigators.

What had happened to Mike Reavis was similar to what had occurred in Kentucky earlier in 1978 with another trainer who was a friend of Charlie Wonder's. William R. Price, a veteran horseman based at Ellis Park that summer, testified before the Kentucky Racing Commission that he had known Wonder "for a long time, and I was just trying to do the man a favor. And for doing that, I got my behind kicked. I did not know, and I'll take a lie detector test or anything you want me to, that I was running a ringer," Price told the panel.

(When punishment was later meted out, Price was suspended for sixty days, the Kentucky commission noting that "Although William R. Price's testimony might strain one's credulity, we are inclined to believe his protestations that he was a dupe, rather than a villain." The commission statement added that "Mr. Price's past record...over a long period of years...was excellent.")

Price informed the commission that it was not uncommon for a trainer who wasn't licensed in a certain state to ask a friend holding a license in that state to run a horse for him.

Wonder had consistently sent Price horses who had won, so Price was not averse to welcoming a couple of more into his Ellis Park barn. "Every horse I ever got from the man (Wonder), I done good with him," Price testified. That summer, Wonder brought in two horses that he said belonged to him, both of which he removed after they had run.

On August 7, Price saddled a horse entered as Prince Sappir in the fourth race. Price's wife was listed on the program as the owner. "Prince Sappir" won by eight lengths. After opening at 20-1, he paid $10.40. "Prince Sappir" was actually a better horse named Jimmy Reb.

Almost a month later, on Labor Day, Price sent out a horse named Eagle Heights. Wonder's wife, Anita, was listed as the owner. Another 20-1 shot in the early action, this one returned $13.60 after scoring convincingly by a length and a half. In fact, "Eagle Heights" was a horse of another, higher, caliber named Beau Bronze.

At the subsequent inquiry, TRPB agent Joseph Fanning told the Kentucky commission that it was the use of counterfeit Jockey Club certificates that had enabled these ringers to get past the Ellis Park officials. The counterfeit papers bore the names of Prince Sappir and Eagle Heights, but the identifying details as well as the lip tattoo numbers were those of Jimmy Reb and Beau Bronze, respectively. It would be very difficult, Fanning said, for anyone looking at the papers to tell that they were phony.

This was the same method that Wonder employed later that year at Hawthorne. After the TRPB alerted Hawthorne track identifier Jim Roche of a possible problem, it was ascertained that the foal papers on "Charollius" were bogus.

Also preceding the Hawthorne caper, the TRPB reported, were ringers on September 24 at the Great Barrington Fair in Massachusetts; another October 29 at Thistledown; and one at Waterford Park November 11.

Another incident involved Wonder shipping out of, not into, Hawthorne with a ringer. At Beulah Park on November 12, Stoned Crow, a recent arrival from the Illinois track, won the tenth race, a $2,000 claiming event. Listed as being owned and trained by Myles Neff, Stoned Crow coasted to a seven-length victory. He paid $13.20 and keyed a trifecta that returned $1,529. In his previous start, at Hawthorne, Stoned Crow had finished twelfth and last in a $3,000 claimer at odds of 94-1. That day he was listed as being owned and trained by Charlie Wonder.

After "Stoned Crow" had run back one week later, another Sunday afternoon at Beulah Park, and won again, Ohio investigators found that the horse, whose registration papers had been signed over to Neff by Wonder, was in reality a bay gelding named Piperazine Pete, winner of a $7,000 claimer at Hawthorne on October 10, his last race prior to invading Ohio.

––––––––––––

It was late in 1978 that the roof began to come tumbling down on this ringer gang. The Kentucky commission acted first, in early December ruling off Wonder "indefinitely." Keene Daingerfield, Kentucky's senior state steward, said that if Wonder "is the quality you have to believe he is, I can't see any time in the future he'd be acceptable to us."

Phar Lap raced just once in North America before dying of colic under mysterious circumstances.

Al Snider would have ridden Citation in the Triple Crown races of 1948, but went fishing one day and never returned.

Red McDaniel (pictured on left, with Clement L. Hirsch and top runner Blue Reading) was America's leading trainer for five consecutive years before he leapt to his death from the San Francisco Bay Bridge.

Ann Woodward (above, with Nashua) allegedly mistook her husband for a prowler when she shot him dead. Her mother-in-law, Elsie Woodward (below, middle), never approved of her son William Jr.'s (below, left) choice of a wife.

William Woodward Jr., with Nashua at Saratoga, inherited Belair Stable from his father.

Dancer's Image led at the wire in the 1968 Kentucky Derby, but was disqualified after an alleged drug positive. Owner Peter Fuller (below) spent years trying to clear his colt's name.

Thomas F. Carey, the current president of Hawthorne, rescued foal papers in a safe from the burning racetrack offices.

Two versions of Hawthorne Race Course: before the devastating 1978 fire (above), and after it was rebuilt in 1980.

The Aga Khan, shown leading in Shergar after the Epsom Derby, refused to capitulate to the alleged extortionists.

David Joost with his family: son Eric, daughter Lauren, and wife Susan. Although authorities concluded that Joost killed his family, then committed suicide, many inconsistencies make that finding implausible, say family members and others.

Lucille Parker Markey, shown with second husband Gene Markey, left Calumet Farm debt-free when she died.

Alydar was a cash cow for Calumet under the management of J. T. Lundy (below, right). But the stallion's death in 1990 precipitated the farm's collapse.

Many theories abound about why top Northern California jockey Ron Hansen plunged from the San Mateo Bridge, including one that he was forced to leap.

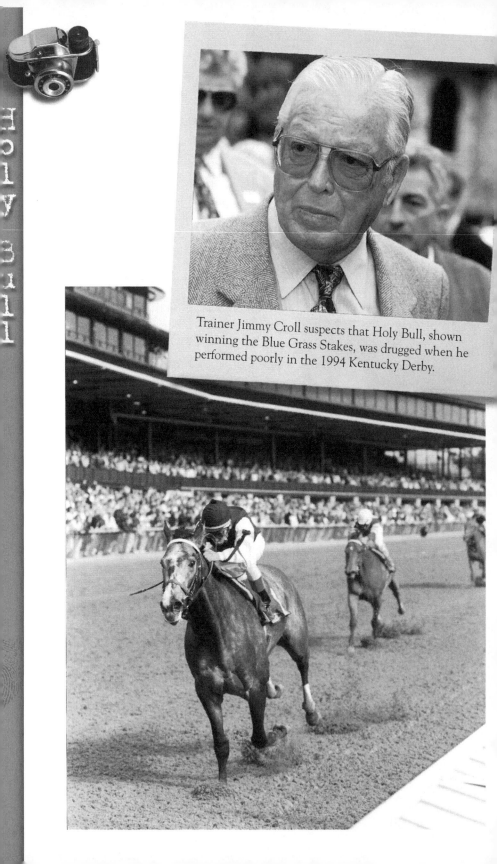

Trainer Jimmy Croll suspects that Holy Bull, shown winning the Blue Grass Stakes, was drugged when he performed poorly in the 1994 Kentucky Derby.

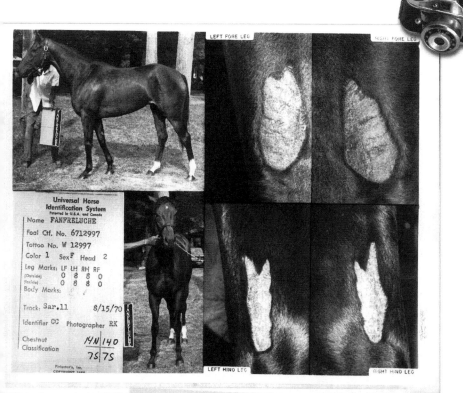

Universal Horse
Identification System
Patented in U.S.A. and Canada

Name FANFRELUCHE

Foal Ctf. No. 6712997

Tattoo No. W 12997

Color 1 Sex F Head 2

Leg Marks: LF LH RH RF
(Outside)   0 8 8 0
(Inside)   0 8 8 0
Body Marks:

Track: Sar.11   8/15/70

Identifier CC Photographer RK

Chestnut
Classification   14N 140
                    75 75

Pinkerton's, Inc.
COPYRIGHT 1969

LEFT FORE LEG   RIGHT FORE LEG
LEFT HIND LEG   RIGHT HIND LEG

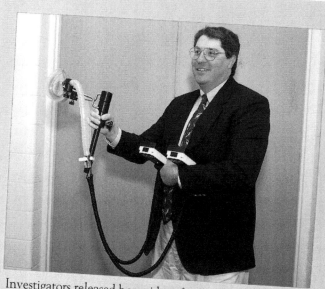

Investigators released horse identification documents for
Fanfreluche when the mare was kidnapped in 1977.
Kentucky Racing Commission vet Robert Holland with a
device to detect the presence of sponges in racehorses.

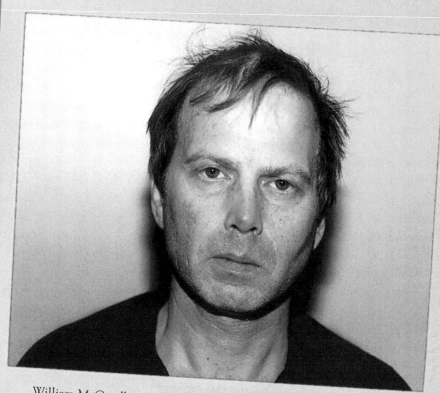

William McCandless, who served time for the theft of
Fanfreluche, was charged in the Kentucky sponging
cases and remains a fugitive.

Illinois acted next, also in December, banning Wonder and Combee for twenty-five years. And in January of 1979, the Ohio commission handed out twenty-five-year suspensions to five men, including Wonder, Combee, and Neff. All the actions taken against Wonder were done so with him in absentia, for he never appeared at any of the hearings that involved him.

The final blow against the gang was struck in December of 1980 when a U.S. District Court in Owensboro, Kentucky, dealt with charges against four men (plus another four unindicted co-conspirators) of running ringers at nine different racetracks between March and November of 1978 — including Hawthorne, on the day before the fire. Nine Federal Bureau of Investigation Field Offices had been involved in the sweeping project. Among those sentenced to incarceration was William Combee, who received one year in federal prison after plea bargaining with the government prosecutor.

Missing from that courtroom scene in Owensboro was Charlie Wonder, described by authorities as "a fugitive from justice who is believed to have fled to Manitoba, Canada," from where he could not be extradited on these charges of "interstate travel in the aid of racketeering."

While guilty of race-fixing in his use of ringers, were Wonder and his cohorts responsible for the Hawthorne fire? Some observers believed so, reasoning that the fire had been started in an attempt to destroy the counterfeit foal papers — a fruitless effort anyway, since those papers were securely ensconced in the fireproof safe that had been rescued from the burning building.

There were other arson theories as well. Illinois state investigators looked into allegations that "syndicate hood-lums," angered by the closing in 1978 of mob-controlled messenger betting services, acted either in revenge, or in an attempt to intimidate potential witnesses in the federal probe of the services. Another faction of conspiracy theorists held that the fire had been set by disgruntled bettors and/or embittered horsemen. But no one was ever charged with committing what was definitely deemed arson.

Was it a bitter bettor, or an irate horseman, who sloshed the accelerant on the old wooden floors, then torched Hawthorne on November 18, 1978?

"That is possible, but in my opinion unlikely," said Chicago attorney Arthur E. Engelland. "Probably," Engelland continued, "the fire was the result of faulty electrical wiring. The track was a tinderbox, a disaster waiting to happen. But if it was a case of arson, I certainly don't believe that anyone connected to Hawthorne had anything to do with it."

A former Thoroughbred owner and breeder, Engelland is a prominent trial lawyer who has represented more racing licensees than any other member of the state bar. One of his prominent clients was Charlie Wonder.

Wonder received his twenty-five-year Illinois suspension over Engelland's objections, the attorney contending that "it was never proved that horse was a ringer. The horse that won the second race that day disappeared. He was never seen again. When you don't have the horse, where is the evidence?" (Engelland is the source of several interesting and controversial theories regarding racing rules, among them his contention that jockeys found guilty of using electrical devices on their horses should not be penalized as severely as they are because they "were trying to win — not lose.")

"Illinois, Ohio, and Kentucky came down the hardest on these guys," Engelland said. "In Kentucky, the racing commission banned Wonder although he was not licensed there. Some states, on the other hand, pretty much whitewashed this stuff."

Summing up his former client, whom he described as being "really, a very very likeable guy and a good horseman," Engelland said that in his opinion, "Charlie may have been involved in this stuff, although I'd say some guys from Florida probably called the shots.

"But did Charlie Wonder burn down Hawthorne? Absolutely not," said Engelland.

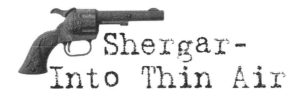

Shergar - Into Thin Air

"...the great Gaels of Ireland
Are the men that God made mad,
For all their wars are merry,
And all their songs are sad."

So wrote poet G. K. Chesterton (1874-1936) in his "Ballad of the White Horse." In characterizing the Irish, Chesterton might well have added a stanza or two about their tremendous affection for horses. Indeed, he might have produced "The Ballad of Shergar" had he lived long enough to learn of the saga associated with that fleet runner.

Perhaps only in Ireland, a small nation the majority of whose citizens are imbued with a love of equines, would such an animal become a target of kidnapping and be held for ransom. In Italy and Germany in the 1970s and '80s, various brigands concentrated on snatching up and holding for money wealthy industrialists, not famous horses. But in Ireland, the target was a five-year-old Thoroughbred, one who ranked as a legend even before he was abducted. That legend then metamorphosized into myth when he was stolen from his stall at one of the country's most famous breeding farms, never to be seen again.

———————

Shergar was a foal of 1978, a well-bred son of Great Nephew out of the mare Sharmeen; he traced to Hyperion on his top side, Tulyar on his dam's. His birthplace was the Aga Khan's Sheshoon Stud in County Kildare, the heartland of Ireland's breeding industry. Sheshoon Stud, located thirty miles southwest of Dublin, borders on the nation's most famous racetrack, The Curragh.

When he turned two, Shergar was sent to the Beech Hurst Stable in Newmarket, England, headquarters of the successful trainer Michael Stoute who conditioned many of the Aga Khan's runners. Shergar adapted well to the change of scenery, but as a very young horse there wasn't much remarkable about him outside of his coloring: the bay colt had four white socks and a very broad and distinctive white blaze on his face. Shergar was far from a standout in Stoute's talent-laden string. English racing writer Julian Wilson in *The Great Racehorses* described Shergar as being "inconspicuous amongst Michael Stoute's magnificent and imposing string." Indeed, Wilson added, "It is meant as no disrespect to either Shergar or my wife — a fair judge of a riding horse — when I recall her initial comment on seeing Shergar: 'Ah, that would make me a nice hunter!' " Because he had not been very impressive in his early training, it was hoped that Shergar might develop into a "useful miler" once he hit the racetrack.

But this all changed as Shergar matured and approached

his career debut, a maiden race at Newbury on September 19, 1980. Shergar had impressed Stoute once the horse had been asked for fast work, and by then Shergar had developed enough physically to impress his rider that day — England's great Lester Piggott, who later described him as "a beautifully built Great Nephew colt with a great big white blaze... whom I rode to victory in his highly promising debut..." That was a one-mile event called the Kris Plate, and Shergar earned all of 2,560 pounds for the Aga Khan. He went off as the 11-8 favorite in a field of twenty-three and won easily by two and a half lengths while setting a course record.

Michael Stoute obviously had great confidence in the colt's abilities. It was considered quite unusual for Stoute to advance a young horse directly from maiden to stakes company, but that is what he did. Shergar's second start came in the William Hill Futurity Stakes at Doncaster on October 25. Although he did not enjoy the best of trips, the inexperienced youngster finished a good second to Beldale Flutter, losing by two and a half lengths. That was the final start of Shergar's juvenile season.

It is well known that some horses make incredible progress from ages two to three. That is what happened with Shergar: when he resumed his career, he was an amazingly transformed specimen. In his three-year-old debut on April 25, 1981, Shergar dominated a good field in the Guardian Newspaper Classic Trial at Sandown, finishing ten lengths in advance of Kirtling, one of the choices. At that point, Shergar was being held at odds of 33-1 for the Epsom Derby.

Next up was the Chester Vase on May 5. With his nineteen-year-old jockey, Walter Swinburn, again applying no pressure whatsoever, Shergar coasted away to win by twelve lengths. This served to make Shergar the 11-10 favorite for the Epsom Derby on June 3, his status enhanced by the absence of the injured Beldale Flutter, his lone conqueror at two. Under Swinburn, the youngest jockey ever to pilot an Epsom Derby favorite, Shergar burst to the lead rounding Tattenham Corner about three furlongs out and proceeded to win eased up by ten lengths — the biggest victory margin officially recorded in the race's 202-year history. That made Shergar three-for-three at age three, with an average margin of more than ten lengths per tally. He was the talk of the European racing world, the most exciting performer to emerge in years.

Shergar returned to the land of his birth for his next race, the Irish Derby on June 27 at The Curragh, near his birthplace. With Swinburn under suspension for a riding infraction at Royal Ascot, Shergar was reunited with Lester Piggott for Ireland's greatest race.

In his autobiography, Piggott wrote that he had been delighted to receive a call from Michael Stoute offering him the mount on Shergar for the Irish Derby. Piggott had ridden Shotgun to a respectable but distant fourth-place finish behind Shergar in the Epsom Derby, so he "didn't have to ponder too long" upon learning of Stoute's offer.

"Shergar," Piggot wrote, "gave me my fifth victory in the Irish Derby, and I have hardly ever had a simpler ride: he so outclassed his opponents that he was literally never out of a canter to beat them. There is no doubting that during the summer of 1981 Shergar…was a great horse."

Piggott noted further that "one aspect of Shergar which inhabitants of Newmarket (site of Michael Stoute's training yard) got to know well was that he could get very fresh, and in that mood do his best to get loose on the gallops — often succeeding with frightening consequences. I remember one particular time when our lads found him walking — alone — down the road which runs by Warren Place. They brought him in, put him in a stable and — having recognized him from his distinctive large white blaze, as well as from the Stoute yard rug he was wearing — phoned his home stable to report him safe and sound. The lad who came to collect him said that Shergar had got loose on the Limekilns and had been galloping all over the Heath."

Taking on older horses for the first time, Shergar, reunited with young Swinburn, kept his win skein going in the King George VI and Queen Elizabeth Diamond Stakes. After temporarily being trapped on the rail, Shergar shot through on the inside to score by four lengths. Following the race, his connections indicated that Shergar's next start would be the Prix de l'Arc de Triomphe on the first Sunday of October at Longchamp in France.

A change in plans, however, saw Sherger contesting the St. Leger at Doncaster on September 12 as a "prep" for the Arc. Rumors abounded that Shergar was not showing his old form in his training, and pre-race backing of him was much lighter than usual. On a heavy course, Shergar ran the worst race of his career, finishing fourth, nine lengths behind victorious Glint of Gold, a horse he had trounced by ten lengths in the Epsom Derby. The Aga Khan then announced the colt's retirement. Shergar concluded his brilliant career with a record of six wins in eight starts and earnings of 320,000 pounds.

After turning down offers for Shergar from American breeders, the Aga Khan syndicated him for $18.3 million (the fourth highest such valuation at the time, but one that was reportedly much, much less than he would have realized had he accepted an offer from the U.S.) and declared the horse would stand in Ireland. The shares were priced at $450,000 each, the Aga Khan retaining fifteen percent (six shares) as the largest single shareholder.

Members of the syndicate included such notables as Lord Derby, Robert Sangster, Captain Tim Rogers, Sir John Astor, Stavros Niarchos, Sheikh Mohammed, and — among prominent North Americans involved — Paul Mellon, John R. Gaines, E. P. Taylor, and Bertram Firestone.

When Shergar returned in triumph from the racetrack to Ballymany Stud, the Aga Khan was on hand to greet him. Pipe bands and dozens of wellwishers also turned out to welcome the conquering hero on this festive occasion.

His first year at stud, Shergar serviced forty-four mares, forty-two of which produced foals — an exceptionally high potency rate (the resulting foals included Authaal, sold for a European record 3.1 million Irish pounds in 1984 and winner of the Irish St. Leger two years later). It was to be Shergar's last year at stud as well.

———————

On the night of Tuesday, February 8, 1983, Shergar was in

his stall at Ballymany Stud in County Kildare, only days away from beginning his second season as a stallion, having been booked to fifty-five mares. At approximately 8:30 p.m., Jim Fitzgerald's family had completed their dinner in their home on the grounds. Fitzgerald, fifty-five, was the head groom at Ballymany. Suddenly, five or more armed and masked men burst through the door and accosted Fitzgerald, his wife, and their five children. The terrified Fitzgerald believed that they were being attacked by members of the Irish Republican Army (IRA).

Fitzgerald was held at gunpoint as his family was locked in another room in the house. He was told he would be killed if he did not cooperate. Then Fitzgerald was ordered to lead the men to Shergar and to load the five-year-old stallion into a horse trailer. Understandably, Fitzgerald followed orders. He placed a bridle on Shergar and led him into the trailer. The gunmen then blindfolded Fitzgerald and ordered him to lie face down on the floor of another van they had brought with them.

Security at Ballymany at that time was minimal. The vehicles — there may have been three all told — made their way unnoticed down the winding drive that led to the Dublin-Limerick road. There was no guard on the farm's unlocked front gate.

The horse trailer bearing Shergar headed in one direction, while Fitzgerald was driven around the countryside in another vehicle. Some four hours passed before he was released several miles from Ballymany, Fitzgerald never having seen the faces of his abductors. After finding a phone, Fitzgerald called his brother, Des, to come and pick him up. Once he had returned home and found his family unharmed, the shaken Fitzgerald was able to inform his boss, farm manager Ghislain Drion, a native of France, that Ballymany's most prized possession had been stolen in the night.

"It (the theft operation) was very neatly done," commented an officer of the Gardai Siochana (commonly referred to as the Garda), Ireland's police force. Also apparent was that the thieves knew the business: the breeding season was to begin that week, with the first twelve of Shergar's scheduled fifty-five mares already at Ballymany.

Shergar's stud fee for non-syndicate members was $93,000, placing his potential annual earnings near $5 million, and he had a productive expectancy span of fifteen to twenty years. The horse had been taken at the peak of his economic potential. It was thus not surprising when, on the day following the theft, farm manager Drion fielded an anonymous ransom demand of almost $3 million.

The massive investigation of the matter was under the direction of Superintendent James (Jimmy) Murphy. A middle-aged, veteran officer, Murphy looked, according to *Sports Illustrated* writer Clive Gammon, "startlingly like a gracefully aged Dick Tracy, right down to his gray fedora with a black band." Murphy stated that he was not opposed to a reward for information regarding Shergar being offered, but that he was adamantly against any ransom being paid. His thought — as well as that of many others interested in the case — was that giving in to ransom demands would serve to encourage acts such as this being repeated in the future.

For days, Superintendent Murphy and his men fielded phone calls from people all over Ireland, as well as suggestions from a couple of eager clairvoyants based in England. Speculation as to the horse's whereabouts ran rampant, as did rumors and hoaxes: Shergar's head had been cut off, or Shergar was hidden away in Northern Ireland, or Shergar was seen running loose across the fields in the southern part of the country. Other callers claimed Shergar had been flown out of the country by cargo plane on an unreported flight from a secret airstrip, or that he'd been removed by boat from an obscure cove along an uninhabited stretch of the Irish coast...The inventive powers displayed were most impressive.

Shergar's value to the thieves seemed to be primarily as a vehicle of ransom, for he would be practically impossible to sell and very hard to hide. As veterinarians noted, the horse's health would demand that he be exercised, even if he was being kept on a low maintenance diet to limit his energy. But his appearance was so distinctive, it was thought doubtful that his captors could risk that. And altering Shergar's appearance would be a daunting task: even if his coat could be dyed and his dramatic white markings somehow disguised, Shergar had a very unusual (and unalterable) amount of white in his left eye. As a writer in the *Irish Independent* put it, "At least one-third of Ireland would know the horse on sight."

Murphy ordered a massive search of the countryside. All the breeding farms in Ireland were examined by squads of police, as well as many other farms, in the days after the horse "went missing." Irish farmers were urged to search every foot of their lands for any trace of Shergar. Not only was national pride at stake — this was the first kidnapping of a famous horse in Ireland — but the act constituted a threat to the economy, for the Irish breeding industry contributed some $135 million to the country's coffers annually. It was feared that some breeders would take their stock out of Ireland, that potential investors would be scared off by this incident. The national concern was expressed by Lord Killanin, former International Olympic Committee president, who spoke on the Saturday following the theft at Leopardstown racetrack outside Dublin. "For God's sake," he said, "I implore everyone in this island to keep a lookout... in the name of Irish racing and of our image in this world."

The Aga Khan initially withheld public comment on Shergar's theft, but one of his relatives commented, "The whole thing seems like a fiction." This was a point not lost on the readers of best-selling mystery writer Dick Francis, the former English champion jockey whose 1967 novel *Blood Sport* had described the theft of a famous (fictional) stallion for use in secretly servicing mares. "I hope they (the thieves) did not get their idea from me," Francis said.

Following the Wednesday ransom call to Ghislain Drion, a call that reportedly was not repeated, a London tabloid, *The Sun*, reported the next day that its veteran racing writer, Peter Campling, had been contacted by a man who said he was one of the kidnappers. If Shergar was to be returned, the caller said, Campling was to travel to a hotel in Belfast, Northern Ireland, and await further word. It was at this point that farce took a role alongside tragedy in the structure of the Shergar story. As *Sports Illustrated's* Gammon recounted the situation:

> There were, it turned out, two other journalist invitees, Lord John Oaksey of *The Daily Telegraph* of London, and Derek Thompson of Thames Television...The threesome took off from London's Heathrow Airport in a departure as private as a Saturday night in Piccadilly Circus. Not surprisingly, the three journalists were joined at the hotel by a gaggle of colleagues, who would later give them an unusual experience, that of being hunted by a pack of journalists.

> The promised phone call from the supposed kidnapper did come through, and Thompson answered it in the hotel lobby with TV cameras and other newsmen in close attendance. Thompson's side of the conversation was overheard by millions on TV, and then the three journalists were smuggled out of a rear entrance of the hotel and into a waiting automobile. But the press pack was soon on their tail as they headed thirty miles south from Belfast to the stables of trainer Jeremy Maxwell in County Down, whence they had been directed by the mystery caller.

> Maxwell and his wife, Judy, it turned out, had already been called by the self-described kidnapper, who was now using the code name of Arkle. (Arkle was a great Irish jumping horse in the 1960s.) The

Maxwell home rapidly filled with police and reporters. The evening produced another phone call…and a weird one it was. The ransom had been reduced to a mere 40,000 Irish punts (about $64,000), said Arkle.

On Friday, Oaksey was ready to admit he had been taken for a ride by a hoaxer. A 'razzmatazz, idiotic media caper,' was how he saw it. The hoax went on the next day. This time, however, the call was more sinister. 'Something has gone dreadfully wrong,' a voice said to Judy Maxwell on Friday morning. 'The horse is dead.' Early that morning, the BBC (British Broadcasting Company) had been called with the same message, though that caller had specified that Shergar had received a serious eye injury in the stall where he was being kept and had had to be put down.

The front-page *Dublin Evening Herald* headline on Friday said SHERGAR IS DEAD-GANG. That the newspaper, a sensationalist sheet, chose to lead its front page with a Shergar story rather than with a horrific London multiple-murder case that had just broken, gives some idea of the importance of the kidnapping to the Irish.

Faced with only unsubstantiated reports, authorities were not about to conclude that Shergar was definitely dead. The search continued, and on Monday the Garda for the first time revealed descriptions — however sketchy — of two of the kidnappers, presumably provided by groom Jim

Fitzgerald: one was "built like a jockey," another was said to have a Northern Irish accent. Superintendent Murphy issued an appeal to the kidnappers: "There are strong indications that Shergar is dead. I ask the men responsible to produce evidence that this is not so."

Also reportedly having contacts with the kidnappers were radio journalist Colin Turner; Shergar's veterinarian Stan Cosgrove (a syndicate member); and Captain Sean Berry, secretary of the Irish Thoroughbred Breeders Association. Captain Berry later told *The Sunday Press* that he had received four phone calls between March 17-27. Different voices were heard in the calls, Captain Berry said, but three of the four people spoke in what he termed "cultured Irish accents." None of these phone contacts resulted in anything useful to the investigation.

Believing Shergar to be dead, police on both sides of the Irish border called off the search for him in May. In mid-June, Lloyd's of London underwriters announced they would pay out $10.5 million to the syndicate shareholders for the loss of Shergar. (The insurance company also denied reports it had ever had any contact with the kidnappers.) Lloyd's spokesmen said they decided to settle the claims after being advised by attorneys that the kidnapping of the horse amounted to its theft. However, another one million in mortality insurance would not be paid to other syndicate members who had not insured for theft, Lloyd's said, unless Shergar was proved to be dead by the time most of those policies ran out in November.

(When Shergar was syndicated, each shareholder was

responsible for obtaining insurance. Some protected their investment against theft, some against death, some against both, some against neither. After the theft, disputes over some of the insurance policies dragged on for years. Famed Irish trainer Vincent O'Brien and fellow partners in the ownership of Coolmore Stud had purchased three shares in Shergar and paid the first installment of 100,000 pounds on each before the horse was kidnapped. Lloyd's insurers refused to pay claims of 200,000 pounds plus interest lodged by the Coolmore combine because these policies covered only against the event of death, not theft. O'Brien and the other Coolmore shareholders sued in a London High Court seeking damages; they contended the insurers were negligent in failing to make certain that the coverage did include theft. In April of 1994, the court ruled that because Coolmore had never specifically asked for theft coverage, the defendants were not negligent in failing to provide it. "Prior to the theft of Shergar," the judge said, "the majority of those concerned in the bloodstock business...did not consider the theft of a thoroughbred stallion a significant risk.")

Another strange twist in the case involved the aforementioned veterinarian, Stan Cosgrove. In early November of 1983, there were reports in the Irish press that the police were probing the disappearance of £80,000 of purported ransom money which was supposed to have been paid to kidnappers of Shergar in July. A package containing the money was given by Cosgrove to a Garda detective; the officer, in turn, handed the money over to a farmer in County Clare, who was to act as intermediary. The farmer said he left the money in the trunk of a car so that it could be collected "if Shergar was returned." When he later went back to the car, the farmer said, the money had vanished, and there was no hint of Shergar or any clue as to his whereabouts.

In a November 12 story in the *Irish Times*, Cosgrove denied that this had taken place, adding that no such sum was ever passed. Subsequently, however, Cosgrove reportedly confirmed that, acting on his own initiative but with the financial support of some fellow syndicate members, he had indeed been the source of the money for this failed venture.

Cosgrove was among the syndicate members who had purchased mortality insurance. Years later — in the winter of 1994 — he was still anxious to obtain proof of Shergar's death so that he could be paid his claim of 150,000 pounds plus some 450,000 pounds in interest that he sought. A woman claiming to be able to produce the bones of Shergar demanded a payment of 40,000 pounds "up front" for her efforts. Nothing came of that, nor of the discovery in April of 1994 of a horse carcass found in County Donegal purported to be that of Shergar.

———————

Who stole Shergar, and what happened to him? Rumors and theories continue to abound.

In his 1984 book *In Search of Shergar*, Colin Turner wrote that "a favourite theory was that it was a kidnap that had gone wrong. According to this version, the kidnappers had taken the horse with every intention of pursuing a ransom demand, but Shergar had been injured and had had to be destroyed...

"Then there were theories that said Shergar had simply been stolen. Several possible reasons were put forward for the theft...(the leading one being that) the horse had been stolen as an act of spite and vengeance against the Aga Khan, a man with many enemies, both spiritual and temporal."

Among those enemies, Turner continued, were Libyan leader Colonel Muammar el-Quaddafi, who reputedly "hated the Aga Khan," and American breeder and bloodstock agent Wayne Murty. Wrote Turner: "Colonel Gaddafi (Quaddafi) was a very serious suspect. He had the necessary ruthlessness and resources: his people had carried out terrorist acts in various parts of the world and had plenty of links with the IRA. Irish terrorists had been trained in camps in Libya alongside PLO fighters and left-wing terrorists from half a dozen countries."

Police officials, Turner wrote, were "pretty well satisfied" that it wasn't a "straight IRA or INLA (Irish National Liberation Army) job, if only because these organizations had never shrunk from claiming responsibility (in the past) for indiscriminate bombings and maimings, torture, executions, knee-cappings or bank robberies...I was convinced," Turner wrote, "that the kidnapping was the work of an international gang, but I didn't believe that foreign thieves could operate in County Kildare, or indeed within the Republic, without the help of the illegal Irish organizations." The IRA's motives, in this scenario, would be to earn money for arms by being paid to kidnap the horse for another party. (Police sources later indicated that the regular IRA was denying any involvement in the theft. The radical arm of that organizations, the Provisional IRA, or "Provos," were always under suspicion of Garda authorities.)

As to Wayne Murty, his feud with the Aga Khan was fairly well known. In early March of 1983 the English newspaper *Daily Star* published an interview with the Kentucky resident, who five years earlier had been involved in a bitter dispute over the sale of horses once owned by French financier Marcel Boussac. Facing bankruptcy, Boussac made a deal to sell fifty-six horses to Murty. Later, however, a French court ruled that the sale was illegal and ordered a new dispersal, one that saw the Aga Khan acquire the horses. Murty bitterly accused the Aga Khan of exercising his great influence unfairly to bring about this result.

In the *Daily Star* interview, Murty said he believed he was a prime suspect in the Shergar kidnapping because of the bad blood between him and the Aga Khan. He said if he could have stolen Shergar in the course of the legal battles over the Boussac horses, he would have done so. But, Murty emphasized, he had definitely not had any involvement in Shergar's kidnapping.

Another possible motive for Shergar's kidnapping was, Turner wrote, "straight theft for gain...Rumours were always starting in racing circles that Shergar was servicing mares in some Middle Eastern stud to help create a new breed of master-horses, or that his sperm was being sold all over the world for secret artificial insemination...The romantics all favoured this theory. Everyone secretly fancied the idea that some unknown colt, with an undistinguished pedigree but maybe just a ghostly trace of a white blaze on his forehead, would come thundering round Tattenham Corner and steal the Derby at 100-1. It's the kind of idea racing folk love..."

Nearly ten years after Shergar's abduction, the London *Sunday Times* created a sensation when it published an interview with a formerly prominent IRA member turned police informant. Sean O'Callaghan, serving a life sentence for two murders, told the *Times* that Shergar was alive for only a few hours after he was taken.

O'Callaghan indicated in the interview that he was part of a nine-man team responsible, a team that included an experienced horseman. He said Shergar became uncontrollable and that he was then shot and buried in a wooded area some 100 miles from Ballymany Stud. The IRA's plan, according to O'Callaghan, had been to raise money via ransom to be used in the purchase of new and more sophisticated weapons.

Irish racing journalist Raymond Smith, in his 1994 book *Tigers of the Turf*, noted that there had been speculation Shergar was buried in a bog in County Leitrim. But, Smith added, Garda sources, "while expressing absolutely no doubt that Shergar is dead, will not go so far as to pinpoint any particular spot in the Republic as the likely place where he was hastily buried."

In Smith's view, this was an ill-conceived job from the start. "The Provos," he wrote, "in demanding a ransom of 2 million pounds made the mistake of thinking that they could get an immediate decision from those with whom they had made contact by phone. They did not understand the machinations involved in the syndication of a stallion. They believed they could get a quick 'Yes' from one individual and that, under threat of Shergar being assassinated, they would be able to collect in double quick time the sum they were seeking." What they failed to take into account, Smith said, was that all members of the syndicate, scattered in nine different countries, would have to be contacted before any ransom could be paid. Perhaps, Smith reasoned, the kidnappers erroneously believed that the Aga Khan, as the single largest shareholder, could act unilaterally. This did "not wash with the kidnappers when it was pointed out to them," Smith wrote, and when they "did not get the reply they wanted" to a final demand, "they used the ominous words, 'that's it.' The rest was silence..."

Smith wrote that in March of 1993,

> Sean O'Callaghan, who in 1983 was a senior figure in the IRA's 'Southern Command,' made a statement while in Maghaberry Prison near Belfast, to the effect that he was told of the fate of Shergar by one of the unit that actually carried out the kidnapping.
>
> The masked gang of six, armed and carrying walkie-talkies, had planned to keep Shergar in the Ballinamore area of County Letrim (where in December of 1983 they held for ransom a prominent Irish businessman who was later safely rescued) 'while endeavouring to gain the 2 million-pound ransom.
>
> But, according to O'Callaghan, the gang never

realized just how highly-strung a thoroughbred sire can be when taken from familiar surroundings. 'The horse threw himself into a frenzy after being disturbed and since they were unable to pacify him, they had to kill him,' said O'Callaghan.

It (became) obvious that Shergar had been killed. Time had run out on his Provo kidnappers. The theory in official circles is that the horse became fractious and that his minders could not control him. They had no other course open to them but to put him down and dispose of the body.

This theory gained credence when the aforementioned O'Callaghan wrote a book entitled *The Informer*. Published in 1998, it detailed his work as an IRA member turned police informant, or double agent. He said the Shergar plot was hatched in prison by a former bookie's clerk and an IRA veteran who headed the special operations team in charge of raising funds and buying arms for the organization. O'Callaghan said unequivocally that Shergar had been killed, "Even though the IRA kept up the pretense that he was alive and demanded a ransom for his return."

Actually, no evidence has been produced to support *any* theory concerning Shergar's fate.

Raymond Smith concluded the Shergar chapter of his book with a respectful mention of Chief Superintendent James Murphy, now retired, "who was a central figure in leading the investigations...and whose grey hat and distinctive style made him known globally overnight as the result of the intense television coverage of every aspect of the case...It can be revealed that Murphy refused a sum of at least 250,000 pounds sterling to give his story exclusively to one British paper. All he was asked to do was sit down and speak into a tape-recorder and a 'ghost' writer would do the rest.

"But the day Murphy retired he made a vow to himself that he would never give an interview about the case or ever talk to any member of the media about it, even on a non-attributable basis. All the financial inducements in the world would not make him change his mind on that.

"The man they came to know affectionately in County Kildare as 'Jazzer' Murphy will carry to the grave his own conclusions on the 'Shergar Affair.' His file is closed.

"That in itself adds another ironic twist to the story."

What Joost Knew

It was called Leisurewoods, a quiet, attractive subdivision some twelve miles southwest of downtown Austin, Texas, just off Interstate 35 on the outskirts of Buda and near the Hays/Travis county line, and the prevailing atmosphere was one of tranquility — until the first weekend of March, 1990. Then violent death came to four residents of Leisurewoods. Discovered shot to death on the morning of Monday, March 5, were forty-one-year-old David L. Joost (pronounced "Yoast"), director of administration of the Texas Racing Commission; his wife Susan, thirty-five, a twelve-year employee of the Texas Railroad Commission; and their two children, ten-year-old son Eric, and daughter Lauren, five —all four members of what was described by many who knew them as "a wholesome, loving family," one headed by a "dedicated employee who was a devoted husband and father."

David Joost died of a single gunshot wound to the chest. Next to his body, which was in the hallway near a bathroom, lay a .38-caliber revolver. His wife had been shot once in the back, their daughter once in the chest; they were both found on the bed in the master bedroom. Eric's body was on the bed in his room; he had been shot in the chest and left shoulder, a total of three bullet wounds. All four Joosts were dressed in nightclothes. All the shots had been fired at close range.

No signs of forced entry into the house were visible, said Hays County Sheriff Paul Hastings, nor any signs of a struggle. Nothing appeared to be missing. No suicide note was found. Hastings noted that both the Sunday and Monday newspapers were in the driveway.

Travis County Medical Examiner Robert Bayardo concluded that all four deaths had taken place sometime between 2 and 3 o'clock Sunday morning. Because David and Susan Joost were state employees, Sheriff Hastings said, he chose to "immediately call in the Texas Rangers" to aid in the investigation (this was done within twenty-four hours of the discovery of the bodies). He also brought in the Department of Public Safety Crime Scene Lab Team to collect evidence.

The cause of this disaster at 108 Killdeer Drive in Leisurewoods, where the Joosts had lived for ten years, has been the subject of contention ever since.

———————

When he was hired by the Texas Racing Commission in December of 1989, David Joost joined a state agency which at that point had no major racetracks to monitor. (G. Rollie White Downs, a minor league plant, was the only track that had opened since the Texas legislature had approved pari-mutuel wagering in 1987.) The fledgling industry was then engaged in fierce competition for much sought-after racing licenses for both horse and dog tracks. The commission, formed in 1987, had been the subject of a state auditor's office report that questioned its accounting practices.

The first of the big Texas tracks to open was Sam Houston Race Park, which hosted its inaugural meeting in 1994. (Retama Park in San Antonio and Lone Star Park near Dallas followed in 1995 and 1997, respectively.) Joost's position had been created during a reorganization of the Commission staff. Joost said at the time, "A big potential exists in the state for the racing industry. I think I have the background and expertise to be able to contribute. I'm getting my feet firmly planted and clearing the desk."

Joost hailed from Moulton, Texas, a cattle and farm town of some 1,000 people located eighty-five miles east of San Antonio. An Eagle Scout and an excellent student, he was valedictorian of his Moulton High School class. Following his graduation in 1967, Joost enlisted in the U.S. Air Force and served for four years, two of them (1969-70) as a staff sergeant with the Military Police in Vietnam, based in Saigon.

After leaving the Air Force, Joost used the GI Bill to go to college, first at Blinn College in Brenham, Texas, then at the University of Texas in Austin from which he was graduated in 1974 with a degree in business administration, his major in accounting. A certified public accountant, Joost held various jobs in state government, including serving as senior auditor in the governor's office and chief financial officer of the State Property Tax Board. He was dismissed from the latter position in October of 1989, victim of what he described as "office politics" involving a new director. He quickly found other work with the racing commission, where as director of administration he supervised a staff of five. Joost's responsibilities included payroll, hiring, and accounting.

Said Joost's brother Daniel, early in 2000, "David and I and our families were together that Thanksgiving (of 1989). He told me he'd lost his job with the tax board. That was the first time that ever happened to him. He said it was because of office politics. He wasn't worried about it at all. He said, 'I'll get another job.' The next month David got hired by the racing commission. I know he had to have a complete background check for that, and it was fine."

Joost made a good impression on his racing commission colleagues from the start. One co-worker described him as "somewhat reserved" but "extremely conscientious...very likable. The staff enjoyed David." Even though Friday, March 2 of 1990 was a state holiday — Texas Independence Day — Joost had put in a full day at the office.

When the ordinarily punctual Joost did not arrive for work on Monday, his co-workers became concerned. It was completely out of character for him to be a "no show." Attempting to track him down, they called the Texas Railroad Commission, where Susan Joost worked. She, too, they were told, had failed to appear at the office that day.

Late in the morning of March 5, Charles Scurlock, an accountant on Joost's staff, drove to Leisurewoods to check on the family. Finding the house locked and eliciting no response with repeated knocking, Scurlock called the Hays County Sheriff's Department. Responding was Constable Billy Reeves. It was Reeves who forced his way into the house through a side door from the garage into the Joost home, and he and Scurlock were the first to see the bodies.

Reeves subsequently wrote in his official report, "Mr. Joost's body was lying on its back in a spread-eagle fashion, with the feet nearest the door and the head farthest from the door. The body was clad in a white T-shirt and white jockey shorts, and I could see a burnt hole in the center of the chest area of the shirt, and a blood stain surrounding the hole."

As news of the slayings spread, residents of Leisurewoods expressed disbelief and dismay. The neighborhood was considered to be safe, although there had been a series of unsolved burglaries in recent weeks. And the Joosts had never struck any of their neighbors as potential targets of violence. David Joost, an assistant coach for son Eric's "Sidekicks" soccer team in the Hays Youth Association, was also a regular attendee at his son's Little League games, as were Susan and Lauren. "We often sat with them at the ballpark," said one neighbor, adding: "They were very pleasant people with beautiful, darling kids."

T. C. Mallet, a former colleague of Joost's, said David "was always talking about his kids, about youth soccer, and about taking them camping." Another friend, Darrell Rupert, told the *Austin American-Statesman* he had known David for nine years. "He was a real conscientious, dependable and honest person. I've know him professionally and personally. I had a tremendous amount of respect for him.

"They were a very happy family."

On Friday, March 9, more than 500 mourners crowded into St. Rose of Lima Catholic Church in Schulenberg, Texas, Susan Joost's hometown, for the funeral Mass. Addressing the throng, St. Rose pastor Reverend Richard Filice said in reference to the tragedy, "It is not easy to understand...in fact, it is impossible to comprehend. David and Susan and Eric and Lauren are in the company of the saints and with Our Lord for eternity," the priest said.

Burial followed in the St. Rose of Lima Cemetery. Pink flowers lay atop the smallest of the two white caskets, Lauren's, while Eric's was decorated with yellow flowers. Red roses were on the silver and gray caskets containing their parents. The four graves were surrounded by wreaths. Affixed to the tombstone shared by David and Susan was a photo of them, both smiling, with the date of their wedding inscribed beneath it. A tombstone in the adjacent row, over the children's graves, bore a recently taken photo of them.

Before the mourners left the cemetery, members of the Veterans of Foreign Wars post from Moulton, David's hometown, presented his survivors with a U.S. flag in tribute to his service to his country.

———————

Although the remains of the Joost family were buried that March morning in south central Texas, numerous questions persisted about the events that had wiped this young family from the face of the earth.

In addition to Father Filice, there were many others who found "impossible to comprehend" the official explanation of the death of the Joost family: triple murder, then suicide. Major among them were Susan Joost's father and brother, Clarence and Robert Besetzny, and one of David's brothers, Daniel, then thirty-four.

Daniel Joost vividly remembers how he learned of the tragedy. "I got home about 5 o'clock in the afternoon that Monday," he recalled, "and a lady in town that our family knew called on the phone. She said 'Daniel, quick, turn on the TV news.' I said, 'What's going on?' She said, 'David and his family are all dead.'

"I could not believe it. And I sure could not believe it when they said David had done this thing."

The ruling of Justice of the Peace Orlena Hehl and the medical examiner had been announced on Wednesday, two days before the funeral. Autopsy results, they said, showed that David Joost shot his wife, two children, and then himself. Sheriff Hastings said that both state and local investigators believed the "pressure of his job" may have pushed Joost to commit the crimes. "Everybody says how stable he was and how it wouldn't be like him to harm anybody," said the sheriff. "But sometimes someone about to commit suicide who kills people he loves is in his own mind protecting them...He doesn't want them to be hurt by what he's about to do."

People who had worked with David Joost did not agree with the sheriff's assessment. Charles Scurlock told the *American-Statesman* that Joost "was not obsessed by his job," and that he had never "had any complaints about his wife or kids." Racing commission Chairman Hilary Doran said Joost had been functioning well in a demanding role, including straightening out budget problems stemming from before his hiring, but that he did not seem anxious or pressured. "I talked to David on Friday," Doran said, and "he was upbeat. I detected no stress or strain or irritability or anything."

Some three months after she had ruled the deaths to be a triple murder followed by a suicide, eighty-four-year-old Justice of the Peace Hehl had second thoughts. "Lingering questions" regarding the case caused her to order a public inquest, which was delayed, then permanently canceled after it was termed illegal by then Texas Attorney General Jim Maddox, who said Hehl had already ruled on the case.

Daniel Joost said he was "bitterly disappointed" by this development. Daniel, who at the time of his brother's death was a U.S. Army master sergeant stationed at nearby Fort Hood, had insisted from the start that his brother was "simply incapable" of causing such carnage. "I knew my brother real well," Daniel said. "Shooting someone else or himself was not in him at all." Three months after the attorney general's ruling, the Joost family and Susan's family hired private investigator David Rains of Houston, a former member of the Louisiana State Police criminal investigation division.

Along with the other members of both David's and Susan's families, Daniel suspected that the four Joosts were killed by professional gunmen and the crimes made to look like murder-suicide, perhaps "because of something my brother knew" regarding corruption in the racing scene in Texas.

"He died the day before he was scheduled to make an important report to the commission," Daniel said.

"I talked to David the Thursday before he died," Daniel Joost said early in 2000. Retired from the Army after a twenty-year career, he works for the Copperas Cove, Texas, water department. "Ever since our mother passed away in 1986," Daniel said, "the two of us had looked after our father a lot. David and I had planned to go to our father's house (in Moulton) that weekend and repair the kitchen sink. David said to me, 'We'll have to do it next weekend instead. I'm real busy this weekend. I'm working on a report I have to give to the commission on Monday. You wouldn't believe some of the stupid shit these people are doing.' That's what he said to me," Daniel said.

One of the documents the newly hired Joost had been scrutinizing was a controversial contract the racing commission had awarded to the national consulting company Deloitte, Haskins and Sells (now Deloitte-Touche) for work in helping to bring about the return of pari-mutuel racing. It was a multi-million dollar contract and its size and terms were questioned by some members of the commission as well as some Texas legislators. The *American-Statesman* quoted a family friend of the Joosts, Bill Baran, as saying David Joost told him he was "worried" about an unspecified contract. "He was going to terminate the contract because they weren't producing," Baran said.

Said Daniel Joost of his brother, "David was as honest a person as you'd ever find. If he came upon something that was wrong, I'm positive he would have been the person to dig into it." The report submitted to the racing commission, the one Joost was to have written, mentioned no irregularities. The fact that the report was not initialed by Joost, as was his custom, caused Joost family investigators to question its authenticity.

(In April of 1993, a federal grand jury subpoenaed files from the commission as part of the investigation into the deaths of the Joosts, but the jury took no action. At the time the subpoenas were served, David Freeman, then the executive director of the racing commission, said he was "mystified" as to what the investigators might be seeking. Freeman earlier had termed as "ridiculous" rumors regarding a so-called "conspiracy theory" involving Joost's death.)

Assisting the Joost survivors in 1990 was the Houston Turf Club, an unsuccessful applicant for a racing license in that city; the franchise instead was granted by the racing commission to the Sam Houston Turf Club. Houston Turf Club appealed that decision and also filed a $1 billion federal lawsuit, claiming that the commission and other state officials, including Governor Bill Clements, had conspired to control the granting of licenses. In 1992 the Houston Turf Club dropped the suit after receiving an out-of-court settlement from Sam Houston Race Park.

Daniel Joost said the family was approached by representatives of Houston Turf Club "and their investigators. They told us there could be something wrong with this situation. We told them to go ahead and ask any questions they wanted. Our feeling was that they might help us to find the truth by helping themselves."

Survivors of David and Susan Joost received some $500,000 from insurance policies, retirement plans, and other assets. They spent about $80,000 of that on private investigators and attorneys and also put up a $50,000 reward for information leading to the arrest and conviction of the person or persons responsible for the deaths of the Joost family.

Said Daniel Joost: "I think the DPS, the Rangers, and the powers behind them thought, 'They're going to go away.' We didn't. Our family and Susan's family came together and spent a lot of time and money. We worked hand in hand. Susan's parents never believed that David did it. Her dad, Clarence, was writing the checks to finance the effort."

In addition to David Joost's stable background and lack of an apparent motive, private investigators David Rains and Randy Cunningham retained by the Joost and Besetzny families zeroed in on several points, including the following:

• No clearly defined, full fingerprints were found on either the gun or the bullet casings supposedly used by David Joost to fire six shots. "Did my brother shoot himself and then wipe down the weapon?" Daniel Joost asked incredulously.

• No traces of blood or tissue were found on the gun despite its muzzle's having been pressed against two of the victims.

• David Joost was right-handed, but there was no gunpowder residue on the back of his right hand — his firing hand. However, gunpowder residue was found on the palms of both hands and on the back of his left hand, suggesting he had raised his hands in defense against a gunman, perhaps trying to twist the barrel of the gun away from his body.

• The majority of suicide victims shoot themselves not in the chest but in the head, and usually when they are sitting or lying down.

• An investigator for the Hays County District Attorney's office stated that the lack of clear fingerprints on the gun indicates it could have been wiped clean. He testified under oath that he believed the homicides were the work of a "professional."

• A forensic expert, employing luminol — a glow-in-the-dark chemical used to show where blood has been — concluded that a five- or six-inch blot of blood had been cleaned off the tile floor near the front door of the Joost home, far from where the bodies were found. Said Daniel Joost, "The people from the undertakers that took away the bodies said they'd wrapped them up tight in sheets so that there was no blood dripping when they took them out. Whose blood was that by the door then?"

In addition, Daniel Joost said that to his knowledge "David had never owned a gun."

• Roland Moore, a security system expert in San Marcos, Texas, said that about a week before the shootings David Joost called him to inquire about security options, specifically a device that would protect him "if someone was in my back yard and I was sitting on the couch and he was looking at me in the window and wanted to hurt me." According to Moore, Joost did not make an appointment but said he "would get back" to him "within a week."

• As late as 1993, Daniel Joost said, no one in his family had been interviewed by Texas Rangers. Susan Joost's older brother, Robert Besetzny, said that he expected family members to be questioned about whether they were aware of any problems in the Joosts' marriage; that never happened, Besetzny complained.

Raising some of the aforementioned points had been reporter Tom Jarriel on ABC-TV's *20-20* in a program aired in May of 1992. The Texas Rangers refused Jarriel's request for them to discuss the case. Three public officials were interviewed on the program: Justice of the Peace Hehl, who repeated her contention that the case should be reopened; Sheriff Hastings, who defended the official investigation, dismissing new evidence as well as apparent inconsistencies in old evidence; and Bob Lipo, an assistant district attorney at the time of the deaths who said a grand jury should have been convened. "I've lost a lot of sleep over this," Lipo told Jarriel. "Could I have done something different? My hands were tied, but it's just not right. It just doesn't pass the stink test."

Reporter Jarriel told the *American-Statesman* that he was "convinced beyond a shadow of a doubt the family was murdered. I think it was a very professional job, and I think David Joost was killed because of what he knew about the racing commission. I strongly suspect that law enforcement authorities at some level were either involved or were so incompetent they should be removed."

Sheriff Hastings fired back in a public statement, defending the official investigation and charging that *20-20* had "meticulously edited to tell the story they wanted to portray." He scoffed at allegations of a "Mafia hit," said the men hired by the Joost family "are the type of investigators who will 'preach it anyway you want to hear it,' for a price…I, like others involved in the case, supported a grand jury hearing after Judge Hehl requested to change her ruling. However, the Attorney General's office found no reason to open the case." Hastings said he was tired of hearing about the case. The Joost family and their representatives, added the sheriff, "are beating the same dead horse."

Regarding the lack of fingerprints on the murder weapon mentioned by 20-20, the sheriff said that in fact "partial latents were found on the gun…The medical examiner's report noted heavy burns on the left palm (of David Joost) and minimum burns on the right hand. This was explained by the examiner as indicating the trigger was pulled with his right hand, while the left hand was holding the gun barrel to his chest," stated Hastings. In his written statement the sheriff did not address the question of how only "partial latents," not full and visible prints, could be on a gun purportedly last handled by a dead man.

As to ex-assistant district attorney Bob Lipo's statement that the case "Didn't pass the smell test," Sheriff Hastings said that was "probably because he (Lipo) was in his usual position of having his head up his own rear."

In 1993, more than three years after the event, the Joost case landed in another venue: an administrative hearing in Austin to determine whether the Texas State Employees Retirement System would pay $214,000 in insurance claims on the Joosts; the claims were being withheld because of the ruling of suicide. Said Daniel Joost, "this fight wasn't over the money. It was my brother's day in court."

Attorneys for Blue Cross Blue Shield of Texas, administrators of the actual insurance policy, threw a new theory on the table: they claimed that David Joost's motive was his "despair" over Susan's alleged affair with a co-worker, one whose wife was a friend of hers. The man vehemently denied such an involvement with Susan and numerous character witnesses refuted this unsupported charge of infidelity. In 1992 the man offered to take a polygraph test to prove that he was telling the truth. It was not until November of 1995 that the DPS gave him the test. He passed, eliciting an apology from the DPS director.

In January of 1994, four months after the administrative hearing on the insurance claims, state Judge Cathleen Parsley dealt the Joosts' survivors the first of three crushing blows when she ruled that their attorneys had failed to prove a "preponderance of evidence" that David Joost was slain. Although there were "several pieces of evidence which indicate that David Joost's death was not a suicide," said Judge Parsley, "the greater weight of the evidence indicates" that it was.

Parsley was critical of what she termed the "bungling of the initial investigation by local authorities." Photographs from the crime scene, she said, showed that Hays County sheriff's deputies had moved items around and "trampled on carpet" that may have contained valuable evidence. Nevertheless, the judge concluded, the Joost family had not presented enough evidence to support convincingly theories of murder.

The next setback for the Joosts came in May of 1995 when

the Texas Rangers, in their first public report on the case, closed the file with this conclusion: triple murder, suicide. (A story in the *Dallas Morning News* noted that the "Rangers could never firmly establish a motive for Mr. Joost's committing suicide.") Texas Ranger Ron Stewart, the lead investigator, wrote that "An investigation surrounding a tragedy of this magnitude will always leave some unanswered questions...This investigation is closed...pending the development of a responsible lead."

After persistent complaints from the family that the Rangers had mishandled the investigation, Texas Department of Public Safety director Colonel James Wilson agreed to review the case. In January of 1997 that agency's investigators concluded that the Texas Rangers were correct in their findings. The long awaited DPS report stated that "The crime scene reveals absolutely no hint of outside involvement and no credible scenario exists to indicate the perfect crime was committed by an outside perpetrator." Addressing the question of motive, the report cited financial pressures (the Joosts had debts of some $16,600) and job stress. "David was having difficulty coping" at work, said the DPS, adding that he was "apparently overwhelmed by life's events as he interpreted them, and this action was his way out." David Joost acted "for reasons that the rational mind cannot comprehend."

David Rains, one of the Joost family's private investigators, labeled the DPS report "an assortment of misstatements, half-truths, errors, and omissions. They grasped at anything they could find to support a conclusion they had already reached." Susan Joost's brother, Robert Besetzny, told the *Dallas Morning News* that "I think they had their minds made up in the beginning." But he said the battle to prove an outsider committed the crimes was over. "We decided to let it rest. There is nothing we can do about it," Besetzny said.

Justice of the Peace Hehl, who in 1993 changed her original ruling of murder/suicide and amended David Joost's certificate to read cause of death "undetermined," commented, "I don't know that it'll ever be over."

In an early 2000 interview, Daniel Joost remained bitter and resentful. "That investigation was botched from the beginning," he said. "If we hadn't pressed on with our own investigation — if we had done nothing — people might have believed that David did it. If he were alive and accused of killing his family, at least he would have gotten his day in court.

"Will the truth ever come out? Only if somebody confesses, or if somebody who knows who did it gets caught in some crime and decides to turn in the real killer or killers. That is really our only hope."

Tragedy struck Leisurewoods and 108 Killdeer Drive "ten years ago this March," Daniel said. He added that to the members of the Joost and Besetzny families, it seemed like only yesterday.

Calamity at Calumet

Kentucky in the spring can pump shots of eager anticipation into the most turgid, winter-ridden, world-weary bloodstreams. Brand new foals frolic in rolling green pastures and redbuds bloom under warming skies. Keeneland Race Course opens its gates, and for devotees of the Thoroughbred horse, the walk up the dogwood-lined avenue to the track's entrance on an April afternoon is shock therapy for the soul. Hope springs.

So did tears on the afternoon of April 27, 1978 — to the eyes of many present in the record crowd of more than 22,000 as they witnessed a unique tableau near the winner's circle preceding the start of the Blue Grass Stakes. What they viewed was the final meeting of a great Thoroughbred and a grand dame of American racing.

The horse was Alydar, in his red blinkers with his rider, Jorge Velasquez, wearing Calumet Farm's famed devil red and blue silks. The woman was Calumet owner Lucille Markey, who was accompanied by her husband, Admiral Gene Markey.

Both in their eighties, both frail and in poor health and usually confined to wheelchairs, the Markeys had been driven to Keeneland from nearby Calumet and given special permission to park near the winner's circle. As the field paraded to the post, Velasquez guided Alydar to the outside rail so the Markeys could observe him more closely. It was Admiral Markey who had given the handsome chestnut colt his name — a contraction of "Aly darling" — in honor of the Markeys' great friend Prince Aly Khan.

Alydar won that Blue Grass by thirteen lengths with the Markeys cheering him on. The trophy was brought to the station wagon in which the Markeys sat. As they were driven away at the end of a memorable afternoon, Mrs. Markey was seen holding the trophy in one hand, her husband's hand in the other.

Two years later, Gene Markey died, and two years after that, Mrs. Markey passed away, leaving a fortune and a debt-free Calumet Farm valued at some $40 million to her heirs. Eight years later Alydar would be dead and Calumet on the verge of financial disgrace. And within hours of Alydar's death the rumors would begin circulating in the Thoroughbred racing community that his demise was not the result of an accident.

———————

Following his victory in the Blue Grass Stakes, Alydar went on to play the gallant foil in the most thrilling extended rivalry in Thoroughbred racing history, one highlighted by a titanic Triple Crown struggle that would forever link his name with that of his conqueror. Say the words

"Affirmed and Alydar" to most any racing fan and the response will be an expression of admiration and fond recollection.

The two horses faced each other ten times in the course of two years. Harbor View Farm's Affirmed won their first meeting, the Youthful Stakes at Belmont Park on June 15, 1977, by a neck, thus establishing the theme of this long-running hit.

Alydar evened the score by three and a half lengths in the Great American Stakes on July 6 at Belmont. Affirmed countered with two straight tallies: the Hopeful Stakes on August 27 by a half-length and the Belmont Futurity by a nose on September 10. Alydar came back with a length and a quarter triumph in the Champagne on October 15, but Affirmed brought the score to 4-2 his favor with a neck decision in the October 29 Laurel Futurity, sewing up the two-year-old championship.

But America's racing fans "hadn't seen nuthin' yet." The rivalry was to reach new heights in the five-week crucible of class, strength, and resolution called the Triple Crown.

They entered the gate for first time in 1978 at Churchill Downs on May 6, eighteen-year-old Steve Cauthen aboard Affirmed, and Velasquez, thirty-one, on Alydar. Affirmed glided home a length and a half to the good of Alydar, who had trailed by as many as a dozen lengths in the early stages of this 104th Kentucky Derby before closing strongly.

Two weeks later at Pimlico, Alydar engaged Affirmed at the head of the stretch in the Preakness Stakes. They matched strides to the wire, Affirmed prevailing this time by the margin of a neck.

The *piece de resistance* came on June 10 in the Belmont Stakes. Hooking up with six furlongs to run in the mile and one-half race, Affirmed and Alydar went head-to-head the rest of the way before a screaming crowd of 65,000. At the wire it was again Affirmed — this time by a head. The added distance of the Belmont, considered by his fervent backers to be all that Alydar needed to win, had not made a difference in the outcome.

Affirmed and Alydar met one more time, in the August 19 Travers Stakes before a record Saratoga crowd of more than 50,000. Affirmed again finished first, this time by nearly two lengths, but he had severely impeded Alydar on the far turn and was disqualified and placed second. Alydar was awarded the decision in their finale.

The final score read Affirmed seven, Alydar three. Five of their meetings were decided by a half-length or less, the entire Triple Crown by two. (Had Affirmed not been there, Alydar would have won the Triple Crown by a combined margin of nearly twenty-two lengths — such was the spread between these two rivals and their other competition). Their ten races totaled ten and five-sixteenths miles, and at the end of those 54,450 feet Affirmed finished ahead of Alydar by only some four and one-half lengths, or approximately thirty-eight feet. The margin would have been less except for the ground Alydar lost when Affirmed cut him off and he was forced to drop back before coming on again in the Travers. No other rivalry in American racing history compares with this one.

Alydar raced six times at age four, winning twice, before an ankle injury forced his retirement in July of 1979. He went home with a record of fourteen wins from twenty-six starts, earnings of $957,195, and the admiration of racing people everywhere for his great talent and resolve. Runner-up to Affirmed in the voting for both the two and three-year-old championships, he qualified as "The Great Contender." There are worse titles.

———————

Alydar returned to his birthplace in 1979 to prepare for stud duties. Calumet was the most famous Thoroughbred farm in Kentucky, and in America, and most probably in the world.

Calumet began operation as a Standardbred farm in 1924, founded by William Monroe Wright, who had made his fortune as head of the Calumet Baking Powder Company. Seven years later Wright's son Warren Sr. converted it to Thoroughbreds. Calumet won just one race the following season, but only two years after that vaulted to seventh in America in money won thanks primarily to the efforts of its first champion, two-year-old filly queen Nellie Flag. In 1941, only ten years after its formation, Calumet Farm ranked as the nation's leading money winner — a position it would hold for twelve years. Calumet was also the leading breeder for eleven years.

Nellie Flag was the first in an unparalleled parade of nineteen Calumet champions. Five of them were voted Horse of the Year; eleven have been inducted into the National Museum of Racing Hall of Fame. Included in this incredible roster are a record eight winners of the Kentucky Derby, seven of which were trained by Ben Jones and his son Jimmy Jones: Whirlaway (the 1941 Triple Crown winner), Pensive (1944), Citation (1948 Triple Crown winner), Ponder (1949), Hill Gail (1952), Iron Liege (1957), and Tim Tam (1958).

When Warren Wright Sr. died at age seventy-five in 1950, Calumet's awesome reputation was described in an obituary in the *Thoroughbred Record* by its editor, Haden Kirkpatrick. "In a sport that has its integrity sometimes questioned," wrote Kirkpatrick, Wright's "was above the reproach of even the most scurrilous critics. The world knew...that when the Calumets went down as they sometimes did, they went down with all turrets blazing.

"That element of uncompromising endeavor," Kirkpatrick continued, "was doubtless Warren Wright's greatest gift to American racing. For the devil red, not merely a symbol of the ultimate aristocracy of the turf, became also the proud banner of the $2 bettors. They believed in it, and they worshiped the horses that bore it. Wherever the Calumets were running, the clerks, the salesmen, the laborers could turn out in full confidence...secure in the knowledge that whether they rode with Wright or against him, his entry was going to blast for all the money, and intended either to get it or crack wide open trying."

Two years after Warren Wright's death his widow, Lucille, married retired United States Navy Admiral Gene Markey. The Markeys would see Calumet win three Kentucky Derbys that decade, but then a decline in the farm's breeding quality set in. Calumet would never again dominate as it had for so many years. There was a lengthy stretch of relative mediocrity until the emergence of Alydar and champion three-year-old fillies Our Mims (1977) and Davona Dale (1979).

Lucille Markey was preceded in death in 1978 by her only child, Warren Wright Jr. When Mrs. Markey passed on in 1982, Calumet was inherited by Warren Wright Jr.'s widow, Bertha, and her four children. One of the children, named Lucille after her grandmother (and nicknamed Cindy), was married to forty-one-year-old John Thomas Lundy, who was chosen by the heirs to serve as president of the new Calumet Corporation, a multi-million dollar, debt-free entity.

J. T. Lundy hailed from nearby Scott County, son of a tenant farmer. He had dabbled in the horse business in the past, although his main passion was auto racing and he counted several famous drivers among his friends. Lundy swung into action, wielding a new broom with a vengeance at Calumet. Fired were several longtime Calumet employees (including trainer John Veitch, who had his "lifetime" breeding right to Alydar taken away by Lundy). Out the window went the farm's tradition of conservative fiscal practices. This was the advent of a high-flying horse market buoyed by high-priced horse flesh, and Lundy quickly positioned himself to be a major player.

Central to Lundy's vision for a revived and energized Calumet was his management of Alydar, who had proved to be an immediate success at stud. Foals from Alydar's first crop sold at Keeneland in 1982 for an average of $827,143, making him the second leading sire at the sale behind world leader Northern Dancer.

Alydar's sons and daughters soon began making their marks on the racetrack as well as in the sales ring. They would include 1988 Horse of the Year Alysheba, who retired as the world's leading money winner with $6,679,242; the 1990 Horse of the Year Criminal Type; and champions Easy Goer, Althea, and Turkoman. The success of Alydar's offspring made him North America's third leading sire in both 1986 and 1987, and second leading sire in 1988 and 1989.

Alydar was never syndicated. He was rarely at rest, either. In 1989, for example, he was bred to 104 mares (an unusually high number at that time, though not out of the ordinary today) all told, including some from Australia late in the year. Alydar made 200 trips to the breeding shed from between early February and early December. This increase in production eventually led to a glut on the market of Alydar offspring.

But in 1984, Lundy, taking advantage of Alydar's enormous commercial appeal, sold fifteen lifetime breeding rights in the horse for $2.5 million each, realizing $37.5 million. But that was just part of Lundy's maneuverings. As the farm's debt load began to balloon, Lundy began pre-selling seasons that Calumet controlled for two and three years in advance. In some circles, Alydar was starting to be referred to as "Lundy's ATM machine."

This all came to a halt on November 13, 1990, when a substitute night watchman, thirty-two-year-old Alton Stone, reported Alydar to be badly injured in his stall in the Calumet stallion barn.

Shortly before 10 p.m. that Tuesday night, Stone said, he found Alydar with a terribly damaged right rear leg, a jagged portion of the cannon bone protruding through the skin. The bottom of the sturdy oak door to Alydar's stall was not flush to the floor but was encased by a bracket containing a roller. The two iron bolts holding the bracket had been sheared off at floor level. The bracket and roller lay loose in the straw — a sight than none of the people arriving later on the scene said they had ever observed before in any horse barn.

After Stone summoned help, the sweat-soaked, distressed horse was stabilized with a temporary cast, sedated, and nine hours later, on Wednesday morning, operated on in the Calumet clinic a half-mile from the stallion barn.

Dr. Larry Bramlage, a nationally renowned specialist in equine bone work, was one of the veterinary surgeons who attended Alydar following the injury. Working with him were Dr. William Baker, the regular veterinarian for Calumet, and Dr. Lynda Rhodes, the farm vet. In the November 24, 1990 issue of *The Blood-Horse*, Bramlage described the efforts to save Alydar:

> The initial fracture was Tuesday night. (Alydar) broke it and was frantic. The procedure is to stabilize the limb and let them realize they are hurt. Once they realize they have a problem, they become more tractable, which he did by Wednesday morning.
>
> Alydar suffered a mid-shaft transverse fracture of the cannon bone, which is a complete break

through the middle of the bone. The accident of overloading the bone was done by him kicking through the stall door. The bone bent sideways enough to break. It is not...like a racing injury.

The bone broke in half and opened through the skin. That is serious, because the cannon is the densest bone in the horse's body. Not many other animals have bones as thick and hard as the horse's cannon bone; a giraffe has a similar bone. The bone is hard with no muscles around to protect it. With exercise (as while racing) it gets thicker and harder...

The bone went through the skin, which allows infection access. That can keep a fracture from healing because the middle of the cannon bone has the least blood supply...The cannon is not spongy bone like upper body bones. It is essentially a cylinder of ivory with blood trickling out through the bone from the inside to the outside.

An injury such as Alydar's is really a tough fracture to handle. First, you try to get the horse stabilized; that went well. Then you have to get him through surgery and back on his feet.

At 9 a.m. Wednesday, we did surgery. We put a small plate through the hole where the injury occurred because we did not want to expose other tissue. Pins were placed across the bone and into the cast so that his weight was distributed through the cast rather than down the bone. If we had put in a big plate, we would have reduced the blood supply more. We used transfixation pins (across the bone into the cast) so he was walking on the cast.

The surgery took about two hours. He lost some pieces of the bone through the fracture, and a bone graft was used from the hip to stimulate healing of the bone.

The cast was placed on, and he went through recovery (in the recovery stall). In about 1 1/2 hours he was back on his feet. About three hours later he was moved to the convalescent stall in the same barn. He was content to eat hay and grass. All his responses were normal.

Alydar recovered from surgery and was in a sling to support his weight. He was restless and bothered by the sling...He began the agitation with the sling...His heart rate went up...He was sedated on and off throughout the night, which caused him to be gassed up and a little colicky...Keeping him sedated was not working well...

On Thursday morning, Bramlage continued,

(Alydar) was less tolerant of the sling. We had to make the decision either to keep him sedated, or let him move without the sling...We all agreed he backed us into the corner (with either the sling or sedation) and we had to try to get him out of the sling.

When we let him out (of the sling) and he moved around, he slipped and fell. He stumbled on a front leg (stubbed his toe) and couldn't catch his balance with his hind leg, and 1,200 pounds went down.

When Alydar fell he broke his femur in the right hind leg, the leg whose cannon bone was already fractured. That was it. Nothing further could be done to save him. At 8:30 on the morning of November 15, he was humanely destroyed via lethal injection.

Concluded Bramlage: "Stallions are used to having things their own way. In spite of how well the surgery went, we didn't win. It's like playing a chess match — the horse makes a move, and you make a move. We gave him a chance...We gave it our best shot."

Alydar's death was a devastating blow to those who had known him best, including John Veitch, who developed the horse but who had subsequently been fired by J. T. Lundy as Calumet's trainer; and jockey Velasquez, who said: "I loved Alydar, and I had a special relationship with him, like I've never had with another horse. I always used to bring him sugar when I'd come to the barn in the mornings. Alydar got so he knew my voice.

"One day at Belmont I got out of my car near John Veitch's barn, and I hid behind a tree. I started calling out, 'Hey Champ, Hey Champ.' That's what I called Alydar. He couldn't see me but he started screaming and kicking and bucking in his stall. Finally, I had to stop hiding and come out from behind the tree, because I was afraid he'd hurt himself."

Velasquez said that in 1986, seven years after Alydar's retirement, he went to visit him at Calumet. "Alydar was out in a field, about 100 yards from where I was standing at the fence. His head was down, he was grazing. I hollered out, 'Hey Champ.' Alydar looked up right away, pricked his ears, and then came charging over to where I was standing. He was the best horse I ever rode," Velasquez said years later after he, too, had retired. "He was the Champ to me."

On November 15 Alydar was interred in the formal cemetery at Calumet, joining the farm's eight Kentucky Derby winners and the farm's foundation sire, Bull Lea. Alydar was buried "whole" — a sign of respect accorded few horses (head, heart, and hooves are the norm). Said Lundy, "It was a heartbreaker to put him in that hole and bury him."

Lexington insurance adjustor Tom Dixon, who had been called to the scene the night Alydar was injured, ruled that the horse's death was accidental. He concluded that Alydar had kicked the corner of his stall door so forcefully that the impact broke his leg. A month later the mortality claim on Alydar was paid by the insurers (primarily Lloyd's of London). It was the largest in the history of horse insurance: $36.5 million. The majority of that record amount, some $20.5 million, was used by Calumet to pay down a debt owed First City Bancorporation of Houston, Texas.

———————

Less than eight months after Alydar's death — on July 11, 1991 — the Wright family-controlled corporation that owned and operated Calumet Farm filed for Chapter 11 under the federal bankruptcy code. The filing listed debts of $118,050,732 — an amount amassed in just nine years since Lucille Markey's death. Before the bankruptcy filing, a number of creditors had sued Calumet, their claims coming to more than $25 million.

Lundy had resigned as Calumet president on April 3, 1991. Nine months later, in Miami, Florida, he declared bankruptcy, listing almost 100 creditors and liabilities of $77 million. Lundy's friends insisted that he and the other Calumet heirs had been whiplashed by economics: a combination of a declining horse market and damaging changes in tax reform laws.

The management team that took over Calumet's operation following Lundy's departure was headed by trainer John T. Ward Jr. Its secretary-treasurer was another Central Kentucky horseman, Ronald Sladon. Even though Calumet had been honored just the previous year with an Eclipse Award as North America's outstanding breeder, the same season that its Criminal Type had been voted Horse of the Year honors, the crash was unavoidable under the circumstances, said Sladon. He termed Calumet's financial arrangements — constructed by the previous, Lundy-led management team — as "an ever widening web." The farm was spending more than $1 million a month, yet the great majority of its 1991 bills had not been paid. (The new management group was astounded to discover a total of just $400 left in a Calumet general account in the Georgetown, Kentucky, bank — an account that had seen some $350 million pass through it during the Lundy years.)

In Sladon's view, Alydar's death served to accelerate the collapse of a "debt-upon-debt" financial structure. Sladon told *The Blood-Horse* writer Deirdre B. Biles that what happened was inevitable: "There was no way they could breed themselves out of it. Alydar's breeding ability was heavily mortgaged, and when he died, a lot of creditors started calling," Sladon said.

Although Sladon declined to criticize the Lundy-era management, he did say, "on the record that...the chief executive was pulling in in excess of $1 million annually in commissions."

————————————

More than 3,000 people assembled at Calumet Farm on March 26, 1992 for the "Absolute Auction" of the property and everything on it (25,000 brochures had been mailed to potential buyers). The winning bidder for the 767-acre main tract at $17 million was prominent owner-breeder Henryk de Kwiatkowski, who continues to operate it.

After resigning as Calumet president, J. T. Lundy dropped from public view. For the next few years, there were numerous unconfirmed reports of Lundy being spotted in various places all over the world. In *Wild Ride*, her fascinating, meticulously researched book on the collapse of the Calumet dynasty, Ann Hagedorn Auerbach wrote that in "a region rich with folklore where storytelling is about as natural as talking, 'J. T. sighting' was almost as much fun as going to the races.

"One reason for the intrigue was simply a matter of arithmetic. For most people, the numbers in the Calumet debacle just didn't add up. So much money flowed into the farm during the Lundy years that no one could understand how it was possible that nothing was left. This image of a gap between money in and money out, in conjunction with the fact that Lundy was bringing into his own coffers millions of dollars in commissions and breeding rights, led to the suspicion that Lundy had stacks of money hidden away — money of his own and money that might be legally construed as Calumet's," Auerbach wrote.

"Using rough estimates of income and expenses," she continued, "some people placed the sum of missing cash at a stunning $300 million...Ron Sladon estimated that...somewhere around $90 million or $100 million (was) unaccounted for."

Meanwhile, rumors continued that Alydar had been killed. Included among those believing that rumor was the notorious Tommy Burns, known as "The Sandman" because he "put horses to sleep" for a living. Burns was apprehended in a wide-ranging federal probe of insurance fraud in the show horse industry. While awaiting trial in 1992, he told Harlan Draeger, an investigative reporter for the *Chicago Sun-Times*, that without having any direct knowledge he nevertheless was positive that Alydar was killed for the insurance. "I read that he broke his leg in a stall," Burns told Draeger. "You think I believe that? Never happens. It was Calumet Farms (sic)...They were in financial trouble."

(Burns was a veritable fount of rumored information. In the same interview, Burns claimed that the body of missing candy heiress and racehorse owner Helen Brach "went to Gary, Ind. and was burned up in one of those steel furnaces there. I know this from a good source," Burns said.)

A year after Alydar's death, a Lloyd's of London agent told

the *Lexington Herald-Leader* that "there was nothing to be gained by killing the horse. The farm couldn't be saved by killing the horse." The agent expressed the view of many in the industry: that Alydar was worth much more alive than dead.

In *Wild Ride*, a contrasting opinion is offered. Auerbach points out "Very few knew that Alydar, despite his stepped-up work schedule, was no longer the cash cow of Calumet...

"Considering Calumet's fragile condition," Auerbach added, "its long list of debts, and its struggle to pay insurance premiums and operational costs, there was every reason in the world to suspect something evil — something that happened in those moments before the first bone broke, something that none of the caretakers, the vets, and all the good people who tried to save the stallion's life could have known about. The motive could easily have been to pay down the First City debt, the most onerous of all Calumet's obligations...The insurance claim...would greatly diminish the $44.75 million debt, making the farm's financial state less onerous to (potential) outside investors...Despite appearances, Alydar was worth more dead than alive." (His stud fee had dropped from $250,000 in 1988 to $165,000 in 1990.)

Could Alydar somehow have been *provoked* into the act that led to his death? One theory popular among the skeptics was that someone had filed off the bracket at the base of the stall door before Alydar was discovered to be injured, thus shoring up the scenario that had the horse kicking the door so hard he broke his leg.

That the leg was broken by a kick — not a crowbar or

another blunt instrument — remains the firmly held opinion of Dr. Larry Bramlage. In a letter written to the author in November of 1999, Bramlage (who was the American Association of Equine Practitioners veterinarian on call when Charismatic broke down during the 1999 Belmont Stakes) said that "extraneous details" might lead people to "consider the possibility" of a blunt instrument being used on Alydar.

"But," Bramlage emphasized, "My opinion remains the same. I believe the horse's fracture was an accident. What I most often said, including under oath, is that 'I saw nothing at the time of the accident, during the horse's treatment, or since that makes me believe the horse's fracture was anything other than an accident.' The medical facts fit an accident best, they do not fit an intentional assault." As Bramlage said in conclusion, "This story won't seem to die."

The same point was made in a letter published in the February 12, 2000 issue of *The Blood-Horse.* Tom Dixon, the insurance adjustor who ruled Alydar's death to be accidental and whose company paid the record $36.5 million claim, wrote that, "countless rumors to the contrary, there was nothing suspicious or mysterious" about the animal's death.

"There is a mystery as to how the original fracture occurred," wrote Dixon, a Lexington resident who retired in 1996, "but after nine years, a grand jury investigation…and continuing FBI investigations, nothing has solved that mystery.

"Good horse people know from long experience that you can put a yearling in a ten-acre paddock with one hole and the yearling will manage to step in it. People with veterinary experience also call the stall a 'horse's worst enemy.' "

Dixon concluded, "Folks, stuff happens. Please, let the horse rest in peace."

Supplying plenty of fuel to keep the rumor mill running was the case of Alton Stone, the Calumet employee who called in the alarm on Alydar on the night of November 13, 1990. In the summer of 1997 a federal grand jury in Houston, Texas, began investigating J. T. Lundy's operation of Calumet as well as the death of Alydar. The following January, the grand jury issued an indictment of Alton Stone. It alleged that Stone, a groom who worked days in the Calumet broodmare division, had lied about the circumstances leading to his working the night shift as a watchman on November 13.

The grand jury issued two counts of perjury against him. He pleaded not guilty.

The grand jury said Stone had lied when he testified that the regular watchman, Harold (Cowboy) Kipp, asked Stone to substitute for him that night. (Kipp testified that he had been ordered to take the night off by an associate of Lundy's.) The second count charged Stone with lying about his whereabouts on the farm in the eighty minutes before he said he found the injured Alydar. Lead federal prosecutor Julia Hyman Tomala, an assistant U. S. attorney, said she was convinced Stone was participating in a cover-up of a plot to kill Alydar for his $36.5 million insurance value.

In July of 1998 Alton Stone was convicted on the perjury counts, and in November of that year was sentenced to five months in prison and five months of home confinement.

Next up in a federal court room in Houston were Lundy and Gary Matthews, who had served as Calumet's chief financial officer during Lundy's years at the helm. Lundy had been taken into custody in Miami on March 3, 1999, upon his return to the U. S. from Venezuela.

Lundy and Matthews had been indicted in December of 1998. Their trial on charges of bank fraud, bribery, and conspiracy began January 18, 2000, before Judge Sim Lake in U.S. District Court, Southern District of Texas. Federal prosecutors said the alleged bribe of $1.1 million went to First City Bancorporation (which declared itself insolvent in 1992) in exchange for $65 million in unsecured loans. The bank's vice chairman, Lundy's friend Frank Cihak, along with four associates, had been convicted on fraud and money laundering charges in 1994.

The Houston trial lasted three weeks. Among witnesses called by the prosecution was Lucille Drinkwater, Lundy's ex-wife, who had remarried after their 1993 divorce. Once a millionairess in her role as a Calumet heiress, she lived in Florida at the time of the trial and was working as a cleaning lady. Although her testimony was not considered particularly helpful to the prosecution, the twelve-member jury took less than three hours to find Lundy and Matthews guilty of bank fraud, bribery, conspiracy and making false financial statements.

The verdict shocked both men. Matthews said he had just been "doing his job," while Lundy maintained "We didn't do anything wrong. We just did our best to do business." They remained free on bond until sentencing that was scheduled for June 8, 2000. Each man faced a minimum of seven years in prison.

Also expressing angry disbelief at the verdict was Matthews' attorney, Dan Cogdell, who offered this interesting take on the nation's court system: "If I was less politically correct, I would say you never put your trust in 12 people who are not smart enough to get off jury duty."

Attorneys for Lundy and Matthews planned to file appeals after sentencing.

U. S. attorney Julia Hyman Tomala, who was promoted to a position with the Department of Justice's fraud section in Washington, D. C., said in February of 2000 that the investigation into Alydar's death would continue.

Most of the speculation and suspicion about that death would never have arisen — and certainly wouldn't persist today — had Calumet Farm used what so many other major Kentucky horse farms do: a security system with video monitors in the stallion barns. But Lundy, despite his enormous expenditures on other items (planes, race cars, and residences) did not invest in such a system, even for the stall of one of the most valuable stallions in the world.

Alydar's right hind leg was broken twice. The second break, incurred in the fall he took the day after his surgery, was witnessed by several people, including the attending veterinarians. The first fracture, the one that set him on the path to his death, was not seen by anyone — as far as is known.

Ron Hansen-The Joker

Anyone who knew him will tell you that jockey Ron Hansen was "one of a kind." With his outstanding athletic ability, lust for life in the fast lane, engaging personality, and roguish ways, Hansen was a unique individual in northern California racing circles, both admired by friends for the way he could brighten their days with his infectious humor, and despised by some bettors who were convinced he was illegally manipulating some of the races in which he rode.

The race-fixing accusations were never proved. Also never established was exactly what happened to the thirty-three-year-old Hansen in the early morning hours of October 2, 1993 — the last time he was seen alive.

For the man some referred to as The Joker, there were three possible explanations regarding his disappearance: (1) Hansen made a major miscalculation in the dark, early morning hours when trying to escape police following an auto accident on the San Mateo Bridge. (2) A deep lode of hidden sorrow or depression ran beneath his upbeat public veneer, causing him to commit suicide. (3) Someone, for whatever reason, didn't find The Joker funny at all — the result being his murder.

———————

Many Americans frequently complain about "The Media" being "too cynical" (which is not the same as skeptical, just as fame is not the same thing as notoriety), but segments of it covering the Kentucky Derby every spring frequently veer more toward the border of gullibility than cynicism.

If you cover only one or two big races each year and do not have exposure to others, and are in desperate need of something with which to fill that gaping space your sports editor is holding for you, you're a prime prospect for having your leg pulled. Doing the pulling to a significant segment of America's sporting press in May of 1990 at Churchill Downs was Ron Hansen. Whatever yarn he came up with — no matter how far-fetched — was dutifully reported by some of the story-hungry media.

Hansen was in Louisville to ride a one-time $40,000 claimer named Video Ranger in the 116th Run for the Roses. Video Ranger, owned by Korean-American clothing exporter Kwon Myung Cho, was stakes-placed; in fact, he had finished second (though well beaten) to eventual Kentucky Derby favorite Mister Frisky in the Santa Anita Derby, but was accorded little respect in the days preceding the world's most famous horse race.

Hansen, however, was another story — or several other stories. Reveling in the attention, Hansen was the star of the morning backstretch interview sessions, producing a succession of outrageous, entertaining, and duly reported falsehoods. This was vintage Hansen: a source of colorful yarns, many comprised far more of hyperbole than fact. But this was the first time Hansen's act had played in a national spotlight.

Hansen told the media that he had met his second (and then current) wife, Renee, when he was returning to the jockeys' room one afternoon following a losing ride and she angrily began to spit on him (untrue.) He said that when their marriage took place a few months later in Las Vegas (true), the principals involved — bride, groom, and minister — were all completely nude throughout the entire ceremony (untrue). And Hansen vowed that, if he won the Kentucky Derby on Video Ranger, he would "strip naked" in the hallowed winner's circle beneath the Twin Spires.

Fortunately, Churchill Downs' protocol-minded President Thomas H. Meeker — a former U.S. Marine Corps officer — didn't have to grapple with the results of Hansen's threat to undress. Video Ranger, at odds of nearly 66-1, ran a decent race but finished fourth in the fifteen-horse Derby field, more than a dozen lengths behind the victorious Unbridled. But his buddies back in the Bay Meadows jocks' room got a huge kick out of Hansen's one and only Derby Week.

"This guy loved to be in the spotlight," recalled one of his friends, Robert D. (Bob) Umphrey. Currently the director of racing at Gulfstream Park and racing secretary at Calder, Umphrey worked in the Bay Area from 1986-93, primarily as racing secretary at Golden Gate Fields.

"He looked a lot like a scaled-down version of Jim McMahon, the quarterback on the Chicago Bears when they won the Super Bowl (1985)," Umphrey continued. "Ronnie was a huge fan of McMahon's and he had the same kind of brash, cocky attitude as the guy they called the 'punky quarterback.' He went to a Bears-Forty Niners game one time, wearing a Bears jersey with McMahon's number on it and sunglasses like McMahon wore. The Niner fans were giving him hell all afternoon, swearing at him, throwing stuff at him in the stands. Ronnie just laughed at them. He had a great time stirring people up."

Regarding Hansen's pre-Derby performance, a riding colleague, Ron Warren Jr., commented, "It was typical Ronnie. There's nothing he liked better than building up a story." Hansen's fellow riders, of course, were quite used to his inventive sense of humor and reveled in the fact that he was "doing his number" on the national scene — the kind of "number" he had done numerous times in the past with them and people they knew. Few of them had ever been to Louisville for Derby Week. They got a vicarious wallop out of the antics of The Joker.

———————

Ron Hansen was born January 5, 1960, in Logan, Utah. He grew up as one of six children on a dairy farm near Lewiston. Hansen's introduction to competitive race riding came early: at age eleven he won a Quarter Horse race at a bush track despite having fractured an arm in a starting gate accident only days before.

Seven years later, Hansen launched his professional career north of the border. He won leading apprentice honors in Canada in 1978 and was rewarded with that nation's

Sovereign Award to mark the achievement. As a journey-man the next year, Hansen led all riders in the Dominion.

Hansen was an immediate success when he shifted his base of operations first to Longacres near Seattle, then to north-ern California, where he would remain for the rest of his career, one that saw him win a total of 3,693 races from 20,422 mounts with purse earnings of $42,635,184.

The five-foot, four-inch, 114-pound reinsman won a record 158 races during Bay Meadows' 1990-91 meet. He set another mark when he posted 164 victories at Golden Gate Fields in 1991. (Both of these records were later broken by Russell Baze). Hansen led the standings at Bay Meadows from 1988-91, at Golden Gate in 1990 and '91, at Pomona from 1982-91. His best single season was 1991: Hansen's mounts earned $4,793,645, and his 342 tallies were good for fifth place in the North American rankings.

Major among the numerous stakes winners Hansen rode was Simply Majestic. In 1989 they combined for victories in the Longacres Mile, All-American Handicap, Kensington Handicap, Silky Sullivan Invitational, and Thistledown Breeders' Cup Handicap.

While Derby Week of 1990 was the period during which Ron Hansen got the most widespread media exposure of his life, it wasn't the first time his name appeared in national racing publications and on news wires that year. The first time occurred when Golden Gate Fields general manager and vice president of racing Peter W. Tunney barred Hansen early in the season for alleged race fixing and bribery of jockeys. Hansen was reputed to be the linchpin in race-manipulating schemes, some of which allegedly burned Las Vegas racebooks for a reported half-million dollars.

Hansen's primary accuser was a fellow jockey named Doug Shrick. He told authorities Hansen had promised him they would "cash a big ticket" if they worked together. Why Hansen would single out Shrick, one of the jockey colony's lesser lights, was unclear, although some held with the theory that Hansen was "holding" horses and "darkening their form" before other riders won on them. What did become clear in testimony at hearings before the California Horse Racing Board, however, was the fact that Shrick had an axe to grind with his more famous and successful colleague: Hansen had stolen Shrick's girlfriend. Evidently convinced that this romantic triangle lay at the heart of Shrick's accusations, the California board cleared Hansen. He resumed riding after the ban imposed by Tunney had lasted six weeks. The board suspended Shrick for ten years.

Not all California racing officials agreed with the Las Vegas assessment of Hansen and his impact on supposedly "suspect" races. Golden Gate chief state steward Leon Lewis told racing author Mike Helm, as recounted in Helm's 1991 book *A Breed Apart: The Horses And The Players*, that he and fellow stewards "had looked into the bribery charges over a year earlier and had not found sufficient grounds to warrant an action." According to Helm, Lewis' view of the Las Vegas racebooks that had been complaining about "northern California 'steam' cashing in on long-shot bets was unsympathetic. 'You don't hear those guys complaining to the media and the FBI and asking for an inquiry when they make a killing and nobody cashes a bet,' " Lewis told Helm. " 'They just think they should never have to pay anything out,' " Lewis added.

Commented John Avello, director of racebook operations at both Bally's and the Paris in Las Vegas and a prominent figure in the gaming industry, in an interview early in 2000, "We've investigated a lot of races over the years. It's one thing to have a guy come in and bet 'steam' — a hot horse, maybe it's the owner betting, or a friend of the trainer, and they believe they've got one ready to win. But it's another thing to have fixed races being bet on," pointed out the Poughkeepsie, New York native who has worked in Las Vegas for more than two decades.

———————————

It is believed by some that the so-called "Hansen factor" prompted the Las Vegas racebooks to enter into the current commingling arrangement with the nation's racetracks — an arrangement that sees the bets made in Las Vegas combined with pari-mutuel pools at the tracks, thus enabling the racebooks to pay track odds. John Avello insisted that the decision to have the Las Vegas racebooks begin to commingle their bets "had nothing to do with Hansen."

David Schorr is customer relations manager for Las Vegas Dissemination Company. LVDC is the "middleman" that beams the races into the seventy racebooks in that city (three books in Reno and one in Laughlin are the only ones in the state that do not commingle). According to Schorr, commingling (which went into effect in March of 1990) was "simply a good business decision, a matter of fiscal responsi-

bility. And it proved to be extremely popular with the bettors. Before commingling, a guy could hit a trifecta that paid
$3,200 at the track but only $320 at the racebook because
there was a cap, or limit, on odds paid out. This just wasn't
good business.

"Pari-mutuel betting," Schoor continued, "is the only kind
of bet made at the casinos that the casino operators can root
for the customers to win. With commingling, the house's
percentage is tied to the takeout, so they don't care if the
players win their bets at whatever odds. Betting at the racebooks escalated tremendously with the advent of commingling," Schorr said.

Well-known Las Vegas odds-maker Michael (Roxy)
Roxborough told writer Rick Snider of *The Washington Times*
in May of 1999 that prior to the 1990 advent of commingling "when somebody was trying to put the money over on
a racetrack, they almost always came to Las Vegas because it
wouldn't affect the track odds." Roxborough, wrote Snider,
estimated that "about twelve" races each year — or less than
one-thousandth of one percent of the nearly 56,000 races
run — come under scrutiny for "unusual wagering" patterns.

Commingling, as Avello noted, "limits our exposure. But
even with commingling we keep an eye on things. We watch
out for somebody coming in and trying to stir (influence)
the pools by betting a horse or horses he doesn't like in
order to drive up the odds on a horse that he does like. Still,
we pretty much take any kind of bet on the major tracks —
$100,000 show bets on Santa Anita races, for example. We
wouldn't do that at a small track. If we got hit with a win-

ning $100,000 show bet at Balmoral Park, for example, there would be a minus show pool and we would have to make up the difference."

Avello pointed out that prior to commingling, "Most of the books wouldn't take big bets from people they didn't know. They wouldn't touch them. The one or two books that did do that back in 1989, well, they got burned."

Another Las Vegas racebook executive, who requested anonymity, downplayed the number of successful betting coups that took place in the late 1980s. "The few times they scored, they supposedly won from $50,000 to $300,000. I don't know about that. Books will never tell you what they lost. Usually in those races the guys doing the major work bet exactas or daily doubles. Hansen would win one of the double races, then maybe finish second or third on the favorite in the other one."

(Some of the alleged betting coups at Golden Gate and Bay Meadows did not involve Hansen, the source confided. "One of the big ones was a race that wasn't 'fixed;' they just got away with one. There was a horse that shipped in from Utah to Golden Gate. He'd won four or five races at the bush tracks out there, but the past performances in the *Racing Form* showed him as a first-time starter. This thing went off at 42-1 and all the action was to win — no exactas; they didn't hook him up with other horses in the double. This horse ran five or six seconds faster than anything else on the program that day. He was halfway down the stretch before the rest of the field turned for home. He looked like Secretariat.")

After being cleared by the California Horse Racing Board, Hansen returned to action at Golden Gate on St. Patrick's Day of 1990. Many of the fans on hand welcomed him warmly. Riding a mare named Naski, Hansen won the second race in a three-horse photo. Passing the finish line, he jubilantly raised his right fist as the railbirds cheered.

One of the Golden Gate stewards, no fan of Hansen's, called for a replay of the finish; he wanted to determine if Hansen's celebrating was in actuality designed to show up Golden Gate executive Tunney, who was seated in the clubhouse. The videotaped conclusion of the race was scrutinized from several angles before it was decided, to the steward's satisfaction, that Hansen had acted out of exuberance, not retaliation. Hansen's supporters were not so sure of that. They took considerable relish in his flamboyant gesture.

If Hansen's arm-pumping was indeed designed to flout authority, it would not have been out of character. California board investigators once were notified that Hansen was drinking alcohol heavily, steadily, and had ridden while under its influence on more than one occasion. Tipped by an anonymous phone caller who said that Hansen was drinking one raceday morning in a bar near Bay Meadows, agents rushed to the scene. They found Hansen grinning at them from behind a bottle of non-alcoholic beer. He easily passed the Breathalyzer test that they then administered. Some of his friends believed Hansen had made the "anonymous" call to the authorities. "It was just the sort of thing he would do," one of them said. Similarly, searches of Hansen's auto for drugs never uncovered any.

The last day that he rode, Ron Hansen did not win a race in eight tries. However, this did not seem to dampen his spirits. After all, the next afternoon — Saturday, October 2, 1993 — he had the mount on the multiple stakes winner Slew of Damascus, one of the choices in the $200,000 Bay Meadows Handicap. Wayne McDonnell, Hansen's good friend and longtime agent, described his client as being in "a terrific mood" following the Friday races.

After leaving Bay Meadows, Hansen visited at least two area taverns as well as the homes of two friends. According to police, he phoned his wife, Renee, sometime in the midst of these wanderings to say that he would not be joining her and their two-year-old son Blake at home that night, that instead he would be staying at the house of one of his friends. This was not an uncommon decision for Hansen; if he was out late on a Friday and was slated to exercise horses the next morning, he often chose to stay with friends who lived near the track.

At about 2 o'clock Saturday morning Hansen walked out of a friend's apartment, saying he wanted to move his car to a different parking spot. He never came back.

Thirty minutes later Hansen drove his white 1990 Jaguar XJS at an estimated 100 miles per hour across the San Mateo Bridge. He was heading east, perhaps toward his Alameda home, when he tried to switch lanes in order to pass a Toyota Celica. As he did so Hansen's car rear-ended the Toyota, sending it crashing into the concrete bridge siding. The Toyota turned over. Hansen did not stop. Fortunately, the people in the Toyota were not seriously injured in the collision.

Hansen then drove his Jaguar about a mile eastward on the bridge from the scene of the accident. His damaged car was later discovered where Hansen had abandoned it, its hazard lights blinking. The car keys were missing, but Hansen's wallet was in the glove compartment. Police tracked down a witness who said he had observed a man walking away from the Jaguar, a little more than a mile from the site of the accident and very close to the end of the bridge. If that was Ron Hansen, it was apparently the last time he was seen alive.

When Hansen failed to show up for the Saturday morning workouts, no alarms were raised, but when he did not appear to fulfill his riding engagement on Slew of Damascus concern began to escalate into worry. (With Tom Chapman substituting for Hansen, Slew of Damascus won the Bay Meadows Handicap, providing Chapman with an unexpected $11,000 pay day.)

Renee Hansen filed a missing persons report on her husband that day. Authorities launched an extensive search of the Bay, using boats and helicopters. They looked most carefully in the shallow waters under the San Mateo Bridge, waters that recede to three feet at low tide. But there was no sign of Hansen. In the days that followed, police received hundreds of tips from callers or correspondents claiming that Hansen had been spotted in Utah, Washington state, and Canada.

Speculation as to Hansen's whereabouts ran rampant in the ensuing weeks. With his reputation for revelry and mischief, almost anything was deemed possible. Some people thought that he was hiding out, fearful of apprehension following the auto accident. Had he crossed "the wrong people" in dealings involving his riding and had they exacted a fatal punishment? Others believed that Hansen had abruptly decided to undergo treatment for substance abuse and had secretly entered a program (in 1988 Hansen underwent treatment in a Salt Lake City facility for cocaine abuse). Since most of these programs require a minimum stay of twenty-eight to thirty days, there was hope Hansen would come home in early November, laughing and cured, The Joker once more having put one over on his friends and fans.

That was the hope expressed in the Bay Meadows jocks' room in the days after Hansen's disappearance. The mood there was somber, lacking as it was both Hansen's laughter and the mirth he caused. One of the riders described the scene as being "kind of like an engine running but missing a spark plug." The backstretch seemed a less lively place, too. Also missed was Hansen's penchant for generosity to those down on their luck; he had been a regular and receptive target for tapped out grooms and hotwalkers.

Writing in *The Blood-Horse* of December 4, 1993, Catherine Chriss noted that this was not the first time that Hansen's driving had "gotten him into trouble. Four years ago, Hansen was convicted of reckless driving, and the following year he was charged with driving under the influence. Dick Smith, a private detective investigating Hansen's disappearance, said the jockey also had been involved in a hit-and-run accident in 1988 in Calgary, Alberta, Canada. Smith said those charges were dismissed.

"If Hansen shows up," Chriss wrote, "the California Highway Patrol wants to press...felony charges...for hit-and-run and driving under the influence. If convicted of a felony, Hansen could lose his racing license.

"With nothing else to go on, close friends have reverted to their favorite theory: That Hansen is hiding out somewhere, probably sipping mai tais on a beach in Mexico. Although Smith said Hansen hasn't touched his credit cards or ATM card, he has many friends who'd be willing to protect him and loan him money.

"Friends suggested that Hansen may have wanted to escape a tangled personal life that involved a girlfriend or two, a paternity suit, and child support for a nine-year-old son in Canada, all the while having a wife and son in Alameda, an affluent island community in the Bay area," Chriss wrote.

One of Hansen's favorite watering holes was The Van's, whose owner, Loring De Martini, expressed the optimistic view shared by many. "You look at Ronnie in a situation like what happened," Martini told Chriss, "and it's like they dropped Houdini in the water. You're waiting and waiting and waiting. Finally, a few bubbles whoosh up and there he is. That's what I expect of Ron."

Also maintaining a positive attitude was Dick Smith, the private investigator, who said there was "evidence" supporting the belief that the jockey was alive, albeit at a "crisis point" in his life. Smith told *Daily Racing Form* correspondent Dale Omenson in early November that, having talked to numerous friends and acquaintances of Hansen, he had concluded the jockey was "burned out. He was tired of being

Ron Hansen, the flamboyant jockey. His ex-wife, Natalie, said he was a country boy who...was thrust into the fast lane. He never had the level of sophistication of other people with the same level of income."

Hansen's former wife, according to Smith, claimed that following Hansen's aforementioned hit-and-run incident in Canada, Calgary police had "bounced him off the wall pretty good. After this (recent) accident, he could have seen the other car flip in his rearview mirror and said, 'Screw this, I'm not going to jail.' He was burned out anyway," Smith told Omenson. "That's why he split and went underground."

October 12 was the birthday of Hansen's mother, Sylvia. When that day came and went without any word from their missing son, Sylvia and her husband, Dale, became increasingly distraught and pessimistic. According to Dale, his son "always" sent flowers to his mother on her birthday, had done so ever since he was old enough to buy flowers. When no floral gift arrived, Ron Hansen's parents were devastated. Hansen's wife, Renee, had also not been contacted by her husband since the night of October 1.

Writing in the October 25, 1993 issue of *Sports Illustrated*, Richard Hoffer said that it seemed "highly unlikely (Hansen) would stay away from his family so long once he knew no one (had been) seriously injured (in the auto accident). 'I know it sounds odd, calling Ron a party animal and a family guy,' " Hansen's friend and fellow jockey, Jack Kaenel, told Hoffer, " 'but he had the energy for both.' "

As the days stretched into weeks and there was still no sign of Hansen, his friends began to fear the worst — especially after November 2, the supposed end of any substance abuse program in which he might have enrolled.

On January 20, 1994, the question of Ron Hansen's whereabouts — subject of such television tabloid programs as *Prime Suspect* and *Hard Copy* in addition to the other widespread media coverage — was answered. A man working in a brine shrimp harvest discovered a partially decomposed body in a salt marsh near the San Mateo Bridge, not far from where Hansen's car had been abandoned more than three months earlier.

The body, found caught up in some rocks, apparently had washed ashore in an area that had been thoroughly searched after Hansen's disappearance. Dental records established that it was Hansen. Dan Apperson, supervising investigator for the Alameda County coroner, said full-body X-rays revealed nothing obvious regarding cause of death. Specimens were retained for the autopsy, but the body was sent, at the request of Hansen's parents, to Utah for burial.

Hansen's death was eventually ruled accidental, the coroner reporting "no signs of foul play." Investigators concluded he either fell over the railing, or jumped over it, in order to avoid being nabbed by the California Highway Patrol which had been summoned to the scene of the accident. Reports circulated among Hansen's close circle of friends that he had been "blitzed" that early morning. Even if not drunk, he may have panicked in his fear of arrest. If Hansen's plan was to jump from the bridge into the shallows and then walk across the marsh to safety, he failed — either by incapacitating himself in the leap, or becoming trapped in the sticky mud and remaining unseen in the dark, unable to extricate him-self, like a person in the clutches of quick sand, when the tide rose.

Unconfirmed rumors circulated that Hansen was racing across the San Mateo Bridge in flight from threatening pur-suers, gamblers angered by his not having fulfilled a promise. Some people suggested he had suddenly succumbed to enor-mous pressures in his private life and, without any hint to friends or family, decided to "end it all" with the kind of fatal leap that Robert Hyatt (Red) McDaniel employed off the San Francisco Bay Bridge, fifteen miles to the north, in the spring of 1955.

But the consensus was that Ron Hansen had made a fatal miscalculation when he jumped from the bridge into what he believed to be safe water while trying to elude arrest.

Holding to that theory was convicted race-fixer Richard Sklar, who claimed to have been "real tight" with Hansen. In a copyrighted article in the July 14, 1997 *Los Angeles Times* written by Eclipse Award-winning Turf writer Bill Christine, Sklar said that he had "heard all the stories about Hansen and the Mafia and the casinos in Las Vegas" and didn't believe any of them. "Nobody killed Ron Hansen. He was drinking and tried to run away from the accident," Sklar told Christine.

At the time of the interview, Sklar, forty-six, was serving a sentence for bribing a jockey to "hold" horses in Arabian races run at Los Alamitos Racetrack near Los Angeles. Richard Pfau, one of the leading riders of Arabians, was implicated with Sklar, sentenced to probation, and his racing license suspended indefinitely.

Richard Sklar was no stranger to the headlines even prior to his conviction for race-fixing. In 1991, on Century Boulevard in Los Angeles near Hollywood Park, Sklar was in a gold Jaguar owned and driven by a well-known gambler named Bobby Unger. Unger reportedly had won more than $70,000 in bets at the track just hours before. Unger was shot to death in his Jaguar, victim of "an unsuccessful" robbery attempt. Sklar was unharmed.

Nearly a year after the 1997 interview Christine again visited the incarcerated Sklar, who on this occasion boasted of what he claimed to be his lengthy association with Ron Hansen. Sklar said that he and Hansen had collaborated in numerous fixed races, Sklar betting and the jockey attempting to orchestrate the outcome of these events, attempts that were not all successful. Sklar was so tight with Hansen, he told Christine, that Sklar bought the rider a cellular phone "so they could stay in contact during race cards." Phone calls between the two were made even from the jockeys' room, Sklar bragged. Sometimes when Hansen contacted Sklar from there he would secretly call from one of the toilet stalls, Sklar said. Sklar said he "always knew when he did that...There'd be an echo on the phone."

Why Richard Sklar would feel compelled to make these allegations against a dead jockey is not known. What is a matter of record is that Sklar at one point in the course of his being investigated declared he had fixed "about 500 races" at the major California Thoroughbred tracks from 1987-97, a claim that California Horse Racing Board investigators labeled "preposterous." Also known was that an FBI agent said that Sklar had failed a lie-detector test.

In the 1998 *Los Angeles Times* interview, Sklar announced that his career as a race-fixer "was over." Professional golf was next on his agenda, Sklar said, adding that he eagerly awaited the day four years hence when he would turn fifty and thus become eligible to try to qualify for the Senior PGA Tour. He was confident he would fare well on those fairways. He told Christine he could "hit a ball as far as Tiger Woods."

One veteran racing man who gave no credence to Sklar's allegations regarding Hansen was Bob Umphrey. He said flatly, "There was no funny business going on with Hansen in the years I was there.

"Hansen's so-called exploits," Umphrey continued, "were greatly exaggerated. He was given much more 'credit' than he ever had coming. He was investigated more than once and never was proved to be guilty of anything."

Umphrey pointed out that Hansen was frequently tabbed to ride stakes horses shipped in by prominent trainers from southern California. "He rode for Neil Drysdale, Bobby Frankel, guys like that," Umphrey said. "When Russell Baze was gone for three years, riding in southern California, Ronnie was the leading rider in northern California by a ton — by fifty winners over his closest competition at those meetings! He did the riding for all the top local stables. I don't know how anybody could conclude that a guy doing that well, being that much in the spotlight, was fixing races. And when Baze came back to ride up there, well you can forget about even the thought of any funny business being carried out by Ronnie or anybody else. Russell Baze wouldn't stand for it.

"If Ronnie ever did any 'business,' " Umphrey theorized, "and I'm not saying he did, it might have been at the Pomona Fair. I heard some of the boys in Vegas got crushed a few times with winning bets on races from the bullring there. But there was no proof of Ronnie fixing races at that track, either."

Summarizing Ron Hansen, Bob Umphrey said, "He was a free spirit. He was no angel, that's for sure. But he was a great guy, very generous. If there was ever a benefit for somebody, any kind of fund raiser, you could always count on Ronnie.

"He also had as much talent as any rider I've ever seen."

Holy Bull
Undone in the Derby

———⟨⟩———

Pari-mutuel betting on the Kentucky Derby was introduced in 1908. The first seventy-one runnings under the new betting system were extremely kind to betting favorites and their supporters: no fewer than thirty favorites won during that period, an outstanding strike rate of forty-two percent. Then the Twin Spires fell in: from 1980 through 1999, nary a single public choice prevailed in the Run for the Roses. (Fusaichi Pegasus broke the streak by winning as the favorite in 2000.) Among the more notable members of that large "beaten chalk" brigade was Holy Bull in 1994. That season's eventual Horse of the Year ran the worst race of his life in the Derby, a departure from form so startling and disturbing as to raise numerous questions in its aftermath. His horrified owner-trainer subsequently became convinced this dismal effort resulted from the fleet gray colt's having been drugged prior to the Derby.

What was to have been Warren A. (Jimmy) Croll's finest hour in horse racing, in which he would become the only man in history to both own and train a winner of the

Kentucky Derby, proved instead to be a disaster. Jimmy Croll suffered what he described as "the greatest disappointment of my career."

————————————

Jimmy Croll has been renewing his trainer's license for more years than most of his rivals have been alive. Born on March 9, 1920, in Bryn Mawr, Pennsylvania, Croll was first exposed to the equine world at hunt meets and fairs in which he rode near his hometown. After a brief stint in pre-veterinary school at the University of Pennsylvania, Croll gravitated to the racetrack. He received his first training license in 1940 at old Havre de Grace in Maryland, won his first race at Delaware Park later that year, and saddled his first stakes winner, War Phar, in 1951 at Bowie. More than sixty-five other stakes winners would follow. In the course of his six decades campaigning a public stable at the Eastern seaboard tracks, Croll became well-known for both his affability and his professionalism.

He has enjoyed some good fortune, too, as he would be the first to tell you. One example of it was his meeting at Gulfstream Park in 1957 with Rachel Carpenter. She sat in a clubhouse box adjacent to Croll's. One day Mrs. Carpenter told Croll she wanted to start a racing stable, and she asked him to buy a couple of cheap horses for her. Among those initial acquisitions was a $10,000 claimer who finished third in Mrs. Carpenter's Pelican Stable colors its first time out, much to her delight; thus began an association that would extend for forty years. The modest, unassuming woman, Croll subsequently learned to his astonishment, was an heiress to the A&P supermarket fortune. "You'd never know she'd had a dime," her trainer once said.

The first champion that Jimmy Croll trained was Parka, America's leading grass runner in 1965. He had also claimed Parka for $10,000 for Mrs. Carpenter. Parka went on to win eleven stakes. Other Pelican Stable runners included major stakes winners Al Hattab (the broodmare sire of Holy Bull) and Herecomesthebride. Croll would also train Forward Gal (champion two-year-old filly of 1970) the 1987 Belmont Stakes winner Bet Twice, and Housebuster (the 1990 sprint king) for other clients, as well as stakes winner and eventual dominant sire Mr. Prospector.

Croll said that never in the four decades that he trained for her did Mrs. Carpenter ever tell him where or when to run one of her horses. This was not the only factor that qualified her as a "dream owner." In 1979 Mrs. Carpenter made out her will. One of her financial advisers later informed Croll that Mrs. Carpenter was leaving all of her horses to him. In the fifteen years that ensued before her death, Mrs. Carpenter never mentioned this bequest to her trainer. When she died of cancer, Croll became the new owner of nineteen of Mrs. Carpenter's horses. "She was a very, very generous person," Croll said.

Croll sold eighteen of those "gift horses," but not a two-year-old named Holy Bull. As the trainer once told *The Blood-Horse* writer Deirdre B. Biles, "I enjoy developing a horse — to me that's the name of the game — and the wheeling and dealing I don't think is a whole lot of fun. If I couldn't get any two-year-olds to train, I would quit."

Croll very much enjoyed developing Holy Bull and saw this son of Great Above—Sharon Brown win his first start in dashing fashion at Monmouth Park on August 14, 1993 — the very day that Mrs. Carpenter passed away at age seventy-eight. His retaining of Holy Bull from his inheritance would eventually result in huge financial benefits for Croll.

Holy Bull went on to win his other three starts as a juvenile, including the Belmont Futurity and the In Reality Stakes at Calder in Florida. He earned $335,760 and an assignment of 125 pounds — one below co-topweights Brocco and Dehere — on The Jockey Club's Experimental Free Handicap. As Jimmy Croll freshened the promising youngster over the late fall and early winter, both he and Holy Bull's regular rider, Mike Smith, were beginning to entertain dreams of a Kentucky Derby triumph.

Performing as the 1-2 favorite, Holy Bull stretched his perfect record to five when he captured the grade II Hutcheson Stakes on January 30 in his 1994 debut at Gulfstream Park. He was the 13-10 choice in his next start, the grade II Fountain of Youth on February 19, but suffered his first defeat. After taking the early lead, as was his custom, Holy Bull displaced his palate — something he would never do again — and stopped to a veritable walk. He finished twenty-four lengths back of the victorious Dehere.

This led to Holy Bull's not going off as the favorite — the first of just two times in his career — when he returned to action in the grade I Florida Derby on March 12. He returned to his old form, too, smashing his opposition by nearly six lengths. When he went wire-to-wire in another easy score in the grade II Blue Grass Stakes at Keeneland on April 16, he solidified his status as Kentucky Derby favorite. And that is what he was when he flopped so abysmally on the afternoon of May 7 at Churchill Downs.

_____

Jimmy Croll did not have a good view of the start of that 120th Kentucky Derby — "some big bozo stood up in front of me and I couldn't see the break," he said — but he wouldn't have liked it. What he was able to observe proved most disheartening as well.

When the gate opened, Holy Bull did not break alertly. According to the *Daily Racing Form* chart, Holy Bull also was "in tight" early, "raced within easy striking distance to the far turn, then tired badly." *The Blood-Horse*'s summary of the race said, "Holy Bull joined the ranks of 14 consecutive beaten Kentucky Derby favorites after having a disastrous start...Holy Bull broke with his hind end under him, then was 'tattooed' or knocked on both sides by horses coming out of the gate."

This confirmed speedster, this devastating front runner, never sniffed the lead, winding up eighteen and a quarter lengths behind Go for Gin, who won by two lengths from Strodes Creek. Holy Bull beat just two members of the four-teen-horse field.

The early portion of Holy Bull's Derby trip was indeed rough, and the race was run over a sloppy strip. But he had been banged before, and in his only other venture over a track labeled sloppy he had won the Futurity at Belmont the previous season. Croll was unhappily surprised and puzzled by the effort. So was Mike Smith, who expressed his frustration this way: "Nothing went right. We got a bad start, and then we got wiped out breaking, and then on the first turn we got wiped out again. It's the Derby. You've got to have the best horse on the day it's run."

Croll said Holy Bull emerged from this debacle with just a nick on his right hind foot. "I have no qualms about running in the Preakness," he said, although he would soon change his mind and pass both the Preakness and the Belmont Stakes with Holy Bull. His reasoning was that "if you don't win the Derby, the other ones don't mean as much." He said he had learned that in 1987 with Bet Twice, who won the Belmont after finishing second in both the Derby and Preakness, but "never got the recognition he deserved."

In the first few days after the Derby, Croll announced that Holy Bull's leg was fine but that there was a slight irregularity in his blood count. Speculation continued as to the colt's Derby failure.

One veteran racing observer, Turf writer Bob Roberts of *The Cleveland Plain Dealer*, was critical of the Churchill Downs stewards for their failure to order a post-race test on Holy Bull. In his column, Roberts quoted chief state steward Bernard J. Hettel (who since 1992 has also served as executive director of the Kentucky Racing Commission) as saying, "We tested the first three finishers and could have tested the whole field if I wanted. Holy Bull wasn't a prohibitive favorite (at odds of 11-5), so I wasn't overly concerned about him."

(How this oxymoronic cliché has wormed its way into racing's lexicon is not known, but it is used repeatedly by television commentators who are apparently unaware that if a favorite were truly "prohibitive," there would not be any betting on him at all.)

Roberts added that "What troubles me about Holy Bull was that he was so lifeless in the (Derby) post parade that the pony person escorting him let go of Holy Bull's reins. Set free, Holy Bull barely picked up his head."

Lexington Herald-Leader sports columnist Billy Reed noted that while being led to the paddock for the Derby, "Holy Bull looked a bit sluggish." The Eclipse Award-winning writer quoted Paul Rogers of WHAS radio in Louisville as saying, "I thought he looked a little lethargic on the track, but I didn't really know because I wasn't sure what he usually looked like." Yet, as Reed pointed out, only "eight days after the Derby, Holy Bull worked a half-mile at Monmouth Park in a blistering :46 4/5."

Holy Bull's first race after the Kentucky Derby was a dazzler. On May 30, he faced a good field of nine older horses (their total earnings at the time exceeded $7 million) in the storied Metropolitan Mile at Belmont Park. He won like breaking sticks.

As Steven Crist reported in *The Blood-Horse*, jockey Smith "was sitting still on Holy Bull, letting Cherokee Run (who would be voted the 1994 Eclipse Award as champion sprinter) draw within a long half-length after six furlongs in 1:09.41, then he just waved his whip and Holy Bull took off again. Holy Bull was two and a half lengths clear at the furlong pole, then finished strongly to more than double his lead…Applause began to rise from the crowd. Holy Bull ran the mile in 1:33.98…He became only the sixth 3-year-old in the last 40 years to win the Met Mile, following Sword Dancer, Arts and Letters, Conquistador Cielo, Gulch, and Dixie Brass."

The Met Mile tour de force served to cast Holy Bull's Derby debacle in an even more puzzling light. So did the four stakes victories that made up the remainder of his sensational 1994 campaign. On July 3, he won the grade II Dwyer at Belmont by nearly seven lengths. On July 31, the scene was Monmouth Park and the margin was a length and three-quarters in the grade I Haskell Invitational. At Saratoga on August 20, Holy Bull answered those who questioned his ability to win at a mile and one-quarter when he courageously held off Concern by a neck in the grade I Travers, "the Midsummer Derby." Preakness and Belmont Stakes winner Tabasco Cat finished third, a whopping seventeen lengths in arrears. Holy Bull's final race of the season saw him again show his heels to older rivals, this time in Belmont's Woodward Stakes; runner-up Devil His Due was five lengths back after Holy Bull zipped nine furlongs in 1:46.89.

Each victory added to Holy Bull's reputation. He was a great story to begin with, a gift horse who could run, and his blazing speed and striking looks fueled his increasing popularity. As Jimmy Croll put it, Holy Bull had become "the people's horse. They cheered him at Keeneland both before and after the Blue Grass, and they even cheered him in New York when we'd lead him into the paddock. Now, that's really something!"

Penny Chenery knew plenty about equine charisma. Secretariat's owner was at Saratoga for Holy Bull's Travers. As she later told *The Thoroughbred Times*, Holy Bull "certainly knows who he is and knows that he is best. I went down to the paddock after the race. It was just as the jocks were put up (for the race following the Travers), and suddenly here was this sweaty gray horse being led back through the paddock. I looked up the way you do when you wonder who a horse is and I was checking his number and I suddenly realized who it was. Holy Bull looked at me as if he were saying, 'Hey, don't you know who I am?' "

Because of a clerical snafu Holy Bull was not Breeders' Cup-eligible. Croll decided not to supplement him to the Classic (at a cost of $380,000), saying that the horse "had done enough" and that a rest was indicated. Croll said he would aim for the Breeders' Cup Classic of 1995.

Holy Bull had trounced fellow three-year-olds, dominated older horses, and underlined his versatility by numbering among his victims both the winner of the Breeders' Cup Classic (Concern) and Breeders' Cup Sprint (Cherokee Run). His record of eight wins from ten starts, with earnings of $2,095,000, garnered him honors as Horse of the Year and three-year-old champion male. Except for the Derby disappointment it was a great season for both man and beast, as Croll was inducted into the National Museum of Racing Hall of Fame at Saratoga Springs, New York.

What was to have been Holy Bull's "Breeders' Cup Year" did not materialize. After beating top sprinters in Gulfstream's Olympic Handicap in his seasonal debut on

January 22, Holy Bull was sent off as the 3-10 favorite in the grade I Donn Handicap three weeks later.

In the post parade for the Donn, Mike Smith let Holy Bull bow toward the enthusiastic crowd of 18,963, many members of which sported Holy Bull tee-shirts and buttons. However, at the half-mile pole of the race, the throng was silenced as Smith abruptly pulled up the big gray. Holy Bull had severely strained the superficial flexor tendon and some ligaments below the ankle. The horse known to his legions of fans as "The Bull" was through racing forever, sadly subtracted from a stage so lacking in stars with national appeal. He was retired with a record of thirteen wins from sixteen starts and earnings of $2,481,760.

Commented Tom Dawson of ESPN's *Racing Across America* series of the sudden retirement of this heavily publicized horse, "I don't think the industry overdid it with Holy Bull. The stars make themselves. It's so hard to get the horse with the talent and charisma…You can hype all you want, but unless the horse has those things it won't make a difference. With Holy Bull, it was the fans who made him a star. He was the real thing."

In an amazing exercise in baton-passing, the winner of the Donn 'Cap was Cigar, who would proceed to become the sport's next big star, dominating the headlines with an historic winning streak that reached sixteen (the Donn was number four).

Holy Bull began his stud career at Kentucky's Jonabell Farm in 1995 and proved immediately popular and effective. Croll retained seventy-five percent ownership of Holy Bull, who stands for a fee of $25,000 and who has been bred to an average of 100 mares per year. He was the leading first-crop sire by number of stakes winners of 1998 and was among the leading second-crop sires by progeny earnings the following year.

A little more than two years after his retirement, Holy Bull was in the headlines again when Croll charged that the crushing loss of the 1994 Kentucky Derby was because "They got to my horse."

In a copyrighted story written by Bill Christine for the April 29, 1997 edition of *The Los Angeles Times*, Croll was emphatic: "I know more than ever that Holy Bull was drugged."

Croll pointed to Holy Bull's brilliant record both before and after the Derby, saying there were valid reasons for his only other career defeats. He said he had been interviewed during the Keeneland fall meeting of 1994 by an FBI agent. Croll said he informed the agent of his suspicions. Nothing ever came of whatever investigation was conducted, however.

To Croll, there was an obvious possible motive for stopping a Kentucky Derby favorite. "Can you imagine how much money there is to be made if you knew — if you knew for sure — that the favorite was going to run off the board?" Croll asked.

In taking the '94 Derby, Go for Gin (who never won another race in nine subsequent attempts) paid $20.20. He topped a $2 exacta with 7-1 shot Strodes Creek that was worth $184.80. The trifecta, completed by 14-1 Blumin Affair, paid $2,351.40.

Present on the Churchill Downs backstretch during Derby Week of '94, Croll told Christine, was a man who eighteen months later would be involved in a federal lawsuit accusing him of illegal involvement with large quantities of a powerful sedative.

Some ten days after *The Los Angeles Times* story appeared, Croll told Frank Carlson of *The Blood-Horse* that he regretted the fact that his remarks were made public. "I would never say anything to embarrass the sport," Croll said, while not disputing the accuracy of the Christine story.

In March of 2000 Jimmy Croll, based at Gulfstream Park with an eight-horse public stable, reiterated his theory regarding Holy Bull. "He didn't work that well before the Derby," Croll said. "He wasn't exactly right; he was dull, not really himself. I should never have run him. It was my own dumbness. And I could have scratched him — he belonged to me; he was my horse. I don't know what I was thinking," he said ruefully.

Croll said Holy Bull "got banged around in the race, but that wasn't why he ran so bad. Mike (Smith), when he got off him, he was as puzzled as me. It took Holy Bull about three days to recover, to get back to himself after the Derby. It was during that time that I started to suspect what had gone on with him. Then when he came back and beat older horses in the Met Mile, well that convinced me something was not right in Kentucky. And he never lost another race all year!"

When Croll was interviewed by Bill Christine in 1997, he refused to name the person he thought had drugged his horse. He still will not. "I know his name, all right," Croll told this author in January 2000, "and I've got my suspicions, but I've got no proof."

Prior to 1994 Croll had saddled two Kentucky Derby starters, neither of which he owned: the aforementioned Bet Twice and Royal and Regal, eighth in Secretariat's 1973 Derby. The '94 Derby was the "biggest disappointment of my career," Croll said. "How many times do you get a chance to win the Derby?"

In an interview in March of 2000, Bernie Hettel gave little credence to Croll's claims. The veteran racing official noted that Holy Bull's workout on the Monday of Derby Week was desultory, especially for him: a half-mile in :50 2/5, out six furlongs in 1:14 3/5. Hettel said, "Maryjean Wall (Eclipse Award-winning Turf writer for the *Lexington Herald-Leader*) mentioned to me that week about how unimpressive Holy Bull was in his work. She told me she was at the rail when he came back and that he was blowing real good. I was a little surprised to hear that, but having learned it I was not all that surprised when he ran poorly on Saturday. I don't think he was fit enough. You got to have them tight as a banjo string for the Derby.

"If Jimmy (Croll) thought something was wrong," Hettel continued, "why didn't he have the horse tested for drugs after the Derby? In all the time since then, Jimmy has never mentioned anything about any drugging to me. He's never discussed the matter with me or any member of the Racing Commission."

Joe Hirsch, executive columnist for *Daily Racing Form* and

the dean of American racing writers, has covered the Kentucky Derby since 1956. He said Holy Bull's poor performance remains a source of perplexity. "Holy Bull was brilliant the race before the Derby (the Blue Grass Stakes)," Hirsch said, "and he was brilliant the race after (the Met Mile). The difference in his form was startling.

"A lot of things can happen to a horse — bad feed, something that throws them off — but Holy Bull had a wonderful trainer, a wonderful caretaker in Jimmy (Croll).

"There have been several mysterious incidents involving the Derby," Hirsch concluded, "and this is one of them."

Bluegrass Conspiracies?

Where is William McCandless?

The central figure in two of Thoroughbred horse racing's more publicized crimes of recent years has been missing since 1998. His whereabouts remained unknown to law enforcement authorities in the spring of 2000, some twenty-four months after he had disappeared.

Has the former U.S. Marine successfully "gone to ground," thus eluding lawmen after his most recent felony conviction involving horses?

Or, as some officials suspect, is McCandless under it — having been silenced by associates fearful of being turned in/exposed for their part in a notorious conspiracy that rocked the Kentucky racing industry in recent years.

One thing is clear: William McCandless has compiled a criminal record unique in the annals of the American Thoroughbred industry.

On June 27, 1977, the Kentucky State Police issued a bulletin from its headquarters in Frankfort under the heading

"Theft by Unlawful Taking." It read: "On Saturday, June 25, a Thoroughbred mare in foal (2 months) was stolen from Paris, Bourbon County, Kentucky. Mare valued at $500,000.

"Description of mare: 10 years old, bay color, tattoo inside upper lip 'W12997', white star center forehead, left and right rear ankles have white stockings, black spots on both rear coronents, and 16 hands high. Was wearing brown leather halter...Anyone having any information, please contact the Kentucky State Police, Dry Ridge, Ky. 41035, telephone (606) 428-1212."

This was news just on the face of it — horse thievery in the heart of the Bluegrass country — and from world famous Claiborne Farm to boot. But the identity of the stolen animal catapulted the story to headline status in publications all over the world. The mare was Fanfreluche, champion three-year-old filly in North America in 1970, the same season she earned Horse of the Year honors in Canada. She was being boarded at Claiborne at the time she was abducted.

Bred by Canadian industrialist Jean Louis Levesque, who had raced her as well, Fanfreluche earned $238,688 while finishing out of the money just twice in twenty-one career starts. At the time she went missing in 1977, she had already made her mark as a broodmare, having produced L'Enjoleur, a two-time Canadian Horse of the Year. In June of 1977, the daughter of Northern Dancer was approximately two months in foal to the great Secretariat.

As a *Sports Illustrated* article put it, Fanfreluche ranked as "the most famous missing female since Patty Hearst." Inquiries as to the mare's whereabouts were made by law enforcement agencies all over the United States and in several foreign countries.

The day of the abduction, a Claiborne watchman said that at 4 p.m., he had counted nine mares in a field, which was the correct number. Four hours later, there were only eight, but the watchman presumed one was out of his sight. It was not until the next morning that a dismantled section of fence was discovered on the 6,000-acre farm and Fanfreluche was declared missing.

Pierre Levesque, son of the mare's owner, told the *Toronto Star* that "Whoever it was didn't pick just any mare out of that paddock. They had to be after Fanfreluche. She's got a really bad temper; she hates people. She would have given them an awful fight." Claiborne farm manager John Sosby had a diametrically opposed view. He thought the thieves may have been after any mare they could nab and "may have gotten Fanfreluche because she was friendly. She would come right up to you," Sosby said.

The younger Levesque was one of the original members of the then-world record $6.08 million syndication of 1973 Triple Crown winner Secretariat. His father had intended to keep and eventually race the Secretariat foal Fanfreluche was carrying. Like the vast majority of owners/breeders at the time, Levesque had not insured Fanfreluche against theft. Her disappearance, however, prompted many breeders to add that provision to the mortality policies they held on their best stock.

In the days following the theft, authorities awaited what they believed would be the result of the crime: a ransom

demand. But none came. Logan Bailey, a Lexington correspondent for *Daily Racing Form*, said the mare could not be
legally sold or any resultant offspring registered by anyone
who took her. "They can't prove ownership because they
don't have the papers. If they intend to do something with
the foal, they would have to falsify the registration," Bailey
pointed out.

Indeed, there was speculation that the thieves might be
planning to create counterfeit registration papers, a difficult
task, and perhaps race the resultant foal under false parent-
age as a "ringer." This sort of hypothesis — which was to
emerge again in 1983 following the theft and disappearance
of the stallion Shergar in Ireland — was popularized by Red
Smith. The Pulitzer Prize-winning sports columnist for *The
New York Times* based his theory on a scenario laid out in
Blood Sport by mystery novelist Dick Francis, a book whose
plot involved valuable stallions being stolen in Kentucky,
then substituted for nondescript studs in California.

Other theories saw the theft as a possible act of revenge
against Claiborne, or as a "prank" designed to shake up the
industry.

As the months passed, no ransom demands ever were
received. A $25,000 reward offered by Levesque and
Claiborne served at first only to elicit useless information.
Some emanated from well-meaning psychics, including one
from California who advised the missing mare was being
housed "in a blue barn" with a mound of horse manure in
front of it.

Less than a month after Fanfreluche's disappearance, the

FBI and Kentucky State Police announced that William Michael McCandless, a thirty-year-old former exercise rider at Midwest tracks and self-described "professional gambler," had been taken into custody as a suspect in the case.

McCandless was born in Paducah, Kentucky, in 1946 as William Michael Rhodes; his mother later married Gene McCandless, an optometrist, and the boy took that name. He had relatives connected to racing — his maternal grandfather, Cleve Thompson, was a trainer, and an uncle was a jockey. After two years of service with the U.S. Marine Corps in Vietnam (he had enlisted at age nineteen), McCandless became an itinerant racetracker, one season (1975) even holding an owner's license in Nebraska. He was described as "a white male, 130 pounds, blue eyes, brown hair and light skin."

After the warrant was issued for his arrest, McCandless — known to his friends as "Mike" — surrendered a week later. He was charged with felony theft, to which he pleaded innocent, and posted a $5,000 bond. He subsequently disappeared, forfeiting the bond, and was sought as a fugitive. Many people questioned whether one man working alone — even a man very familiar with horses — could bring off a theft of this sort, but McCandless was the only person ever charged in the case.

On the afternoon of December 8, 1977, the widespread search for Fanfreluche came to a happy conclusion near Tompkinsville, Kentucky, some 200 miles southwest of Claiborne Farm, near the Kentucky-Tennessee border. Although she had a shaggy winter coat, the FBI had no trouble recognizing the mare standing in a fenced-in lot on a three-acre farm owned by Larry McPherson. "Some of our people would know her anywhere," said an elated FBI agent. A check of the mare's lip tattoo confirmed her identity. Examination by a veterinarian established that Fanfreluche had been well treated, was in fine health, and was still carrying a live foal.

McPherson, an employee of the Tennessee Valley Authority, kept horses as a hobby shared with his wife and sons on the small farm. He told authorities that late that June he had found the mare standing in the road, Ky. 53, that ran past his property. She appeared to have rope burns on her neck and ankles. "You're always finding stray horses and cows in the road in our part of the country," he said. McPherson later mentioned to two lawmen he knew that he had rescued a stray mare off the road, but neither he nor they suspected her to be the famous Fanfreluche. McPherson was aware that a valuable horse had been stolen in Kentucky, but said he assumed she had been taken out of the country.

The McPherson family gave the mare a home and, as McPherson put it, "waited for the day somebody would come claim her." They took a great liking to the stranger, naming her Brandy and frequently riding her. The half-million dollar mare boosted to four the number of horses on the McPherson property, joining a pony, a Palomino, and a Quarter Horse whose combined value was estimated at $600.

The recovery of Fanfreluche was the result of a tip from "individuals we have had dealings with in the past," said an

FBI agent. How the mare came to be abandoned nearly 200 miles from her Claiborne farm was never determined, although some officials assumed that the thief or thieves panicked under the weight of widespread publicity and turned her loose.

On the night of February 16, 1978, at Claiborne Farm, Fanfreluche foaled a bay colt. Fanfreluche and son were presented to the press the following day. Eventually named Sain Et Sauf ("Safe and Sound" in French) by Levesque, he was one of what would be eighteen foals out of Fanfreluche, but not one of the five stakes winners or three Canadian champs. After an eighteen-race career that encompassed only three wins and earnings of $34,836, Sain Et Sauf was sold to India as a stallion in 1989.

Not until June of 1983 — six years after the abduction of Fanfreluche — did McCandless come to trial for that crime, before Judge Henry C. Prewitt, in Bourbon County Circuit Court, some five miles from Claiborne. At the time McCandless, who had been apprehended in Nashville, Tennessee, in August of 1981, had already begun serving a ten-year sentence in the federal prison in Memphis for directing a major interstate tractor-theft ring that operated in Kentucky, Tennessee, Illinois, Alabama, and Florida.

During the three-day trial in the Fanfreluche case, twenty-one witnesses testified for the prosecution. One of them placed McCandless in the area the day of the theft, saying that a man driving a truck with a horse trailer behind had asked directions to Claiborne. The witness identified McCandless (who was at that time a fugitive) from a ten-picture photo line-up. Three other witnesses placed the truck and trailer on a road near the field from which Fanfreluche was. The first of the three witnesses testified he saw the truck heading toward Claiborne with its trailer empty; the other two said they later saw the same truck traveling away from Claiborne with one horse in it. A friend of ·McCandless', a trainer, said the accused had told him he had a buyer (never identified) who was willing to pay $100,000 for the mare.

The final day of testimony saw prosecutor Gentry McCauley call four witnesses to the stand, each described as a friend or associate of McCandless. All four told the court that McCandless on separate occasions had admitted to stealing Fanfreluche.

The jury found McCandless guilty of "theft by unlawful taking." Judge Prewitt sentenced McCandless, then thirty-six, to four years in prison, a sentence to be served concurrently with a one-year term for jumping bail. He would serve his Kentucky sentence after completing his term in the federal facility in Memphis for the tractor thefts. McCandless did not appeal the verdict.

————————

When William McCandless was returned to prison in 1983 after his conviction in the Fanfreluche case, the question remained: what was the point of the crime? The same sort of question popped up seventeen years later when McCandless emerged as the major figure in another Kentucky horse industry criminal plot.

In the late spring of 1996, one of the most innocuous

words associated with horses took on a sinister meaning. The term "sponging" is normally used to describe the traditional hygienic act performed upon a horse after exercise. Suddenly, sponging came to mean a cruel and harmful act perpetrated with malicious intent.

A Kentucky Racing Commission investigation that began in June determined that five horses which had competed in races at Churchill Downs had been "sponged" — in other words, had small pieces of sponge inserted in their nasal cavities. Since horses breathe only through their noses, the sponges worked to reduce air flow and make running more difficult. The five horses, all claimers, were found to have a sponge in one of their nostrils, each thereby losing between forty and fifty percent of its normal oxygen supply.

The sponges had been detected by endoscope after the horses' trainers noticed unusual nasal discharge or a powerful, foul odor. Veterinarians removed the sponges, which were approximately the size and shape of a chicken egg. One veterinarian compared the sponge effect on a running horse as similar to a "car not getting enough gas when it's being driven." Laboratory tests did not detect the presence of any drugs on the sponges.

Stopping horses by the insertion of sponges to impair their breathing was nothing new. There was a series of such incidents at New York tracks in the 1930s (in fact, they prompted that state to become one of the first to institute a system of pre-race veterinary examinations) and in Australia after that. What made the Kentucky situation unique was the fact that never had so many cases of sponging been discovered at one track, Churchill Downs, though only one of the sponging victims, as it would turn out, was stabled at the Louisville oval; the others were all shipped in from training centers or other tracks.

Another odd thing was the absence of evidence of any gambling coups involving the races in which the sponged horses ran. Many trainers thought this was a scheme to slow down horses so they could be thrown out of exotic betting combinations. But a study conducted by *Daily Racing Form* and state investigators concluded that no discernible "betting pattern was used." Only one of the horses had been favored, and the resulting mutuel prices did not suggest gamblers had pounded away on other members of the field, confident the "chalk would fail."

The racing community reacted immediately with attempts to halt these attacks. A reward that would eventually grow to $50,000 was put up through the combined efforts of horsemen, jockeys, the state's racetracks, and a horse van company. The FBI was brought in to assist the Kentucky Racing Commission and the Thoroughbred Racing and Protective Bureau in the investigation.

Most industry observers speculated that the spongings were being carried out by someone familiar with horses and racetrack backstretches. Supporting this theory was the fact that as the number of sponged horses rose to nine, a pattern emerged. All of the equine victims were discovered with sponges lodged in their right nostrils, meaning these foreign objects would not be detected during the typical endoscopic examination for bleeding or other thoracic ailments because the left nostril is almost always used in such probes.

Veteran horsemen also thought that there had to be more than one culprit: at least one person to hold the horse and another to insert the sponge deeply enough so that it would not be blown out. It was estimated that it would take at least a few minutes to do this.

At first, this massive detection effort by authorities failed to pay off. Three more spongings were discovered, bringing the June-July total to eight. A ninth horse was discovered to have been sponged in November. (Two other sponging incidents were deemed to be hoaxes.)

After a seven-month hiatus, a new sponging case was discovered in June of 1997. It involved a horse named Early Conquest, beaten fifty-two lengths as the second choice in a June 8 Churchill race. This prompted the Kentucky commission on June 13 to order pre-race testing of all scheduled starters each day. Employed on a random test basis since March 1997 had been the recently developed Air Flow Measuring Meter, a device designed to detect discrepancies in a horse's airflow.

Unfortunately, one day later, after the order to test all starters was issued, another horse was sponged — in both nostrils. A week later the Air Flow Measuring Meter was scrapped; it was deemed ineffective when both nostrils were obstructed. It was replaced by examinations conducted with a flexible, fiberoptic endoscope approximately the width of a pencil. This procedure involved the endoscope's being inserted eight to ten inches into a horse's nose, its camera serving to reveal any obstruction therein. The procedure was described as minimally invasive and "definitive" by Kentucky Racing Commission veterinarian George Mundy.

The new detection program was hailed in an editorial in The Louisville *Courier-Journal*, which said that "Nothing (and that includes competition from other gambling venues) could cause racing greater harm than doubt about its honesty…'Sponging' is monkey-business, but it's also serious business. We're glad Kentucky's Thoroughbred industry has shown such strong resolve to protect the integrity of the sport."

The latest sponging victim was Class O Lad. Sent off as the 7-5 favorite in the first race at Churchill on June 14, 1997, he was pulled up in distress in the stretch. His failure to finish in the money led to some large payoffs, but again no suspicious betting patterns were identified. As Kentucky Racing Commission executive director Bernard J. Hettel put it when interviewed early in 2000, "Crimes are designed to produce something. When a robber goes into a bank, he's after the money. That's what made the sponging thing so unusual — where was the crescendo? The culmination? What were they after?"

Class O Lad proved to be a very sad story. Claimed out of the June 14 race for $7,500, the six-year-old gelding, a career winner of fifteen races and $186,320, not only never raced again but died that September, a victim of laminitis which, veterinarians said, could have resulted from the sponge-related stress he'd undergone. (A request by his new owners to void the claim because Class O Lad had been tampered with was rejected by the Kentucky commission, which said it was "sympathetic" but that no rules were on the books to cover such a situation. The owners were reimbursed half of the claiming price — $3,500 — thanks to a Kentucky Horsemen's Benevolent and Protective Association insurance program.)

Despite the $50,000 reward and the expensively intensive efforts of all the investigative agencies involved, no suspect emerged for nearly two years after the initial sponging incident. Then came forth a familiar name, that of William McCandless.

As bizarre as the whole sponging episode was, so were the events that led to McCandless being charged. In May of 1998 it was revealed that former Thoroughbred owner and trainer George Isaacs, who had been imprisoned in Wisconsin on drug charges, provided information pointing to McCandless.

Isaacs, fifty-four at the time, was one of several Kentucky residents nabbed during a 1992 raid that saw police seize more than a half-ton of marijuana grown on a dairy farm in the Badger State. Isaacs pleaded guilty to growing and possessing marijuana. He had served four years when he was released early in May of 1998. Isaacs "agreed to testify to certain matters in court," in the words of an assistant U.S. attorney, and was released from five years of probation after helping the FBI collect evidence against McCandless.

Only days after the decision to lift Isaacs' probation, McCandless was indicted by a federal grand jury in Louisville on charges of attempted race-fixing via the sponging of horses. The six counts were divided equally

between wire fraud and "interstate travel in aid of racketeering." Maximum possible punishment on the half-dozen
charges was thirty years in prison and fines totaling $1.5
million.

The indictment said that McCandless — who had not
been located or taken into custody — had traveled from the
Nashville, Tennessee suburb of Hendersonville, where he
lived with his widowed mother, Frances McCandless, to
participate in the sponging of Kentucky racehorses.

According to the indictment, McCandless inserted
sponges into the nostrils of one or more horses prior to
three Churchill Downs races. On May 30, 1996, there were
two sponged horses in the fourth race: 19-1 shot Great
Judgement, who finished fifth, and 6-1 shot Nothing by
Chance, the seventh-place finisher. The fourth race on
June 8, 1997, involved Early Conquest, who ran out of the
money as the second favorite. The third race cited in the
indictment was that of the ill-fated Class O Lad.

In an interview with *Lexington Herald-Leader* reporter
Valarie Honeycutt after the indictment was made public,
McCandless' mother said that law enforcement officers had
searched their home several weeks earlier and had asked her
son to "rat on somebody. He's not a person who would rat."

McCandless, his mother told Honeycutt, "was divorced
and had been able to hold few jobs after he returned from
service with the Marines…She said he thought he had been
exposed to the chemical defoliant Agent Orange — used to
clear jungles — and had contracted an (associated) illness.

"Frances McCandless said she doesn't think her son is

guilty of the racehorse sponging or that he is a heavy gambler...(Her son), she said, 'would never hurt a horse.' " (Law enforcement authorities reportedly maintained a schedule of periodic checks on the McCandless home after his disappearance.)

Four months after he was indicted, William McCandless was featured on the Fox Network's television program *America's Most Wanted*. Among those interviewed was an old family friend, trainer Marion Thomasson, who said of the accused, "He was a young boy who had dreams of having racehorses...He did like to gamble." Another friend, his identity shielded, described McCandless as a lifelong loser at the racetrack. The Kentucky Racing Commission's Hettel labeled McCandless a "bum" and a "loser."

At the end of the program, viewers were asked to "Help us bring in McCandless tonight." It did not happen. *America's Most Wanted* claimed a thirty-eight percent success rate in bringing hundreds of fugitives to justice.

Nearly two years after the show was telecast, McCandless remained at large, his whereabouts unknown. What was known was that in the period of more than two decades his effect on Kentucky's horse industry was significant and wide-ranging. It can be divided into three parts:

(1) The 1977 Fanfreluche case led almost immediately to an increase in awareness of the need for better security measures on breeding farms. It also resulted in far more insurance policies being written to cover theft of horses.

(2) As a result of the sponging incidents nineteen years later, there was a notable increase in racetrack security

measures across the state.

(3) In 1998 the Kentucky General Assembly passed legislation that made horse tampering — formerly a misdemeanor — a felony punishable by up to ten years in prison.

Authorities are certain that in William Michael McCandless they have identified the right man as the culprit in the Kentucky sponging cases. They're just not sure whether he has gone to ground — or is under it.

Chris Antley's
Troubled Finish

All it took was one look and a few minutes of conversing with him to know that jockey Chris Antley was a special person. His piercing eyes, the color of blue ice, seemed to see straight through you as he talked or listened. And his honesty, particularly when speaking of his own trials and tribulations, was disarming. He didn't seem to have a filter.

Brain chemistry is very fragile, however, and the space between unnerving honesty and manic behavior can be wafer thin. For nearly all of his thirty-four years, Antley carried around with him the profound sadness of a difficult childhood, the unbridled drive of a superstar athlete, and a likely chemical imbalance in his brain. His well-being was often thrown out of whack by his thoughts, making him emotionally ill-equipped to deal with the success he achieved at an early age, or the darkening doubts as he grew older. He seemed to be perpetually riding a roller-coaster of dizzying highs and depressing lows. He fought substance abuse, often unsuccessfully.

Antley ironically reached his peak of popularity in defeat, hailed as a hero in 1999 for helping to save Charismatic's life by keeping him calm after the horse had fractured a leg while running in the Belmont Stakes. The iconic photo of Antley, near tears, lifting Charismatic's leg to keep him from further damaging it, has been seen by millions.

And yet Antley couldn't save himself. In the year after winning the Kentucky Derby and Preakness Stakes with Charismatic, he slipped back out of riding, losing his career and livelihood in what had become an all too familiar pattern. And beset by severe health issues, including a diagnosis of being bipolar, Antley, just eighteen months removed from his second Derby triumph, was found dead in his million-dollar Southern California home.

Law enforcement officials couldn't come to an agreement on what happened on December 3, 2000. Was Antley murdered? Did he commit suicide? Or did his end come by some horrific accident? We will likely never know the definitive answer. His brief life only raises more questions.

Chris Antley made his first appearance in 1966, born in Florida and the eldest of three siblings. When he was seven, his family moved to Elloree, South Carolina, an area known for raising and developing performance horses because of its mild winter climate. The Antley family, though, was tearing apart. Chris' parents separated when he was a young teen, and his father moved to Columbia, an hour away, for work with an oil company.

Chris and his younger brother and sister were having problems adjusting to a broken home and a lack of financial wherewithal. Chris would wander to a neighbor's pond to fish and be alone.

"I wanted to be a football player," Antley remembered during an interview in early 2000. "But I weighed 75 pounds. I really wanted to fit in at school. But I was small, and my family didn't have a lot of money. So it was difficult to gain status."

Antley one day rode his bike to a horse stable that was on land adjacent to that fishing hole, seeking to work and make money. Franklin Smith, a horse trainer of sizable repute in the area, gave the youngster a job mucking stalls, raking, pushing the manure cart, and cleaning out feed tubs. Chris was able to pocket some money, buy some clothes, and go out on weekend nights like his classmates. He also found his life's calling.

"He took to the horses right away," noted Smith. "It took his mind off other things going on in his life, and he came out here every day as soon as school was out."

Antley knew nothing about horses, but he quickly realized that his work at the stable gave him a purpose. Slowly, the cowboys who worked there taught him how to handle horses. Antley came to realize that his slight build, which had kept him from his football dreams, was actually a benefit when riding horses.

"People began telling him he looked like a jockey, and that started to fascinate him," said Smith. "Next thing you know, he was riding around the barn on an old pony, and from then on you couldn't keep him off a horse."

Antley and horses were a match made in heaven. They gave an avenue in which to channel love. He made a connection with one particular two-year-old, who he rode to victory in the Elloree Trials before the horse was shipped north to his racetrack trainer. Antley decided to follow him.

"I went straight to my room and started packing an old Army trunk. My mom came in and asked what I was doing, and I told her I was going north. She said, 'No you're not.' And I said, 'Watch me.' I went to Bubba Fogel's gas station on the corner, got a map, and headed to Delaware Park."

He was fifteen at the time and looked about half that. The stable gate guard at Delaware Park laughed him away, since Antley was unaware he actually needed a license to gain access to the track. Fortunately, Franklin's brother Hamilton Smith was training at Delaware, helped Antley get the necessary paperwork, and gave Chris got a job galloping horses in the mornings.

"My brother said the kid was a born natural on a racehorse, and it turned out to be true," said Hamilton Smith. "He was a good-hearted boy, do anything for anybody. He worked hard and was conscientious about horses. Didn't smoke or drink at that time. Only thing the boy ever wanted to do was ride horses."

Antley began riding occasional races, and after a year he ventured to Monmouth Park in New Jersey. As a newly turned twenty-year-old, Antley blossomed and led the nation by riding 469 winners in 1985. He was riding at Monmouth Park and Philadelphia Park during the day, and at the Meadowlands at night. In 1986 he scored 391 times, and made the winner's circle 340 times in 1987. That year, he became the first jockey to win nine races in a single day. And he was riding—and winning—grade 1 stakes races with Single Blade in the Gazelle Handicap, Bordeaux Bob in the Philip Iselin Handicap, and Without Feathers and Maplejinsky in consecutive runnings of the Monmouth Oaks.

At age twenty-four, Antley had established himself in New York, rising to the top to lead that jockey colony in victories. In

1989, he won at least one race for a record 64 straight days, drawing comparisons to the New York Yankees' legendary star Joe DiMaggio, who had hit safely in 56 straight games.

Antley had money and was gaining fame. He was also getting himself in trouble. Before the decade ended, Antley had been suspended twice for drug use and began battling to make weight.

"I was young, and everything happened fast and easy for me," Antley said. "I was in the big world, but I didn't know where to go. People are hanging around you even though you know the friendship isn't there. It was easy to get lost."

As long as he was in the saddle and guiding a Thoroughbred to the finish line, he was a fully functioning star. It was when he climbed down off a horse's back that trouble seemed to lurk around every corner.

In 1991, Antley got back on the beam. Coming back from suspension, he began riding at Gulfstream Park in Florida, and found a fresh haven in which he felt he belonged, which was so key to his well-being throughout his life. He renewed a friendship there with trainer Nick Zito, whom he knew from riding in New York, and got the mount on Strike the Gold after he'd run a disappointing third in the Florida Derby under Craig Perret.

Antley rode Strike the Gold in the Blue Grass Stakes at Keeneland, a major prep race for the Kentucky Derby. Strike the Gold was a tricky horse to ride because of his come-from-behind style. But Antley and Strike the Gold scored in the Blue Grass, and now Antley was on to the Kentucky Derby, the biggest prize in American Thoroughbred racing. During his high-flying days in the late '80s, Antley had ridden in his first two Derbys in 1988 and 1989, finishing off the board.

Would the third time prove to be the charm?

"I had the confidence that we could win it, but with a horse that runs from the back, you also hope you get lucky and the holes open up for you," he said.

Strike the Gold was sent off as the third choice at odds of 9-2, and as usual displayed no early speed, settling into 12th position in the field of 16. Antley began to move as the field entered the second turn, and Strike the Gold moved up into sixth place. Antley guided him outside, and he circled the horses in front of him shortly after entering the stretch.

Strike the Gold prevailed by 1¾ lengths over the California star Best Pal. Antley had achieved what is a lifelong dream for anyone connected to Thoroughbred racing—a win in the Kentucky Derby.

"When I watch it, I get chills," Antley said. "I was thinking, 'Did this really happen?' Because winning the Derby is an immortal thing to any rider."

Antley may have reached the summit of the racing world, but that just meant there was only one way to go. Instead of using the Derby win to propel his life forward, within two years he was seeking to escape the East Coast and its many distractions. By 1993, the rider moved to Southern California looking for a fresh start, and that seemed to work for a while. Antley scored stakes victories with horses such as River Flyer, Individual Style, and Stuka. He brought home 204 winners in 2004, and he became part of the top echelon of riders in the very competitive Southern California colony.

Antley was unable to continue building on that momentum, however. Riding infractions and a shoulder injury led to absences. He also was unsatisfied with a personal life that failed to include a significant other. It doesn't take much for a jockey to lose business. There are no contracts for riders, and trainers and owners want to go with the hot hand. Antley was growing less popular. He began to lose the battle to make weight, and his enthusiasm for his profession slowly ticked away.

Antley was also fighting depression, and around this time he was diagnosed with bipolar disorder, popularly known as manic depression. The condition would haunt him for the last five years of his life and is characterized by mood swings ranging from depressive lows to manic highs. There is no cure, but treatment includes psychotherapy and a lifelong combination of medications such as antipsychotic, antidepressant, and anticonvulsant drugs.

By 1996, there is no doubt that depression had set in, and "personal reasons" caused Antley to intermittently stay away from the racetrack. In 1997, he decided he'd had enough, and returned home to South Carolina. Three years later, in an interview that took place at Santa Anita Park in a trailer used by the Winners Foundation, an organization that helps substance abusers, Antley was able to put that time period in perspective.

"At this level, you have to show up and play the game correctly," he said. "There's no slacking off. You're as good as what you've done lately. I fell off mentally. My discipline faded. It wasn't fun anymore, and I got depressed. I thought my life was over at thirty. I didn't want to live anymore."

South Carolina, at first, did not provide any easy answers. Antley gained thirty pounds, forcing himself to think about a life after riding. He had published a stock market newsletter called the "Ant Report" that went out to 350 subscribers. But after much soul-searching he decided he wanted to take another crack at riding. It was what he knew best, and it is what had always come easiest to him.

Antley started running every day. As the pounds melted away, he got healthier—both physically and mentally.

"I had a glow in my eye. I cared about myself again. I told my Dad as a joke I was going to win the Derby again," he said. "After 18 months away, I walked into the jocks' room at Santa Anita in February, 1999, and I was the fittest S.O.B. in that room."

There was one last peak for Antley to climb, an incredibly steep one. You couldn't throw a rock inside the jockeys' quarters at Santa Anita at that time without hitting a Hall of Famer. Laffit Pincay Jr., Chris McCarron, Eddie Delahoussaye, Kent Desormeaux, and Gary Stevens were the cream of the crop, and Antley wasn't going to step right in and get top mounts. But he made the most of his chances. In April, he won a race for trainer D. Wayne Lukas, and received an unexpected bonus when Lukas told him to watch a horse named Charismatic, who was running in the Lexington Stakes the following day.

"Tell me what you think," Lukas told Antley. "He's probably going to the Kentucky Derby, and you can ride him if you want."

Charismatic was no superstar. Up to that point, he'd won twice in thirteen races. Antley watched the Lexington Stakes on television. Charismatic stepped away from a modest field and won by 2 ½ lengths, and Antley felt a chill of excitement. It was still a longshot chance, but it was a chance just the same, and

Antley was game to grab it. He was going back to the Kentucky Derby.

Charismatic didn't have a lot of backers. His Derby odds of 31-1 were the third-longest of the nineteen horses in the field. Considering that Antley did not lay eyes on Charismatic in person until he got to the saddling paddock before the race, he and his mount worked well together. They ran toward the first turn four-wide in mid-pack. Antley kept his mount wide up the backstretch and then launched a bid into the final turn, churning away up into third place. Only one horse—Menifee—was coming from behind. The wire was coming up, Antley pushed, and Charismatic won by a neck. Together, they had made it back from oblivion.

"I was numbed out," Antley said. "It was spiritual, like the hardest dream coming true. That whole journey. I was so warm inside it made me cry. To get there through all that."

Two weeks later, Antley and Charismatic teamed up again to win the Preakness Stakes. Antley would have a chance to win the first Triple Crown in twenty-one years, since Affirmed and Steve Cauthen in 1978. Antley kept Charismatic close to the pace and less than a length off pacesetting Silverbulletday in the Belmont Stakes. Charismatic went to the lead at the top of the lane, but was passed by the eventual winner, Lemon Drop Kid, and wound up third.

Antley, however, had felt Charismatic bobble near the wire, and took him to the outside of the racetrack, where he jumped off the colt's back, lost his balance, and hit the ground. Quickly recovering, he reached for Charismatic's injured left foreleg and lifted it off the ground to prevent the colt from putting weight on it. Medical staff arrived, and Charismatic was driven back to Lukas' barn for evaluation. He would undergo successful surgery for a condylar fracture and never race again.

Because of his heroics in helping the horse, Antley, too, was celebrated even though he and Charismatic had failed to win the Triple Crown.

Back at Lukas' barn later that day, Charismatic's owner, Bob Lewis, told Antley, "How you tried to assist the horse and hold him up was just magnificent on your part. I can't begin to tell you how proud we are to have you in our association."

Seemingly as a reward for his good deeds, Antley went on a burner for the remainder of that summer. He was aboard stakes winners such as River Keen, Joe Who, A Lady From Dixie, Doneraile Court, and Forestry. He seemed poised to take his place among the top riders in California, with plenty of blue sky ahead.

But the good times never seemed to roll very long for him. Bothered by injuries to his shoulders and knees, along with the struggle of making weight and the return of his depression, Antley was gone from the track by autumn of 1999. He briefly returned at the beginning of 2000 to Santa Anita, but then left the racetrack for the final time. As always, he was searching for something more, something that remained outside his grasp for most of his life. An ABC Sports producer named Natalie Jowett had done a piece with Antley the year before, and the two got married in a Las Vegas ceremony in the spring of 2000. It was hoped that marriage would prove to be the answer to Antley's problems. It wasn't.

Holed up in his home, Antley stopped taking or returning

calls from racetrack friends. With bipolar disorder, it is critical that patients follow a strict protocol of medicine to achieve normality. Failing that, there are episodes of megalomania, delusions of God-like status, and befriending of strangers that anyone with any sense should be avoiding at all costs.

Jockey Gary Stevens, one of Antley's best friends on the racetrack, went to Antley's home several times to try and talk him into entering a drug rehabilitation program. But there is no getting through to victims in the throes of manic depression, and Stevens couldn't move his friend toward help. Not even the impending birth of his daughter could lift Antley out of his final downward spiral.

The signs were clear. On December 7, 2000, CBSNews.com reported that on July 26, Pasadena police arrested Antley for drunk driving. His .26 blood alcohol level was well above the legal limit, and Antley admitted he'd been drinking vodka. Two months later, according to the same news report, Antley's wife, who was living on the East Coast, became concerned when she couldn't reach Antley by phone. She called the Pasadena police department and asked them to go by his home. Police found Antley and Timothy Tyler Jr. at the home along with a gram of methamphetamine and equipment to manufacture that drug. The equipment was located in the room that Tyler had been staying in at the house. Both men were arrested.

The report continued to state that on October 7, a 911 call came from the house, but the caller quickly hung up. When police came to the home, they found Tyler but not Antley. Tyler described Antley as having gone into a rage the day before. Police found broken glass on the floors of every room, furniture tipped over, and "bizarre drawings on walls." There was also broken electronics equipment.

In mid-November, Stevens saw Antley, and told the *Los Angeles Times* that, "He seemed depressed. I had the feeling when I left that he was not going to be around much longer."

Antley's brother flew out to the West Coast to check up on his brother on December 3, 2000. It was just seven months since Chris had completed his incredible comeback by winning the Kentucky Derby. Yet, that happy day seemed worlds removed. At 11 p.m., Pasadena police received a 911 call describing a man who "was lying inside the house, who may possibly be dead." Paramedics and police descended on Antley's home near the famed Rose Bowl. They pronounced the 34-year-old jockey dead at the scene with what was described as "severe trauma to the head," according to the December 4, 2000, *LA Times*.

"We do not believe that this was a random act, and so detectives are looking into all possible suspects," said police commander Mary Schander.

Paramedics told police the circumstances of Antley's death appeared suspicious. The Associated Press termed it an "apparent homicide." According to the AP report, a neighbor of Antley's named Jerry Holt said he was awakened that night by a "screaming car leaving the premises."

Tyler, whose address was listed as Dana Point, CA, but who clearly had been staying with Antley over a period of time, was brought in by police the following day and held in lieu of $45,000 bail on three outstanding drug and DUI warrants, according to the *LA Times*. Police termed him "an associate of Antley's." While they never described him as being a suspect, they knew from previous incidents that he and Antley were involved in drugs together, and had argued. Schander, as quoted by the LA Times and AP, said that "There is no one else we're actively seeking at the moment."

However, after questioning, Tyler was never charged in connection with Antley's death. Because numerous lacerations, contusions, and abrasions were found on Antley's body by police, they initially believed the wounds were consistent with him being struck with an object. However, that is a theory they were not able to prove. The Los Angeles County coroner began an investigation into Antley's demise.

Five weeks later, on January 11, 2001, as Natalie Jowett went into labor to give birth to the couple's daughter, Antley's death was ruled an accidental overdose by the L.A. County coroner. The report attributed his death to multiple drug intoxication. Neuropathology reports conducted by the coroner determined that none of the cuts found on Antley were serious enough to be the cause of his death. It found no significant trauma or any fractures of the skull.

ABC News reported that coroner spokesman Scott Carrier said that "Lacerations were caused by him perhaps falling down and being under the influence. No foul play is suspected, and the Pasadena police concur."

The report also detailed Dr. Louis Pena, deputy medical director with the L.A. County coroner's office, having returned to the scene with Pasadena police sometime after December 3 and recovering a number of gel medication tablets scattered about the premises. He also found numerous areas with blood splattered about. The coroner's report said that Antley apparently became delusional from a combination of drugs and fell in various locations around the house, causing the superficial cuts to his head.

The coroner's report found the presence of four drugs in Antley's system at the time of his death, according to the *Bloodhorse* magazine of January 11, 2001. Clobenzorax, a weight-control drug popular with jockeys, but which was unavailable legally in the United States, was found. Why Antley would be taking that months removed from riding horses is a mystery. The coroner also found methamphetamine; Tegretol, an anti-seizure medication; and Paxil, an anti-depressant, in Antley.

"By taking amphetamine, a person can develop a psychosis and become delusional, and that was consistent with the scene found by Pasadena police the night of the death," Carrier said. "In addition, the heart can develop arrhythmia from amphetamine."

No one, other than possibly Timothy Tyler Jr., if in fact he was in the car heard speeding away from Antley's house the night of his death, knows what actually happened on December 3, 2000. What is evident is that, rather than controlling his medical condition with the proper medications, Chris Antley was ingesting a cocktail of substances that inhibited his capacity to reason effectively. And that such behavior occurred over a period of several months.

The coroner's report, although it disagreed with the first impression expressed by police on the scene, is correct in this aspect: By whoever's hand Chris Antley actually died, he killed himself. It was ruled accidental as far as the final circumstances of his life, but his dissatisfaction with himself, his inability to remain happy about his accomplishments, and his proclivity for getting into trouble had been slowly killing him for most of his life. There was an imbalance in his brain that just didn't allow him to function in a manner or in a range we call "normal." And it is hard to succeed in an occupation as difficult as riding Thoroughbreds unless you are 100 percent present and in control of all faculties.

That Antley achieved as much as he did in his brief career is a testament to his ability and talent. Winning at life can be even trickier, however.

"He always seemed to be searching for something," said his friend Stevens. "Everybody has their ups and downs, and unfortunately Chris didn't respond well to the downs. He had a troubled life."

Big Brown's
Impossible Loss

By 2008, the idea that any Thoroughbred racehorse could achieve the sport's ultimate goal—capturing the Triple Crown—seemed just a sweet dream. For the past thirty years, they had come, one after another, to Belmont Park for the Belmont Stakes after having won the Kentucky Derby and Preakness Stakes, and one by one they had gone down to defeat over the testing 1½ miles of the Belmont Stakes, the third and most elusive jewel in the Triple Crown series.

Affirmed had become a mythic hero, as his Triple Crown heroics of 1978 had gone unmatched since. No one in the late 1970s would have imagined such a scenario, as that decade saw three Triple Crown winners in just a six-year span, with Secretariat and Seattle Slew earning legendary status as well. But after Affirmed, the Belmont had eaten up the Triple Crown tries of Spectacular Bid, Pleasant Colony, Alysheba, Sunday Silence, Silver Charm, Real Quiet, Charismatic, Funny Cide, War Emblem, and Smarty Jones.

It was like the "Peanuts" cartoon where Charlie Brown kept believing he could kick the football, but Lucy pulled it away every single time. Many questioned if the Triple Crown could ever be achieved again.

And then there appeared on the scene a robust bay colt given the name Big Brown by owner Paul Pompa Jr., who worked in the trucking industry and honored United Parcel Service by using its nickname for his Boundary colt. Big Brown was so dominant that the entire Thoroughbred business became Charlie Brown for a few magical months in 2008. This time the football would remain in place. This time the kick would be good. Finally, here was a colt who would join Affirmed and become the twelfth winner of the Triple Crown. This was as close to a lock as you could dial up.

Big Brown went off as the prohibitive 3-5 favorite in the Belmont Stakes on June 7, 2008. The racing world waited, confetti in hand. Glasses raised. Big Brown just needed to navigate twelve furlongs against an overmatched field of foes. The gates opened. The crowd of 94,000 roared. Then Lucy swiped the football. Charlie Brown fell on his ass. Not only did Big Brown not win the Belmont, he didn't even finish the race.

What happened? That depends on who you talk to, but the mystery of Big Brown's abject failure will never be solved, because only he knows. And he's not talking.

Big Brown began life on Dr. Gary Knapp's Monticule, a farm near Lexington in the heart of the Bluegrass region. His dam, Mien, was a modest racemare by the potent stallion Nureyev, and his sire, Boundary, was a grade III-winning sprinter who didn't distinguish himself as a stallion. Boundary, in fact, had been pensioned from stud duty by the time Big Brown made it to the races.

Big Brown sold as a yearling for $60,000 and was entered for sale once again the following year. Pompa was racing a horse named Snake River Canyon who had just won for him, and his cousin and racing manager, Jerry McClenin, noticed that Snake River Canyon's half-brother was being offered at Keeneland's April auction of two-year-olds.

"I told Paul we should look into him," McClenin said. "He checked out well, and we bought him for $190,000. We were happy. He was a nice, big horse, and we sent him to Pat Reynolds to train. It was Labor Day weekend at Saratoga in 2007 when he first ran, and Pat told Paul to wear a nice suit, meaning he'd be taking a picture in the winner's circle.

"The race was incredible. He won by 11¼ lengths. I told Paul that by the time we got home, the phone would be ringing off the hook with offers to buy him. Paul didn't think so, because the race had been on grass, but that didn't matter. When a horse runs like that, going two turns in his first start, people notice."

McClenin was right. The phone was ringing. Darley, a world-wide Thoroughbred conglomerate, offered $3 million for Big Brown. But Pompa wanted to stay in for a piece of the horse, so he entertained an offer by International Equine Acquisitions Holdings Stables (IEAH), which paid Pompa $3.5 million while allowing him to keep 25 percent of the colt.

IEAH moved Big Brown to trainer Richard Dutrow Jr., himself a controversial figure. Already plagued by drug problems, suspensions, and the murder of his daughter's mother, Dutrow was nevertheless the son of a noted trainer and knew his way around a horse.

Dutrow knew what to do with Big Brown, but he needed to summon considerable skill to keep the horse sound. A quarter crack, which is a hoof injury, prevented Big Brown from racing again as a two-year-old, so he had just the one Saratoga victory to his credit as he turned 3. In Florida in early 2008, Big Brown endured a second quarter crack, and it wasn't until March 8 that he made his sophomore debut. It was worth the wait, as Big Brown cruised to a 12¾-length victory in an allowance race at Gulfstream Park. Having shown such promise, Big Brown forced himself onto the Kentucky Derby trail, even with his lack of seasoning.

"This horse has taken control of the game, and we're just innocent bystanders riding along with him," said Dutrow. "He's absolutely unstoppable right now."

Sent to the Florida Derby, a grade 1 prep for the Kentucky Derby, Big Brown shot to the lead from his outside post position. Wearing glue-on shoes to help his fragile feet, Big Brown ran off to a five-length decision, and it was on to Churchill Downs.

In the Derby, Big Brown left from the far outside in a field of twenty horses. Under jockey Kent Desormeaux, he rated off the early pace in sixth position, then commenced his rally a quarter mile from the finish and powered home by 4¾ lengths, becoming the seventh undefeated Kentucky Derby winner. The full-throated hype of conquering the Triple Crown was in full gear considering how easily the colt was topping off his races. And physically, he was imposing, with a broad chest that seemed ready to bully aside anything in his path. He wasn't just defeating his classmates; he was annihilating them. A man among boys.

Nothing much changed two weeks later when the scene shifted to Pimlico Race Course in Baltimore for the Preakness
Stakes. Because of bad weather back in Louisville, Big Brown
only galloped three times in that fortnight. He arrived at
Pimlico three days before the Preakness, but the rains followed
him there, leading to Dutrow waiting until the morning of the
race to breeze Big Brown a quarter mile, a move that might have
been common fifty years before, but was rare in the modern era.
It was a homecoming for Dutrow, who was raised in Maryland,
and for Desormeaux, who began his riding career there. Big
Brown appeared to be at home as well, as Desormeaux kept him
outside of horses in the clear while sitting in third place in the
field of twelve. Big Brown, the prohibitive 1-5 favorite, cruised
past Gayego and Riley Tucker on the turn for home and won by
5¼ lengths, with Desormeaux actually easing up on the horse in
the stretch to conserve as much energy as possible for the
Belmont Stakes in three weeks.

Big Brown's legend was growing as large as his margins of victory. No other horse had come close to even challenging his
supremacy, and it all seemed so easy.

"I've seen the great ones who were not in my era on tape, and
I rode horses that I considered great ones, but I've never seen
anything like this," former jockey Gary Stevens told the
Bloodhorse's Steve Haskin. Although Stevens was serving as an
adviser to IEAH, his observations were hardly outside the norm.

Dutrow gushed, "I swear to God, I've never been around a
horse like this."

Mike Iavarone, one of the principals in IEAH, added, "I'm
awestruck. That was mind-boggling."

And so, it was on to New York, Iavarone's home base. Big Brown's connections displayed a swagger that matched New York City. They dressed in dark suits and sunglasses, travelled with well-muscled bodyguards, and leaned toward brashness and bravado. Dutrow bragged that he had the best horse. He wasn't one to downplay the talents of his star pupil when he could extol his virtues. This wasn't an 'Aw shucks' kind of crowd surrounding Big Brown. His connections did everything but erect a neon arrow over his stall, pointing to the star of the horse racing world.

The first crack—literally—in Big Brown's armor appeared on May 24, one week after the Preakness and two weeks before the Belmont Stakes, when another quarter crack was discovered on the inside of his left front hoof. Big Brown, already in New York, did not go to the track over the three-day Memorial Day weekend, and the lack of activity was making him testy around the barn.

"He has been kind of aggravated," Dutrow said on May 27 after taking Big Brown out for a 1½-mile jog. "I felt going to the track was good for his conditioning and also good for his mind."

The day before that jog, farrier Ian McKinlay, acknowledged to be the top man in the field of hoof lameness, treated the three-quarter-inch crack and stitched it up with stainless steel wire, drawing the crack together in an attempt to draw out the inflammation. McKinlay, who had also treated Big Brown for a similar problem the previous year, noted that the foot was showing improvement, and Dutrow termed it, "A little hiccup. It could actually be a good thing because he burned his heels in the Preakness. This will give him time to get over that."

The week of the Belmont Stakes proceeded along the lines of a well-choreographed coronation. Pompa, Iavarone, and IEAH's Richard Schiavo went to the New York Stock Exchange May 28, held a press conference, and rang the bell to commence trading. On June 1, Desormeaux was at Shea Stadium to throw out the ceremonial first pitch before the New York Mets tangled with the Los Angeles Dodgers. The network morning news shows did stories on Big Brown and his human connections, ginning up general interest for the Belmont. The *Bloodhorse* magazine cover dated June 8 bears the headline, "Is the Wait Over?" Thirty years after the last Triple Crown winner, the racing world was more than ready to anoint a new king.

While most experts gave Big Brown little chance of disappointing, there were undercurrents of potential doubt, if one chose to look closely enough. McKinlay was a constant presence around Big Brown in the days leading up to the race. And there was the matter of Big Brown's being on the anabolic steroid Winstrol, or Stanozolol, to increase muscle strength.

Just as in baseball's steroid era, steroids at the time were legal to administer to racehorses, and Dutrow made no bones about the fact that Big Brown was receiving Winstrol. But with the breakdown and subsequent euthanasia of the filly Eight Belles, who finished second to Big Brown at the wire of the Kentucky Derby, horse racing was put under a microscope as far as drugs in horses. Perhaps because of this, or because Dutrow wanted to prove a point that Big Brown didn't need steroids to win, the trainer decided to take him off the medication before the Belmont Stakes. What, if any, effect that had on the colt's subsequent performance is impossible to determine.

Of more immediate concern was Big Brown's training schedule, which was light by any standards. The inclination, when you have a seemingly super horse that does things so easily, is to think that he can do anything, no matter if it goes against all conventional wisdom. Even Secretariat, by all measures one of the two greatest horses of the twentieth century, proved fallible when he was sent into battle at less than 100 percent, whether it be fighting a mouth abscess in the Wood Memorial, a fever in the Whitney, or a lack of training in the Woodward. He lost all three of those races. But his connections kept thinking he could overcome anything because he was Secretariat.

Big Brown did not breeze between the Kentucky Derby and the Preakness Stakes except for that two-furlong blowout on Preakness morning. But that is only a two-week break between races, and horses that run hard in the Derby tend to run themselves into shape without needing much more before the second jewel of the Triple Crown. It is, however, a three-week gap between the Preakness and the Belmont, which, at 1½ miles, is the longest of the Triple Crown races, and likely the furthest any of these horses will run in their careers. And they need proper training to stay fit for this test. Secretariat, before winning the Belmont by 31 lengths, had three timed workouts between the Preakness and the Belmont.

Big Brown, on the other hand, was being handled with kid gloves because of the quarter crack in his hoof and was sent out for one five-furlong work four days before the Belmont. For those who thought him so thoroughly superior to his competition, this light training regimen meant little to nothing. Others, albeit in the minority, thought it would be his downfall.

Iavarone, thinking back thirteen years during a 2021 interview, remembered another factor that could have hampered Big Brown's Belmont performance.

"Big Brown's home base was at Aqueduct; that was his normal training spot," said Iavarone. "But the New York Racing Association wanted the horse at Belmont to help with the buildup to the race and all the media hype. But Belmont in June can be a tricky track, and in the weeks leading up to the race, the track was rock hard and lightning fast. Horses were running six furlongs in 1:08 like it was nothing.

"Coming off the quarter crack, Rick was really concerned about training over the track, and he asked NYRA to do something about the hardness. So, they added a bunch of sand to the track and slowed it down. And ironically, I think that bit us in the butt, because we missed a bunch of training and then the track was tiring for our horse."

Nevertheless, going into the race, the confidence level in Big Brown's camp was still sky high. After all, Big Brown had won for fun in all his races, and there was no obvious horse to be scared of in the Belmont field, particularly after the scratch of Casino Drive, a Japanese-trained colt who was a half-brother to Belmont winners Jazil and Rags to Riches. Casino Drive had stepped on a stone walking around the Belmont Park barn area, injuring a foot, and was taken out of the Belmont on the morning of the race.

"Even though we had missed ten days of training, at least we got a work into him," said Iavarone. "His first race that year at Gulfstream Park, it rained, and the race was switched from the turf to the dirt. Rick said he was uncomfortable about where Big

Brown was conditioning-wise, because a mile on the dirt is more demanding than on the turf. He didn't think he had him ready. And the horse ran off the screen and won by 12. He won the Derby for fun while 12-wide. So, yes, we were still confident going into the Belmont. I figured his will would carry him through the race because he was better than those horses. And that's how we went into the race."

More than 94,000 fans showed up at Belmont Park June 7, 2008, on a hot, humid New York day to see the coronation of a Triple Crown winner. During the afternoon, with temperatures soaring above ninety degrees, a water outage hit the facility. The track, known as Big Sandy, to begin with, was getting sandier because of the compromised water supply, which may have affected how much water was spread over the track by the watering trucks throughout the day.

Another troubling sign occurred when Big Brown, normally a calm horse, began "bucking and kicking and acting up in the holding barn before the race, and sweating between his legs, which he never does," according to Iavarone.

Having drawn the rail post position in the field of nine, Big Brown was distracted either by the starter, who was standing on the track, or someone in the infield, and ducked to the outside as the gates opened. His back right foot was hit by Guadalcanal, the 25-1 longshot in the next gate, and part of his shoe separated from his hoof sometime during the race.

Desormeaux, not wanting to be boxed in along the rail, tugged on Big Brown to bring him outside of Da' Tara, who had shot to the front immediately. But Tale of Ekati was already in that spot, and Desormeaux had to wrangle Big Brown back inside until they neared the first turn, where he again tugged on Big Brown to go outside. This time, Big Brown bumped into Anak Nakal, but finally found a position out wide and in the clear behind Da' Tara and Tale of Ekati.

"The inside post was the one thing that drove me crazy," said Iavarone. "But when Kent finally got him off the rail and to the outside going up the backstretch, I thought he'd win by ten lengths."

Indeed, the pair looked poised to overtake the leader, whom Big Brown had defeated by 23½ lengths in the Florida Derby, anytime they wanted. With five furlongs to go, Desormeaux asked Big Brown, who sat about 2½ lengths behind Da' Tara, to pick it up. At that moment, the legend of Big Brown deflated.

"He didn't proceed whatsoever. I chirped at him, I started spanking him, kissing at him, screaming at him, but the more I encouraged him, the more he slowed down," Desormeaux said in an ESPN video several weeks after the race. "He was not travelling (like he was) sore. I didn't know what the problem was."

As the field hit the final turn, with Big Brown spinning his wheels, Desormeaux made the controversial decision to ease the horse out of the race rather than continue riding him to the wire. This caused great consternation coming on the heels of Eight Belles's fatal breakdown, because the first inclination of everyone watching was to believe the horse was injured, perhaps badly. And horse racing could not afford to see its biggest star go down the same path as Eight Belles and, years earlier, Barbaro, with the world watching.

"I was crying, my family was crying," said Iavarone. "Was this Barbaro all over again? I don't think Kent meant to do anything wrong. Maybe he was embarrassed for the horse and did it out of respect for the horse."

To everyone's relief, Big Brown was found to be healthy when he got back to his barn after post-race testing. But Desormeaux, who had already been fined multiple times in California for not riding losing mounts through to the finish line, was forced to defend his actions. Clearly, Big Brown was not going to win the Belmont Stakes, but it is still highly unusual for a jockey to pull a horse out of a race for that reason alone. In fact, it is unheard of.

"They weren't in the saddle with me," Desormeaux said of his critics. "I had no more horse. The tank was empty. I'll pat myself on the back for pulling him up."

Nevertheless, Dutrow was enraged at Desormeaux after the race, blaming him for the defeat.

"He was so upset, I couldn't understand what he was saying," said McClenin, Pompa's racing manager. "He was blaming Desormeaux."

It certainly was less than a perfect ride, given the eventful trip even before the horse hit the first turn. But that alone doesn't account for the defeat. Why Big Brown ran such an uncharacteristically poor race is an ongoing mystery. An enhanced video of the race emerged sometime later showing Big Brown's shoe separated from his foot, which certainly would have compromised him. But experts are split into two camps: those who feel he lost all chance before the race even began, and those who think he was defeated by the events that took place on the track.

Billy Turner, who trained 1977 Triple Crown superstar Seattle Slew, told the *Bloodhorse* that the lack of training up to the race is what did in Big Brown.

"I've studied the Belmont for decades, and the successful trainers knew when to lean on a horse and get to the bottom of him," he said. "Good horses like Majestic Prince and Canonero II, who couldn't drill before the Belmont, got beat. If Big Brown could win the Belmont off that training, he was not mortal."

Iavarone agreed. "The real issue was the quarter crack and the time he missed. But what are you going to do when you're running for the Triple Crown? Are you going to say, 'We're not running in the race because we're a work short?' We had no choice. It wasn't optimal, but I felt once he got out there and began running, the adrenaline would take over."

Andrew Cohen, one of the four IEAH investors who owned Big Brown, added, "He wasn't himself that day. He wasn't right. Kicking the stall before the race; he never did that. He is the sweetest horse you'd want to meet. It was hot, but it was hot for everybody. They talk about his shoe coming off. I don't know. It just wasn't his day."

Frank Lyons, a former trainer who was an analyst for the TVG horseracing network in 2008, was living in Dutrow's home the week of the Belmont. "It was a combination of things that got him beat, not one thing," opined Lyons. "First, he couldn't train because of the quarter crack. Second, the track really became Big Sandy that day because they couldn't put water on it. He got tired. And the other horse stepped on his hind foot and twisted his shoe."

None of Big Brown's connections blamed his being taken off his steroid regimen as the reason for his defeat. "Rick probably didn't think he needed them," said Iavarone. "He didn't care what the media said or what I said. But I don't think it was the steroids. We never put him back on Winstrol, and he came back and won two more races.

"He just wasn't ready to run a mile and a half that day."

Indeed, Big Brown returned to the races in the Haskell Invitational Stakes, a grade 1 event two months after the Belmont, but he was all out to get by Coal Play to win by 1¾ lengths. The following month, he won the ungraded Monmouth Stakes, albeit against older horses, by a neck. He was no longer the dominant force he had been previously. He was never the same horse after the Preakness Stakes. And he was retired after hurting himself before the Breeders' Cup that November with a record of seven wins in eight starts and more than $3.6 million in earnings.

But that one loss sticks out, not only because it occurred on the biggest possible stage of North American racing, but because of the ignominious sight of a potential Triple Crown winner galloping and then walking to the finish line after his eight foes had completed the race.

Steroids? Quarter crack? Heat? Lack of training? Uncharacteristic behavior? Lack of water on the track? Separated shoe? Bumping with other horses? Bothered by the starter and the inside post? Poor ride? Take your pick and take your chances. All we can say for sure is it took another seven years before American Pharoah finally solved the puzzle of the

Triple Crown after a thirty-seven-year wait. Seven years after the horse who couldn't lose, lost.

"I've seen a million things happen in this sport," said McClenin. "Great horses run bad races all the time. It's all part of the game."

References

—Books—

Amory, Cleveland. (1960). *Who Killed Society?* New York: Harper & Bros.

Auerbach, Ann Hagedorn. (1994, 1995). *Wild Ride.* New York: Henry Holt and Company.

Braudy, Susan. (1992). *This Crazy Thing Called Love.* New York: Alfred Knopf, Inc.

Chew, Peter. (1974). *The Kentucky Derby, The First Hundred Years.* Boston: Houghton Mifflin Company.

The American Racing Manual. Daily Racing Form, Inc.

Day, John I. and Underwood, Tom R., eds. (1946). *Call Me Horse.* New York: Coward-McCann, Inc.

Dunne, Dominick. (1985, 1999). *The Two Mrs. Grenvilles.* New York: Ballantine Books.

Helm, Mike. (1991). *A Breed Apart, The Horse and the Players.* New York: Henry Holt and Company.

Piggott, Lester. (1995). *Lester, the Autobiography of Lester Piggott.* London: Partridge Press.

Robertson, William H. P. (1964). *A History of Thoroughbred Racing in America.* Englewood Cliffs, N.J: Bonanza Books, a division of Crown Publishers.

Smith, Raymond. (1994). *Tigers of the Turf.* Dublin: Sporting Books Publishers.

Turner, Colin. (1984). *In Search of Shergar.* London: Sidgewick & Jackson Limited.

Wilson, Julian. (1998). *The Great Racehorses.* New York: Little, Brown & Co.

—Newspapers and Periodicals—

The American Weekly; Austin American-Statesman; The Blood-Horse; Chicago Sun-Times; Chicago Tribune; The Cleveland Plain Dealer; Daily Racing Form; Daily Telegraph; Dallas Morning News; Irish Independent; Irish Times; Kentucky Derby Souvenir Magazine; Lexington Herald-Leader; The Los Angeles Times; Louisville Courier-Journal; Newsday; The New York Post; The New York Times; New Zealand Referee; San Francisco Chronicle; San Francisco Examiner; San Marcos Daily Record; The Sporting Globe; Sports Illustrated; The Sun; Sydney Daily Mirror; Thoroughbred of California; Thoroughbred Record; Thoroughbred Times; Turf Monthly; Washington Times.

Index

Photo Credits

Phar Lap (*The Blood-Horse*) • Al Snider (Bert Morgan) • Red
McDaniel (*Fred Purnery/Santa Anita Park*) • Ann Woodward
(*Pimlico*) William Woodward Jr. with Elsie Woodward
(*The Blood-Horse*) William Woodward with Nashua (*The Blood-
Horse*) • Thomas Carey, new Hawthorne (*Matt Goins/EquiPix*)
old Hawthorne (*Hawthorne Race Course*) • The Aga Khan and
Shergar (*Sport & General*) • David Joost (Daniel Joost) • Gene and
Lucille Markey (*The Blood-Horse*) • Alydar (*Anne M. Eberhardt*)
J.T. Lundy (*James Nielsen*) • Dancer's Image, Peter Fuller
(*The Blood-Horse*) • Ron Hansen (*Shigeki Kikkawa*) •
Jimmy Croll, Holy Bull (*Anne M. Eberhardt*) •
Fanfreluche (*Pinkerton's New York Racing Security Service, Inc.*)
Dr. Robert Holland and sponging detection device
(*Anne M. Eberhardt*) William McCandless
(*Kenton [Ky.] County Police Department*).

Acknowledgments

Acknowledgments, John McEvoy

The author is grateful to many people who provided valuable assistance that led to the completion of this book, including: Gus Blass II, Tony Chamblin, Jacqueline Duke, Ray Freeark, Don Grisham, Ann Healy, Joe Hirsch, Ira Kaplan, Anne Lang, Judy L. Marchman, Wayne Monroe, Peter Tonkes, Phyllis Rogers, and Neal Yonover.

Acknowledgments, Lenny Shulman

John McEvoy was not only a prodigious writer who combined his love of horse racing and mysteries to craft wonderful stories, he was also a kind man who was quick to compliment his peers and offer words of advice and kindness. He is missed by all who were fortunate enough to know him.

About The Authors

John McEvoy (1936–2019), a graduate of the University of Wisconsin, was a former newspaper reporter and college English teacher who subsequently served as Midwest editor, then senior writer for Daily Racing Form. He wrote the 1995 book *Through the Pages of the Daily Racing Form*, an historical overview of American Thoroughbred racing based on material that had appeared in that newspaper's first 100 years. He also published a book of poetry, *Legacies*, a profile of the iconic racehorse Roundtable for Eclipse's Thoroughbred Legends series, and the Jack Doyle series of horse racing mysteries with Poisoned Pen Press. He lived in Evanston, Illinois, with his wife of fifty-nine years, Judy.

Lenny Shulman is an Emmy Award-winning writer who has worked extensively in TV and film, as well as for magazines and newspapers across the country. For twenty years he has served as features editor for *BloodHorse* magazine, the Thoroughbred industry's foremost trade publication. He is the author of *Head to Head: Conversations with Horse Racing Legends*, *Ride of Their Lives: The Triumphs and Turmoil of Today's Top Jockeys*, and *Justify: 111 Days to Triple Crown Glory*.